1977

This book may be kept

FOURTEEN D

CHILDREN AND LANGUAGE

Children
and Language

Readings in Early Language
and Socialization

EDITED BY
Sinclair Rogers

LONDON
OXFORD UNIVERSITY PRESS
1975

Oxford University Press, Ely House, London W1

GLASGOW NEW YORK TORONTO MELBOURNE WELLINGTON
CAPE TOWN IBADAN NAIROBI DAR ES SALAAM LUSAKA ADDIS ABABA
DELHI BOMBAY CALCUTTA MADRAS KARACHI LAHORE DACCA
KUALA LUMPUR SINGAPORE HONG KONG TOKYO

ISBN 0 19 437007 0

*Printed in Great Britain by
Western Printing Services Ltd., Bristol*

Contents

SECTION FOUR   Language and Meaning

SECTION FIVE   Language and the Environment

Introduction

Although the study of the acquisition of a first language has been split by a controversy between the *innatists* and the *behaviourists*, neither group has given enough consideration to the relationship between language development and all the other developments of the child—social, cognitive, perceptual. This collection of readings links the development of language to the broader societal and functional aspects of language actually being used. Theories about language acquisition have almost always ignored the actual context and use of language.

At times the controversy between the innatists (Chomsky, Lenneberg, McNeill, Menyuk) and the behaviourists (Bloomfield, Skinner, Sapon, Jenkins and Palermo) has produced more heat than light, as each side believes it has a missionary role in converting the other. The innatists seek to limit the influence of the social context in the acquisition of language by stressing the innate mechanisms which

> describe the child's acquisition of language as a kind of theory construction. *The child discovers the theory of his language with only small amounts of data from that language.*
> (Chomsky 1968, p. 66, my italics)

Notice the use of the phrase 'theory of his language' by Chomsky. He is not saying that the child acquires the means of *using* his language. He is concerned, as are most of the innatists, with describing the potential knowledge of language of children—the child's competence, particularly that aspect of competence dealing with syntax. The behaviourists, on the other hand, have been concerned with the role played by the environment and experience in the process of acquisition. But much of their work has been concentrated on differentials between the language of children of different social classes or children brought up in institutions, and so on.

The very early linguistic and social and cultural environments have clearly marked effects on both the acquisition process and on what is actually acquired. This can be seen especially in section 3 of this book. It is time now for a different approach—an examination of the roles and functions of children's language in society; for with development in language ability goes increased language use which leads to an increased awareness of the world and the child's society and his place in it. It is impossible yet to say which development triggers off another, but what must be clear is that any development in language is not simply a consequence of linguistic factors only, but involves perception, cognition, social environment and others. The over-all aim of this collection of readings is to bring together, from a wide spread of disciplines, articles which give body, social and personal context to the study of child language.

The Sections

The readings in this collection have been selected on the basis of how much information they give of the societal and functional aspects of language in use. The first section contains three readings each of which in its own way, attempts to relate the requirements of a theoretical approach to language acquisition to the necessity of realizing just how much of the actual linguistic situation has been left out of previous theoretical discussions. The development of the functions of language in use in society is the concern of the rest of the collection. As I see it, the book pivots around Halliday's article *Relevant Models of Language*. This makes it abundantly clear that children have a much greater range of uses of language than adults, who tend to think of language as primarily a medium for carrying messages; children on the other hand use it to learn and understand the world, society, about themselves, they use it to play with and so on. This second section is devoted to the ways in which the child attaches meaning to such concepts as 'self', 'non-self', to other people, behaviour, physical events and so on, using language the whole time as a mediating and expressive medium.

The third section discusses how the developing language of the child allows him to discuss what he perceives. This 'talking about' is essential in any thinking or learning process as it enables the child to make links and comparisons between what he has already learned and the new material. It is only when the new is thoroughly related and made part of the old by internal or external discussion, that it can be used as a springboard to the next new information. Clearly language is critical in all this.

Section 4 covers the area of how language is used to give meaning to behaviour and the experiences the child has of the world. The role of language here is one perhaps mainly of a medium of discussion and comparison again. Concepts such as 'small', 'big', 'somebody else's property', 'good manners' can be easily coded in language which can then be used for discussion and reference.

Section 5 deals with the influence of background on linguistic and other developmental processes particularly from the point of view of the disadvantaged child. This is an area of increasing concern as so-called linguistically deprived children have many problems when at school. A major part of the section is given to Basil Bernstein's article in which he discusses the problems of differing linguistic developmental schemata.

SECTION ONE
The Social Contexts of Language

The general thesis linking this book is that the acquisition and development of language involves a much wider perspective of developments
in the child. If this thesis is held, then it means that one ought not to
consider language acquisition merely in terms of language. The three
readings in this section put the case for and against the social context. I
have perhaps declared my bias by including two readings which stress
that the whole context of the child's situation should be considered, to
one, by McNeill, which does not see any particular usefulness accruing
from including the context. The article by Campbell and Wales and
the later one by Bloom approach the question of context from different
points of view. Each of the readings has arisen out of certain drawbacks
that the authors have found in previous research and are endeavouring
to put right in their own. Campbell and Wales concern themselves
especially with the widening of Chomsky's 'competence'. This, briefly,
is not the rather restricted competence in the Chomskian sense but
the 'ability to produce or understand utterances which are not so much
grammatical but, more important, *appropriate to the context in which
they are made*' (Reading 1, p. 7). The authors suggest that the acquisition of this communicative competence, much more than any other kind,
is dependent upon the whole communicative environment.

1 ROBIN CAMPBELL and ROGER WALES
The Study of Language Acquisition

1. The first attempt we know of to record the linguistic development of a child was that of the German biologist Tiedemann (1787) and his interest was in initiating the collection of normative data on the development of children. The greatest stimulus to the serious and careful study of the acquisition of language by children stems from Darwin's theory of evolution, which suggested the continuity of man with other animals. Darwin himself contributed a pioneer study (1877), as did Taine (1877). But it was in the superb, detailed study of the German physiologist Preyer (1882), who made detailed daily notes throughout the first three years of his son's development, that the study of child language found its true founding father. With Sully (1895) and Shinn (1893) following closely on Preyer, a substantial tradition of careful descriptive work was established, easily traceable from the early decades of this century in the journal *Pedagogical Seminary*, through the massive work of the Sterns (1924, 1928) and Leopold (1939–49), up to the exciting recent attempts to refine the descriptive process by appropriating the tools developed by the generative grammarians (e.g. Brown and Fraser 1963). This tradition was largely unaffected by the behaviourist movement in psychology.

It seems appropriate to begin this chapter by referring to the historical origins of the study, because there is currently a tendency to forget that the scientific study of child language has an important and thoroughly respectable heritage of observation and theoretical discussion. Recognition of the existence of this tradition and its influence may not only save us from the mere reworking of old questions but may also lead us to adopt a more moderate and informed position with respect to a number of contemporary claims and controversies. For example, the contemporary practice of vilifying behaviourism for its misleading and inept attempts to

Robin Campbell and Roger Wales: Extract from 'The Study of Language Acquisition' in John Lyons (ed.) *New Horizons in Linguistics*, Penguin, 1970, pp. 242–60. © John Lyons 1970.

explain language acquisition seems largely irrelevant. The important issue is how to go beyond the achievements of Leopold and
the Sterns, scholars who owed nothing to behaviourism.

Let us therefore allow Sully to describe the kinds of questions
and issues which continue to determine the range and nature of
our interest in child language:

> To the evolutionary biologist the child exhibits man in his
> kinship to the lower sentient world. This same evolutionary
> point of view enables the psychologist to connect the unfolding
> of an infant's mind with something which has gone before, with
> the mental history of the race (1895:8). If, reflects the psycholo-
> gist, he can only get at this baby's consciousness so as to under-
> stand what is passing there, he will be in an infinitely better
> position to find his way through the intricacies of the adult
> consciousness. It may be, as we shall see by and by, that the
> baby's mind is not so perfectly simple, so absolutely primitive
> as it at first looks (1875:7). In this genetic tracing back of the
> complexities of man's mental life to their primitive elements
> in the child's consciousness, questions of peculiar interest arise.
> A problem, which though having a venerable antiquity is still
> full of meaning, concerns the precise relation of the higher
> forms of intelligence and of sentiment to the elementary facts
> of the individual's life experience. Are we to regard all our
> ideas as woven by the mind out of its experiences, as Locke
> thought, or have we certain 'innate ideas' from the first. Locke
> thought he could settle this point by observing children. Today
> when the philosophic interest is laid not on the date of the
> appearance of the innate intuition, but on its originality and
> spontaneity, this method of interrogating the child's mind may
> seem less promising. Yet if of less philosophical importance
> than was once supposed, it is of great psychological importance
> (1895:7–8). The awakening of this keen and varied interest
> in childhood has led, and is destined to lead still more, to the
> observation of infantile ways. Pretty anecdotes of children
> which tickle the emotions may or may not add to our insight
> into the peculiar mechanism of children's minds (1895:10).
> The observation which is to further understanding, which is to
> be acceptable to science, must be scientific. That is to say, it

must be at once guided by foreknowledge, specially directed
to what is essential in a phenomenon and its surroundings or
conditions, and perfectly exact. If anybody supposes this to be
easy, he should first try his hand at the work, and then compare
what he has seen with what Darwin or Preyer has been able to
discover (1895:11).

Thus from the first the study of language acquisition was set in
the context of the investigation of the child's total development.
Further, the original interest arose out of serious questions about
the nature of man and his behaviour: there was more at stake than
mere description. Nevertheless, priority was given to the careful
description of what the child was doing. This was followed by
attempts to elucidate what sort of thing language acquisition was,
and only then by speculation about the explanations of these
phenomena. We will now use these aims as a platform from which
to discuss contemporary issues.

In the pursuit of these aims Leopold (1948) and those before
him took the communicative act as their basic psychological unit.
Description was a matter of accurately recording not only the
form of a child's utterances, but also the context in which they
were made and the meanings (so far as they could be determined)
of the constituent 'words'. Perhaps because of this, but more
probably because they did not have such clear ideas about syntax
as we have today, these early workers tended to terminate their
accounts at about the beginning of the third year of the child's life,
by which time most children have begun to produce utterances of
two or three distinct words.

The principal focus of more recent research, however, has been
the period stretching from the beginning of such syntactically
structured speech. This reorientation is due almost completely
to Chomsky's work in syntactic theory. The main aim of this
chapter will be to argue that an extremely important guiding
principle of the early work has been sacrificed in this reorientation
and to suggest some ways in which it might be restored to its
former methodological prominence. Limited space prevents us
from giving a detailed review of empirical work on language
acquisition, but many excellent reviews are available elsewhere: cf.
Richter (1927), Leopold (1948), McNeill (1966, 1969), Ervin-Tripp

(1966). Details of much recent work can also be found in the following collections of articles: Bellugi and Brown (1964), Smith and Miller (1966), Slobin (1970), Reed (1970), Hayes (1970).

Contrary to what one might expect, our knowledge of language acquisition has not been greatly advanced by the recent spate of empirical work. Furthermore, it is our belief that no real theoretical understanding of the acquisition of syntax will be obtained unless, paradoxical as this may seem, the methodological distinction between *competence* and *performance* drawn by Chomsky (the man who, more than any other, has shown the shallowness, indeed the irrelevance, of almost all behaviourist accounts of language acquisition) is drastically revised. We will now indicate how and why we think this distinction should be revised.

2. In the first half of Fodor and Garrett (1966) there is an excellent discussion of the distinction between competence and performance, in the course of which the authors distinguish one clear sense of the distinction which they, like us, regard as 'eminently honourable'. This is the sense in which competence in any sphere is identified with capacity or ability, as opposed to actual performance, which may only imperfectly reflect underlying capacity. This sense of the distinction has been honoured by psychologists in the past (e.g. Lashley, Hull, and many psychologists concerned with education) and likewise by certain social psychologists concerned with the study of attitude and opinion, etc. (e.g. Lazarsfeld). It applies in the construction of so-called 'performance' models of language users; that is to say, 'performance' models are in fact models of competence (in this weak sense of competence). However, when Chomsky talks of competence he is usually referring to a far 'stronger' notion, although it is not clear exactly what is meant by this stronger notion. We shall try to clarify the stronger notion in what follows.

The diverse capacities of human beings are subject to a variety of limitations, and some of these limitations may be described as 'non-essential'. For instance, our arithmetical capacity is limited by the amount of information we can store and manipulate at any one time; our capacity to walk is limited by the amount of time we can go without food or rest. In both these cases, the limiting factors are very general, applying, in the case of the former, to all mental activities and, in the case of the latter, to all physical activities. Hence we may, if we so choose, omit these limiting factors from our theoretical account of arithmetical or locomotive abilities: they are non-essential (i.e. non-specific) to these abilities. Similarly, by omitting any account of the role of memory or the various low-level sensori-motor capacities involved in the perception and production of speech, we can considerably simplify our characterization of linguistic abilities, and thereby arrive at the stronger notion of linguistic competence.

We have distinguished two senses of the term 'linguistic competence', the 'weaker' and the 'stronger'. We shall refer to these as $competence_1$ and $competence_2$ respectively. So far our discussion has been relatively uncontroversial, and it would be generally agreed that the clarification of the notion of 'competence' has far-reaching consequences for the psychological investigation of language and for the study of language acquisition in particular (cf. Moravcsik 1967, 1969). But we must now distinguish a third sense of 'competence'.

Although generative grammarians, in particular Chomsky, claim that their work is an attempt to characterize the nature of $competence_2$ (that is, the nature of those human abilities that are specific to language), their main effort has in fact been directed towards a more restricted sort of competence, which we will call $competence_3$, from which by far the most important linguistic ability has been omitted—the ability to produce or understand utterances which are not so much grammatical but, more important, *appropriate to the context in which they are made* (on this point, the crux of this chapter, see also Schlesinger 1971). By 'context' we mean both the situational and the verbal context of utterances. It is interesting to note that in at least one place Chomsky allows that part of this ability belongs properly to linguistic competence: 'an essential property of language is that it provides the means for . . . reacting appropriately in an indefinite range of new situations' (1965: 6). In passing, it is also worth remarking that the gloomy, negativistic and questionable conclusions of Fodor and Garrett (1966) on the nature of the relationship between grammar and 'performance' models lose their relevance once it is realized how crucial this notion of contextual appropriateness is to the use of language, since neither the type of grammar motivating the empirical studies they discuss, nor the studies themselves, incorporate contextual information.

Of those linguistic abilities explicitly accounted for by recent transformational work, it is the ability to produce and understand indefinitely many novel sentences that has received the greatest attention. Chomsky frequently refers to this ability and for him at least it is this productivity and creativity implicit in the normal use of language that most needs explaining. Chomsky's many remarks on this point are well grounded, and he has quite properly criticized twentieth-century 'structural' linguistics and behaviourist psychology for ignoring this important aspect of language use. But one can go too far in the opposite direction. Much of what we say and write is constrained, in important ways, by the particular circumstances in which we are speaking or writing. Recent work on language acquisition and use has tended to neglect this fact.

Before continuing, we should emphasize that it is not our intention to question the productivity or creativity of language use: what we are insisting upon is the limited nature of the productivity to be explained. Nor do we wish to take issue with the validity of choosing, as a methodological decision, to limit the study of language to the level of context-less sentences. It should be recognized, however, that although a limitation of this kind may serve linguistic ends, its inevitable effect upon the psychology of language is as stultifying as that of the much-abused behaviourist approaches. The history of psychology shows that there is a very great danger of leaping from one extreme position to another when in fact the correct view of the phenomena lies somewhere in between. (A good recent example might be the incremental v. all-or-none learning controversy: cf. Simon 1968). We are therefore arguing that an adequate psychology of language must take account not only of the creative aspects of language use but also of the important role played by contextual factors.

At this point it is worth while referring to a related issue which has been grossly oversimplified in recent psycholinguistic literature. It is only too easy to infer from a casual reading of Chomsky's devastating review (1959) of Skinner or Bever, Fodor and Weksel's (1965) critique of Braine that not only have traditional learning theories very little to say on the subject of language acquisition, but also that no learning is involved at all in the process of acquiring a language and that everything is accounted for by innate predispositions. We are beyond doubt innately predisposed to 'structure information' in certain ways. As Chomsky (1965) has pointed out, even the most militant brand of empiricism presupposes some sort of innate determination. However, it is equally certain that every behavioural acquisition depends to some extent on the interaction of these predispositions with the environment. It is a matter of methodological emphasis whether one directs attention to the environmental variables or to the predispositions. However, it seems clear to us (and to this extent we are in line with traditional approaches) that it is the environmental variables that should be made the primary object of study, since they are more accessible to investigation.

There are considerable parallels between the two issues just discussed: in each there is a question of emphasis at stake, not a question of fact. In both cases it is necessary to take account both of the contribution of the individual and the contribution of the context or environment in which he acts or learns.

For the sake of future reference, let us call the two restricted types of language competence referred to above *communicative competence* (corresponding to competence$_2$) and *grammatical competence* (corresponding to competence$_3$). The rest of this chapter will be devoted to considering how the acquisition of communicative competence can be described and explained. We claim little originality for the view that communicative competence is the primary goal of the psychology of language—in this respect we are the heirs of a long tradition. This theoretical commitment is also in accord with current developments in psychology and linguistics. It can be related, for example, to the numerous recent attempts to enlarge the notion of 'grammaticality' by taking into account such contextual matters as relations between speaker and hearer (e.g. Fillmore 1968; Boyd and Thorne 1969) and referential relationships (e.g. Postal 1968; Dik 1968). It can also be related to the current tendency for linguists to describe the deepest levels of grammatical structure in semantic terms (cf. Chafe 1967, 1968; Anderson 1968; McCawley 1969). Clearly, semantically based transformational grammars hold out greater promise for the characterization of communicative competence than do grammars of the type discussed in Chomsky (1965). From these very general considerations, we turn now to more specific issues. We will begin by considering how the preceding suggestions might affect the way in which communicative competence is studied from a developmental point of view. We will then deal with the controversial issue of explaining its acquisition.

3. Many recent descriptions of syntactic development, notably that of Roger Brown and his associates (e.g. Brown and Fraser 1963; Klima and Bellugi 1966) have failed to take account of situational variables and freely admit this as a defect. Even if one's goals are limited to describing the range of grammatical structures that a child is capable of producing at a particular stage of development, there is still no escape from the necessity of specifying contexts. We can see this in the following way. Let us suppose that during a particular period of development a child is never observed to produce any passive sentences. Suppose further that certain contextual considerations are satisfied whenever such sentences are produced by adults (not an implausible suggestion: for a discussion of some of the factors relevant to the choice of the passive in English see Svartvik 1966). Then the absence of passive sentences from our sample of the child's language at this stage may be attributable either to a lack of capacity to produce this particular structure or to the absence of occasions for its production. Without the relevant contextual information, there is clearly no possibility of deciding between these two alternatives. Some support for this observation is provided by an unpublished analysis of comparative expressions in the speech of a group of pre-school children aged three-and-a-half to four. The corpus consisted of daily observations in the experimental nursery of the Edinburgh S.S.R.C. Cognition Project over a period of six months. From this analysis it is clear that comparative expressions occur much more frequently in 'comparative' situations where two or more children are vying with each other in various tasks—for example in threading strings of beads, building sandcastles, etc. Clearly, the language of a single child at home is less likely to show such structures.

The approach we are recommending would therefore involve sampling not only as much speech as possible but also as diverse a range of situations as possible, some sort of situational record being made at the same time as the speech record. The obvious alternative to this would be to construct different situations experimentally rather than simply wait for them to develop 'naturally'. Here we come up against serious problems. We cannot decide in advance what contexts are most likely to provide suitable occasions for the utterance of a particular structure. We can, however, study children's comprehension in various situations and note whether it approximates to adult comprehension in all of these; and, to the extent that it does, we can then try out eliciting contexts which work with adults with the hope that they will be close to the appropriate eliciting context for children.

At Edinburgh, we have made a detailed study of comparative expressions in pre-school children following roughly these lines. Unfortunately, the finding quoted above came too late to be used experimentally in an 'eliciting' context. In one study the eliciting context was a series of cardboard soldiers of increasing or decreasing stature. The child was first presented with two soldiers and asked to tell the experimenter about them. Questioning followed until some mention was made (or, failing that, provided by the experimenter) of their different sizes. On addition of each subsequent soldier to the series the child was asked 'And what about him?' This technique produced a full range of adjectival forms—so-called positives or absolutes (*He's big, He's a big soldier*, etc.), full comparatives (*He's bigger than him*, etc.), superlatives (*He's the biggest soldier*, etc.) as well as several 'functional' comparisons (*He's too big, He's wee enough*, etc.) which would not have been appropriate adult utterances. In another study the eliciting context involved the justification of a choice of one from a set of depicted objects varying in size for a particular purpose. Here the range of expressions was more restricted: most of them included superlatives, but 'functional' comparisons and so-called absolute adjectives were also found. Notably, almost no full comparatives were found. We say 'so-called' absolute adjectives, since another study of comprehension of expressions containing absolute adjectives has shown convincingly that, even at the age of three or so, children interpret such constructions comparatively. The details of these various studies are not relevant here (cf. Donaldson and Wales 1970; Wales and Campbell 1970; Wales 1970). These results have been mentioned merely to illustrate the effects of varying the 'eliciting' context. So far as we know, studies of this type have not been conducted in the past.

There are two kinds of investigation which we would wish to distinguish from our own. Firstly, a few recent studies (e.g. Fraser, Bellugi and Brown 1963) have tested children's production and comprehension of grammatical contrasts like singular v. plural, past v. present, etc. Strictly speaking, this technique does not measure production at all, since the child has merely to choose between two proffered oral descriptions of a picture: he does not have to describe it himself. Nor does this technique test comprehension satisfactorily, since the child has to choose between only two alternative 'depictions' of each expression. Our approach, by contrast, has been to take a particular structure, and to vary both its lexical content and the context in which it is to be comprehended.

The second group of studies we wish to refer to and compare with our own are those associated with the name of Piaget. It is often said that many studies of children's thinking in the tradition of Piaget could be reinterpreted as studies of their linguistic comprehension. While we subscribe to this general view, we would point out that one could in principle distinguish such studies in terms of the differing demands they make on cognitive and linguistic capacity. In those studies traditionally regarded as testing cognitive capacity it is assumed (possibly quite often wrongly) that the demands made upon linguistic capacity are correspondingly slight. At any rate, we are very much aware of this difficulty and for that reason we have endeavoured to make our tasks as simple as possible. Using this method with pre-school groups, we have discovered many facts which appear surprising in a Piagetian framework. For instance, expressions containing *more* are understood in the same way as the corresponding expressions containing *less*. For example, children confronted with two model trees on which model apples can be hooked tend to respond in the same way to the instruction 'Make it so that there are less apples on this tree than on this one', as they do to 'Make it so that there are more apples on this tree than on this one' (cf. Donaldson and Balfour 1968). In a classification task we have also observed that expressions containing *the same . . . as* are interpreted in the same way as the corresponding expressions containing *different . . . from.*

By defining communicative competence (competence₂) as only those human abilities that are specific to language, we have made the assumption that, although it is difficult to distinguish linguistic from cognitive competence, this is an important issue. This follows equally from Chomskyan notions of linguistic competence. The success of formal linguistics certainly buttresses the assumption that linguistic capacity is theoretically separable from other cognitive capacities. The experimental study of children's linguistic comprehension seems to provide an excellent testing-bed for this assumption.

4. We turn now to the problem of explaining the acquisition of communicative competence. As will be clear from the preceding sections, we believe that much more attention must be paid to the linguistic environment (construed here as the communicative environment) of the developing child than has been given in the recent past, without however reverting to arid stimulus-response formulations (e.g. of behaviourist explanations). Although some studies of phonological aspects of the communicative environment and their relationship to the child's phonology have been reported, very few studies of syntactic or semantic aspects have been made (we shall refer to them below). Among the questions that might be investigated are the following: (a) Is there a tendency among parents to simplify their speech when addressing children? And, if so, what form does this simplification take? (b) How do parents react to non-comprehension or mis-comprehension and how do they modify their subsequent questions or constructions? (c) What sources of information are available to the developing child about the well-formedness and appropriateness of his utterances or the accuracy of his comprehension? (d) How often does this or that construction occur in the speech of parents? (e) In what contexts are these constructions used? (f) To what extent do parents correct, repeat, expand or elaborate the speech of children and what form does their intervention take? Clearly, one could go on asking questions of this type indefinitely.

In some cases we have partial answers, in others the answer has been assumed. For instance, in a brilliant paper, Brown used as his starting-point such assumptions about the use of everyday common nouns in concrete situations as the following (1958: 15): 'the frequencies to which we are now appealing have not, of course, been recorded. We are explaining imagined preferences in names by imagined frequencies of names.' As an example, he suggests that 'when pineapples are being named, the word *pineapple* is more frequent than the word *fruit*'. On the other hand, Bresson (1963) has argued that the early learning of what such nouns refer to cannot be satisfactorily explained by appealing to the situational pairing of these nouns with their referents, since such words are rarely used in the presence of the object they refer to: one tends instead to point to the object or to use a more general term or a pronoun. If either of these apparently contradictory assumptions is correct, it must impose important constraints on the way in which we learn language; but we cannot know whether either of them is correct until some kind of empirical tests have been carried out.

Almost alone among current students of child syntax, Brown, in his more recent work, has shown a clear awareness of the importance of describing the communicative environment (cf. Brown 1968; Brown and Hanlon 1970). He has shown, for example, that, for the families on which he has data (Brown and Hanlon 1970), approval and disapproval are not primarily linked to the truth value of the proposition which the adult fits to the child's generally incomplete and often deformed sentence. . . . While there are several bases for approval and disapproval they are almost always semantic, or phonological. Explicit approval or disapproval of either syntax or morphology is extremely rare in our records and so seems not to be the force propelling the child from immature to mature forms.

Consider now question (c) above. It has often been suggested in recent psycholinguistic literature that the major source of linguistic information open to the child (the 'primary linguistic data' in the sense of Chomsky 1965: 25) is the corpus of utterances to which he is 'exposed' and that this set of utterances is meagre and fragmentary. On this assumption, it is quite understandable that so much innate predetermination has been claimed. But we feel that the 'primary linguistic data' is merely one among many such sources of information; and that it may be of relatively minor importance. For instance, Lenneberg (1967) notes that normal children of congenitally deaf parents are very little retarded in their linguistic development (although the speech of their parents is highly abnormal). This might be taken as evidence that there is a considerable innate predetermination; it seems to us to show merely that certain sources of linguistic information have been overvalued.

What then are the other sorts of information? The most salient perhaps is feedback from the child's everyday communicative acts. If his questions, wishes, demands, and so forth are comprehensible and appropriate to the occasion, they will be followed by the desired consequences. There is, however, an important methodological difficulty here: it is no straightforward matter to determine what is a wish, demand or question in the speech of children. As Chomsky (1959) pointed out with respect to Skinner's (1957) analogous notion of *mand*, it is fatuous to attempt to define such communicative acts in terms of their consequences. We must somehow divine the speaker's *intentions*.

This point is relevant to another observation made by Brown and Hanlon (1970): that there is apparently no relationship between the well-formedness of children's utterances and comprehension on the part of the parents. In fact, Brown only succeeds in distinguishing comprehension or misunderstanding, on the one hand, from lack of comprehension, on the other. Clearly we need to find ways of distinguishing correct interpretations of the child's utterances from incorrect interpretations. Brown himself seems to regard this difficulty as probably insuperable, since 'any message the investigator can make out, the family can also make out, and so the child will in fact already be communicating any idea we can be sure he has'. That is, where true misunderstanding occurs it is unlikely that we, as investigators, will be able to spot it, since the parent has failed to do so. But the child presumably can. It may well be, therefore, that we should examine all three components of the communicative act: the child's question or demand, the parental response to this and the child's response to the parent's action. Brown implicitly suggests a second possible approach when he remarks that he was only able to identify one instance of genuine misunderstanding in his corpus: Child: *What time it is?* Parent: *Uh-huh, it tells what time it is.* In view of his comments quoted above on the difficulty of spotting instances of genuine misunderstanding, it is surprising that Brown fails to see the significance of his identification of this exchange as such an instance. Clearly, it is only because he has succeeded in isolating a class of utterances of the above type as primitive question forms corresponding, in this case, to the well-formed *What time is it?*, that he has identified this interchange between child and parent as an instance of misunderstanding. It will be clear from this example how complex the study of language acquisition must be, if it is to be conducted in an informative manner.

Despite his largely negative findings (which need to be qualified in the light of the remarks we have just made about misunderstanding), Brown still holds the view that 'the empiricist position has possibilities that have not yet been explored' (1968: 290). He discusses three-termed 'interaction patterns' consisting of a question or demand from the child (or mother), a response by the mother (or child) indicating partial or complete incomprehension, and a complete or partial restatement of the original question or demand by the child (or mother). At Edinburgh we have examined similar data, obtained from transcripts of many experimental sessions with pre-school children. Brown argues that the middle-term of the exchange, *Eh?*, *What?*, etc., is understood by the child as a directive to repeat what he has just said. This is not borne out in our data, where the 'repeated' version of the first utterance is normally significantly altered (cf. Child: *Isn't a torch got a battery not a different as that?* Experimenter: *Eh?* Child: *Isn't a battery in a torch not the same as that?*) The child is attempting to produce a paraphrase or to correct his syntax or to elaborate in some way on what he previously said. The value of the resulting information (when comprehension is finally secured) is far from clear, since it depends on what the child is attempting. But it does illustrate some interesting possibilities.

Clearly, there are many ways in which a child might learn whether his utterances are well-formed or not (apart from the rather unlikely one of comparing them with stored representations of model utterances to which he has been 'exposed'). The current neglect of environmental factors in favour of 'innate ideas' (cf. Chomsky 1969) is doubly unfortunate in view of the common tendency to equate linguistic universals with innate predispositions and to overlook the possible contribution of similarities of environment and upbringing. The proper course to adopt in the investigation of language acquisition is to specify first the nature of the linguistic environment, and thus identify the possible sources of information available to the child about his language, and then to discover, presumably by experimentation, which of these possible sources are used. When that has been done, and not before, it will be time to speculate about the genetic contribution of the individual to language acquisition.

5. In the previous section we limited our discussion of language acquisition to external environmental factors. In this final section, we shall discuss briefly the role of internal factors in the development of the system of language in children. This area of cognitive psychology has been neglected until recently, except in the work of Piaget (cf. Flavell 1963), who has long urged the necessity of recognizing certain, presumably innate, principles of internal organization ('processes of equilibration', to use his term) in all areas of cognitive development.

Of course, as we have just emphasized, before claiming that a certain change of behaviour is the expression of an endogenous reorganization of some kind, it is methodologically desirable to demonstrate that it is not the result of learning (in the conventional sense). However, there is a certain type of developmental progression frequently observed to occur in young children which effectively guarantees that the development in question is not the result of learning. These are progressions where the child first of all does something 'correctly' and then, with every appearance of systematicity, later proceeds to do it 'wrongly'. Clearly, this development cannot be explained by environmental factors, since there is no adult model for the wrong behaviour. Nor can it be considered simply as one of a series of approximations to the adult model, since the erroneous behaviour is preceded by a stage in which the child behaves correctly. Perhaps the best-known example of such a progression is the over-regularization of the rule for past-tense inflection in English, which has been noted by many of the earlier workers mentioned in section 1 and recently by Ervin (1964). If one examines the child's acquisition of the past-tense forms of the strong verbs in isolation from the rest of the verb system, they can be seen to display this particular developmental sequence. However, although it is in such sequences that the existence of innate principles of organization is most clearly revealed, it seems to us that whenever we find that the child's use of language is (a) systematic (that is, reasonably constant and predictable over a period) and (b) anomalous (that is, strikingly different from the adult usage), we have evidence of the workings of such innate principles. We can see this by asking why the child's communicative competence has developed in this particular way. It cannot be the direct result of external factors, because of the anomalies, so it must be the result of some sort of endogenous systematic change. The particular form of the anomalous usage then tells us something about the character of these endogenous processes.

It is not hard to find the above characteristics. For example, a frequent topic in traditional work on language acquisition was the interplay of extension and restriction of the range of application of the child's earliest words (cf. Sully 1895; Lewis 1951; Leopold 1948: 149). It often happens that a child's usage of a particular word is initially over-extended as compared with adult usage. Each such over-extension, when systematic, tells us something about the way in which the child organizes his experience. The subsequent changes in the application of such words are a potentially rich source of information about organizational principles. The older writers quoted many cases of endogenous restriction: it was often noted that when a new word, with a range of application overlapping that of a previously acquired word, was learned, the application of the earlier word became restricted, *without benefit of instruction or correction*. Although this principle works efficiently with incompatible terms, it leads to interesting over-restrictions when one term is a hyponym of the other. (By 'hyponymy' is meant the inclusion of the meaning of one term in the meaning of another: e.g. *tulip* and *rose* are hyponyms of *flower*. cf. Lyons 1968:453.) Such over-restrictions are clear expressions of endogenous change, since they satisfy our definition of systematic error.

At Edinburgh we have obtained some data on the development of a sub-system of English adjectives, the adjectives used to describe variations of size (i.e. *big*, *tall*, *fat*, etc., and their antonyms).

The adjective *big* stands in a peculiar semantic relationship to the others. Although the relation between each of *tall, fat, long,* etc. and *big* is not strictly one of hyponymy it has similar properties, since the range of application of these terms is smaller than that of *big* and the range of application of *big* overlaps with each of their ranges. Now we have observed an interesting progression in the application of these adjectives with a number of children (too small, unfortunately, on which to base hard and fast conclusions). Initially, *big* (or its antonym *wee*) is used with reference to almost all differences of size. As the other more specialized adjectives are learned, however, *big* may fall out of use or may be restricted to cases of complex differences in size (e.g. to cases where the objects being compared both vary along two or more dimensions).

If our interpretation is correct, a further question arises: suppose that this over-restriction of the range of application of superordinate or quasi-superordinate terms is the result of an innate organizing principle which resolves overlapping ranges in this way, how does the child progress to adult usage? This is a serious problem, since, while over-extension of the range of application leads directly to overt errors, over-restriction does not do so. We have no clear ideas about this and our speculations have already run too far ahead of the facts. However, it is interesting to note that Piaget has often argued that an understanding of class-sub-class relationships is a crucial acquisition which marks a funda-mental reorganization of the child's thought and occurs usually around seven to eight years of age. Moreover the type of diagnostic test which he favours for assessing this understanding consists in, for instance, showing the child three tulips and five roses and then asking *Are there more roses or more flowers?* At lower age-levels children tend to reply that there are more roses. If children typically organize their vocabulary in the way we have suggested, then this result is hardly surprising.

This brings us right back to our remarks in section 3 on the sub-ject of distinguishing linguistic abilities from other cognitive abilities. The generative grammarians have insisted upon the methodological advantages for linguistics of making such a dis-tinction. We have argued that in any study of the acquisition and use of language this distinction needs to be revised in various ways—in ways which give explicit recognition to the communicative function of language. In doing so, we have been attempting to bridge the gap between traditional views of language acquisition and views that are dominant at the present time. We have also tried to relate the psychology of speaking to the psychology of thinking.

References

Anderson, J. M. (1968) 'On the status of "lexical formatives" ' *Foundations of Language*, 4.
Bellugi, U. and Brown, R. (1964) *The Acquisition of Language*, Monograph of the Society for Research in Child Development, 92.
Bever, T. G., Fodor, J. A. and Weksel, W. (1965) 'The acquisition of syntax: a critique of contextual generalisation' *Psych. Rev.*, 72, 467–482.
Boyd, J. and Thorne, J. P. (1969) 'The semantics of modal verbs' *Journal of Linguistics*, 5, 57–74.
Bresson, F. (1963) 'La signification'. In J. de Ajuriaguerra *et al. Problèmes de Psycholinguistique*, Paris: Presses Universitaire de France.
Brown, R. (1958) *Words and Things*, Glencoe, Illinois: Free Press.
— (1958) 'How shall a thing be called?' *Psych. Rev.*, 65, 14–21.
— (1968) 'The development of *wh*-questions in child speech' *J. Verb. Learn. Verb. Behav.*, 7, 279–90.
— and Fraser, C. (1963) 'The acquisition of syntax'. In C. N. Cofer and J. K. Musgrave (eds.) *Verbal Behavior and Learning*, New York: McGraw-Hill.
— and Hanlon, C. (1970) 'Derivational complexity and order of acquisition in child speech'. In Hayes 1970.
Chafe, W. L. (1967) 'Language as symbolisation' *Language*, 43, 57–91.
— (1968) 'Idiomaticity as an anomaly in the Chomskyan paradigm' *Foundations of Language*, 4, 109–27.
Chomsky, N. (1959) Review of *Verbal Behaviour*, *Language*, 35, 26–58.
— (1965) *Aspects of the Theory of Syntax*, Cambridge, Mass.: M.I.T. Press.
— (1969) 'Remarks on nominalisation'. In R. Jacobs and P. S. Rosenbaum *Readings in English Transformational Grammar*, Waltham, Mass.: Blaisdell.
Darwin, C. (1877) 'A biographical sketch of an infant' *Mind*, 2, 285–294.
Dik, S. (1968) 'Referential identity' *Lingua*, 21, 70–97.
Donaldson, M. C. and Balfour, G. (1968) 'Less is more: a study of language comprehension in children' *B. J. Psych.*, 59, 461–72.
— and Wales, R. (1970) 'On the acquisition of some relational terms'. In Hayes 1970.
Ervin, S. M. (1964) 'Imitation and structural change in children's

language'. In E. H. Lenneberg (ed.) *New Directions in the Study of Language*, Cambridge, Mass.: M.I.T. Press.

Ervin-Tripp, S. M. (1966) 'Language development'. In L. W. Hoffman and M. L. Hoffman (eds.) *Review of Child Development Research*, Vol 2, New York: Russell Sage Foundation.

Fillmore, C. J. (1968) 'Lexical entries for verbs' *Foundations of Language*, 4, 373–93.

Flavell, J. (1963) *The Developmental Psychology of Jean Piaget*, New York: Van Nostrand; London: Macmillan.

Fodor, J. and Garrett, M. (1966) 'Some reflections on competence and performance'. In J. Lyons and R. Wales (eds.) 1966.

Fraser C., Bellugi U. and Brown R. (1963) 'Control of grammar in imitation, comprehension, and production' *J. verb. Learn. verb. Behav.*, 2, 121–35.

Hayes, J. R. (1970) (ed.) *Cognition and the Development of Language*, New York: Wiley.

Klima, E. and Bellugi, U. (1966) 'Syntactic regularities in the speech of children'. In J. Lyons and R. Wales (eds.) 1966.

Lenneberg, E. H. (1967) *Biological Foundations of Language*, New York: Wiley.

Leopold, W. (1948) 'The study of child language and infant bilingualism' *Word*, 4, 1–17.

Lewis, M. M. (1951) *Infant Speech* (2nd Ed.), London: Routledge & Kegan Paul.

Lyons, J. (1968) *Introduction to Theoretical Linguistics*, London: Cambridge University Press.

— and Wales, R. (1966) (eds.) *Psycholinguistic Papers*, Edinburgh: Edinburgh University Press.

McCawley, J. D. (1969) 'Concerning the base component of a transformational grammar' *Foundations of Language*, 4, 243–69.

McNeill, D. (1966) 'Developmental Psycholinguistics'. In Smith and Miller (eds.) 1966.

— (1969) 'The development of language'. In P. A. Mussen (ed.) *Carmichael's Manual of Child Psychology*, New York: Wiley.

Moravcsik, J. M. E. (1967) 'Linguistic theory and the philosophy of language' *Foundations of Language*, 3, 209–38.

— (1969) 'Competence, creativity and innateness' *Philosophical Forum*, 1, 407–37.

Postal, P. M. (1968) *Aspects of Phonological Theory*, New York: Harper & Row.

Preyer, W. (1882) *Die Seele des Kindes*. In H. W. Brown *The Mind of the Child*, New York: Appleton.

Reed, C. (1970) (ed.) *The Learning of Language*, New York: Scribners.

Richter, F. (1927) *Die Entwicklung der Psychologischen Kindersprachforschung*, Münster.

Schlesinger, I. M. (1971) 'Production of utterances and language acquisition'. In Slobin (ed.) 1971.

Shinn, N. W. (1893) *Notes on the Development of a Child*, Berkeley: University of California.

Simon, H. A. (1968) 'On judging the plausibility of theories'. In B. van Rootselaar and J. F. Staal (eds.) *Logic, Methodology and Philosophy of Science III*, Amsterdam: North Holland.

Slobin, D. I. (ed.) (1971) *The Ontogenesis of Language*, New York: Academic Press.

Smith, F. and Miller, G. A. (eds.) (1966) *The Genesis of Language*, Cambridge, Mass.: M.I.T. Press.

Stern, C. and Stern, W. (1928) *Die Kindersprache*, 4th Edn. Leipzig: Barth.

Stern, W. (1924) *Psychology of Early Childhood*, London: Allen & Unwin.

Sully, J. (1895) *Studies of Childhood*, London: Longman.

Svartvik, J. (1966) *On Voice in the English Verb*, The Hague: Mouton.

Taine, H. (1877) 'On the acquisition of language by children' *Mind*, **2**, 252–9.

Wales, R. J. (1970) 'On comparing and contrasting'. In J. Morton (ed.) *Language with Psychology*, London: Logos Press.

— and Campbell, R. N. (1970) 'The development of comparison and the comparison of development'. In F. d'Arias, M. L. M. Levell (eds.) *Advances in Psycholinguistics*, Amsterdam: North Holland.

The Contribution of Experience

In this reading extracted from his book, *The Acquisition of Language*, McNeill puts in a clear and well-argued way the reasons why the context and the environment surrounding a linguistic event should not be included when considering language acquisition. One of his most important contributions can be seen in Smith and Miller (1966) in his article *Developmental Psycholinguistics* in which he, for the first time, collates and relates empirical evidence from three different research projects into the language acquisition process.

We would now most probably say that however justified theoretically McNeill's approach is (and remember that it is a theoretical justification only) it has certain drawbacks:

(a) It has the implicit belief that the developmental pattern of language acquisition which emerges from the study of a few children will be almost universal.

(b) The children were chosen from a restricted background—highly educated middle-class homes where the parents were intimately involved in their own and their children's educational development.

(c) The contexts in which the utterances were used were not considered important. This led to two further problems:

(d) The syntactic structure of each utterance was not related to the range of possible meanings and functions the utterance could have in the context. This weakness is especially criticized by Bloom in the next reading.

(e) The immediate linguistic context of the utterance was not thought to be of particular significance. We now realize that utterances do not occur in a vacuum but have some over-all relationship to the whole of the verbal interaction.

In the few years separating his article and the book from which this reading is taken there is no fundamental shift in McNeill's position. As he says in the reading (see **p. 34**):

There is a disappointing inconclusiveness to what can be said concerning the contribution of experience to language acquisition.

This has to be seen as an attack, even at a late stage, on the behaviourist point of view; it is not an attack on the work of such men as Bernstein or Labov whose works show that social background (or the experience of it) can affect what type of language the child acquires and what range of functions and use of language is available.

We now have what appears to be a general principle: Children form relationships with ease, but require time to learn the restrictions on relationships. The contribution of experience will therefore be largest in those regions of grammar where general rules apply least. The meanings of individual words are merely the most extreme form of linguistic information not covered by general rules; there are many less extreme cases and we can draw a continuum between the lexicon at one end and the most general rules at the other for each language separately. If the principle suggested is correct, the order of acquisition will correspond to the order of rules along this continuum, with the most general rules being learned first and dictionary entries being completed last. The observations of C. S. Chomsky (1969) show this order of acquisition.

A natural assumption is that the relationships which children form with greatest ease are the universal types of transformation. Rules that use these relationships with the fewest restrictions will be the first a child acquires. As noted, there are only about a half-dozen universal types of transformations; the complexity of the actual transformational rules of a language arises through the combinations of and restrictions on these universal types. It is not unreasonable to regard the universal transformational rules as being an aspect of man's capacity for language. They describe relationships for which we have a special sensitivity, and hence are maximally able to discover. One of the universal transformational relationships is permutation. It is involved, for example, in the derivation of wh-questions. Young children have great difficulty in copying the left-to-right order of arrays of objects. Usually this difficulty is interpreted as showing an absence of something —a schema for order, for example. But equally it shows an ability to permute order. Languages exploit this ability in the form of a universal transformational relation. That adults are less open to such confusions, having well-established schemas for order, may be one aspect of their declining capacity for language (cf. Lenneberg 1967, for a discussion of critical periods in language acquisition).

However, even adults show a special sensitivity to permutation in particular situations. In solving anagrams, for instance, two parallel processes of permutation can take place. One is conscious, deliberate, overt, and typical of adults; the other is unconscious, spontaneous, covert, and presumably typical of children. The following is the record of one adult solving LEKISTL, an anagram for a common kitchen utensil: ketsil, setkill, siktell, teksill, ell, sell, lel, kell, ketsill, kitsell (the subject saw the solution at this point), silklet, skillet. She tries out various combinations, following a strategy that often produces a solution. However, in this example the last of the deliberate permutations (kitsell) bears little resemblance to the answer, and the sequence from ketsil to kitsell represents almost no movement. Rather than deliberate permutation, a second covert process of permutation was taking place, and reached the solution first.

The present chapter describes what is known of the way a child's linguistic experience contributes to his acquisition of language. What is known is largely negative: learning does *not* take place through imitation; overt practice with linguistic forms does *not* play a role. More positively, we can identify 'training situations' that arise during the interactions of adults and children where information about transformations is, as it were, put on display.

Since the role played by experience is greater with rules that carry more restrictions, we should focus attention on these most restricted cases, but it is not possible to do so. Ironically, most efforts to show the contribution of experience to language acquisition, which have had the goal of establishing a place for learning theory, have concentrated on the simplest cases, i.e., the ones where experience plays the least role. As a consequence, nothing much can be said about even the basic questions. What amount of exposure, for instance, and what kind of material, is necessary to learn restrictions on general rules? How does the necessary amount of experience depend on the kind of restriction being learned?

Imitation

One traditional view of language acquisition has the process advance through imitation. It has not always been clear precisely what this theory means. The word 'imitation' possesses two quite different senses, and only one can be applied to language acquisition. In one sense, 'imitation' refers to resemblance—one person comes to resemble another more and more closely. The trait on which the resemblance develops must necessarily be arbitrarily variable within broad limits. Resemblance in height is not the result of imitation, but etiquette and driving on the left side of the road in England are. In this sense, language also is acquired through imitation. In the second, more technical sense, 'imitation' refers to a process whereby behaviour is acquired by copying the behaviour of a model. Such a view was applied to language acquisition by Allport (1924) and has occupied a place in psychology ever since. It is in this second technical sense that language cannot be said to result from imitation.

There is no question that children imitate the speech of adults. In fact they do it a great deal. Fully 10 per cent of children's speech at 28–35 months is imitative in the records collected by Brown (unpublished materials). There are, for example, such exchanges as the following (different adults and children are speaking):

ADULT	CHILD
Oh, that's a big one	big one
But, he was much bigger than Perro	big a Perro
Salad dressing	salad dressing
That's not a screw	dat not a screw
Are they all there?	all dere?

The fact that children imitate the speech of adults does not mean that the process of acquisition is imitation. *It runned, allgone shoe*, and *a that man* have no models in adult speech but are grammatical within a child's system. The system in which these forms are grammatical clearly could not have been derived from imitation.

It is possible, however, that adult forms are introduced into a child's speech through imitation. As long as a child's grammar is not fully developed he might produce such utterances as *a that man* but enrich his grammar through the imitation of well-formed examples. In this case, imitations will be 'advanced' grammatically relative to spontaneous speech. Ervin (1964) looked into this possibility by comparing children's spontaneously occurring imitations to their spontaneously occurring free speech. The grammatical organization of the imitations was identical with the organization of the free speech. Only one child in Ervin's sample of five was an exception, and in her case imitation went in the wrong direction and was more primitive.

The result reflects a general characteristic of child speech. There is a strong tendency among children to include nothing in the surface structures of sentences that cannot be related to deep structures—i.e., nothing for which there is no transformational derivation known. The principle encompasses spontaneous speech as well as imitation. If a child does not yet include the progressive inflection *-ing* in his speech, he will not imitate *-ing* in the speech of adults, particularly if the adult model is long relative to his memory span. *Adam's nose is dripping* might be imitated *Adam nose drip* but probably not *Adam nose dripping*. It is for this reason that imitation can be used as a test of children's productive capacities.

The resistance of children to new forms sometimes goes to extravagant lengths. Consider, for example, the following exchange between one mother and her child (from McNeill 1966a):

Child	*Nobody don't like me*
Mother	*No, say 'nobody likes me'*
Child	*Nobody don't like me*
	(*eight repetitions of this dialogue*)
Mother	*No, now listen carefully;*
	say 'nobody likes me'
Child	*Oh! Nobody don't likes me*

It is possible to instruct children to imitate, as Slobin and Welsh (1967) and Fraser, Bellugi, and Brown (1963) have done. Under these circumstances, a child's imitations may depart from his grammar. But enforced imitation is not typical of the ordinary circumstances of child speech, and phenomena observed here cannot be extended automatically to the actual acquisition of grammatical structures.

Rather than serving a didactic purpose, imitation often seems to be carried out in play. It is the opposite of instruction, therefore, if indeed it has any effect at all. A child manipulates the grammatical system already at his disposal, often in fantastic ways, but he does not go beyond it. The effect, if any, would be to reinforce the primitive structure. Take as an example one of Brown's subjects, who, starting from an ordinary imitation, went on in a fugue-like manner (mentioned by Slobin 1964; also McNeill 1966a):

Adult	*That's the tattooed man*
Child	*Tooman. Tattoo man. Find too tattoo man.*
	Tattoo man. Who dat? Tattoo. Too man go, mommy?
	Too man. Tattoo man go? Who dat? Read dat.
	Tractor dere. Tattoo man.

Weir (1962) found many examples of similar grammatical play in the pre-sleep soliloquies of her two-and-a-half-year-old son. The child selected a particular paradigm—sometimes grammatical, sometimes phonological—and then elaborated on it with a stream of examples. The following uses a syntactic paradigm. It might be considered the linguistic equivalent of building up and knocking down a tower of blocks.

go for glasses
go for them
go to the top
go throw
go for blouse
pants
go for shoes

We thus arrive at a negative conclusion: The contribution of parental speech to language acquisition is not to supply specimens for children to imitate.

Overt Practice

One implication of the phenomenon of inflectional imperialism is that overt practice has no influence on whether or not a form remains in a child's grammar. The regular past-tense inflection in English was so rare in the speech of Ervin's (1964) children that it appeared first on the frequent strong verbs. These verbs, in contrast, had been used for months with their correct irregular inflections. This extensive practice added nothing to the stability of the irregular inflections, which were swept away by the regular inflection, when it appeared. Obviously overt practice is not essential for developing restrictions on general rules, since it is the conflict with a general rule that in this case removes the correct and well-practised inflection.

Reinforcement by Approval

Behaviourist psychologists define a reinforcer as an event that increases the probability of a response. There is no arguing with such a circular definition, except to point out the circularity, but one can look at particular cases and see if they fit the definition. An event commonly alleged to be a reinforcer to young children is parental approval. Brown *et al.* (1968) examined all the instances of approval that appeared in the records of their three subjects, and found that its occurrence depended only on the truth value of what the child said. Grammatical form was irrelevant. A child could say *that's Popeye's* and be told 'no' if it was Mickey's, but he could say under the same circumstances *that Mickey* and be told 'yes'. Obviously, approval, if it is a reinforcer, will increase the probability of grammatically incorrect forms as much as it does grammatically correct ones. By the usual circular definition, therefore, approval cannot be a reinforcer of grammatical form.

Training Situations

As already noted, imitation fails to affect child language because of a strong tendency in children to assimilate adult specimens to their current grammars. One way to avoid assimilation is to place the burden of introducing new forms on adults. Brown *et al.* (1968) discuss three situations that could conceivably have this result, 'expansion', 'modelling', and 'prompting'.

An expansion is an imitation in reverse. An adult, repeating a child's telegraphic sentence, typically adds the parts he judges to have been omitted. There is usually a number of possible adult sentences available as expansions. *That mummy hairband*, for example, could be expanded to become *that's mummy's hairband, that was mummy's hairband until you dismantled it, that looks like mummy's hairband*, etc. But often one sentence will best fit the extralinguistic situation, and that sentence becomes the expansion. If the child's meaning is correctly grasped, an expansion presents a surface structure that expresses the deep structure the child has in mind. The expansion is necessarily experienced by the child in contiguity with his intended meaning and can be effective when the child notices the way the two are related.

Cazden (1965) looked into the effectiveness of this training situation by deliberately increasing the number of expansions given to children. The children were two-and-a-half years old, spent each weekday in a nursery school, were from working-class homes, and received in the normal course of events few expansions either at school or at home. (Expansion is something middle-class parents, especially, do.) In Cazden's experiment every child spent one-half hour a day, five days a week, looking at picture books with an adult who systematically expanded everything the child said. At the beginning and at the end of the experiment, three months later, the children were given a specially devised test of linguistic performance (covering, for example, NP and VP complexity and the imitation of various syntactic forms). These children were compared to two other groups of children, in the same nursery school, who received in one case what Cazden called 'models' and in the other no special treatment at all. 'Modelling' is commenting—everything said by a child is commented upon, rather than improved upon, as in expansion. If a child said *doggie bite*, for example, an expansion might be *yes, he's biting*, whereas a model might be *yes, he's very mad*. Children in the modelling group also spent one-half hour a day, five days a week, looking at picture books with an adult.

The results were clear cut. Modelling was better than expanding. Relative to the group of children who received no special treatment there was a modest gain in linguistic performance among the children who received expansions but a large gain among those who received models. A greater variety of syntactic and lexical forms is required for modelling compared to expanding child speech, as Cazden pointed out. In expansion an adult is closely led by a child—he must use the child's words and something like the child's syntax—while in modelling he must avoid the child's words and often his syntax. Apparently, it is not helpful for linguistic development when a child's utterances constrain the structure and content of adult speech; however, it is this very fact that should make expansion advantageous.

Cazden apparently has shown that modelling assists linguistic development (an opposite result will be mentioned below), but it is not clear that she has shown that expansions do not. Middle-class parents expand about 30 per cent of the speech of their children. One can ask why this rate is not higher, say 50 or 70 per cent. One reason must be that not everything said by a child is interpretable in the extralinguistic context. In such circumstances adults would tend not to expand. In Cazden's experiment, on the other hand, the rate of expansion was by design, 100 per cent. Young children might not pay attention to expansions in the face of such an avalanche (Brown *et al.* 1968). And even if they do pay attention some utterances in Cazden's experiment must have been inappropriately expanded (McNeill 1966b). When an expansion goes astray a child could formulate a rule that does not exist in English. He might, for example, relate the meaning of 'that's mummy's hairband' to *that looks like mummy's hairband*. The poor showing of expansion in Cazden's experiment is, therefore, to be expected even on the assumption that expansions are the only method for the acquisition of transformations. A study by Feldman and Rodgon (1970) compared 'contingent' expansions (only clear utterances expanded) to 'non-contingent' expansions (all utterances expanded) and found, as expected from the argument above, that contingent expansions helped more than non-contingent. What was surprising, however, was that *both* kinds of expansions were superior to modelling. Feldman and Rodgon's subjects were similar to Cazden's in age (two-and-a-half) and background (poor urban black families), and had had similar school experiences (day care centres). The test of linguistic ability were not identical in the two experiments but were at least similar. It is not clear why a different result appeared with modelling. The relative effectiveness of expansion and modelling remains an open question.

Brown *et al.* (1968) have looked at expansion in another way. As noted before, to calibrate linguistic development they use mean length of utterance rather than, as usual, chronological age. When the calibration is carried out in this way the fastest of Brown's three subjects is Sarah, the next fastest is Adam, and the slowest is Eve. We can compare this order to the order of expansion by the children's parents, which gives Adam, Eve, and Sarah. Sarah, who is most advanced, therefore, was the one who received the fewest expansions. Let us focus on the contrast between Eve and Sarah, for they present the sharpest differences. It so happens that at any given utterance length Eve used fewer modal verbs, inflections, prepositions, articles, and other superficial sentence forms than did Sarah, while Sarah used fewer nouns, verbs, and adjectives. Thus, at any given utterance length, Sarah's speech was syntactically more like adult English, as Brown *et al.* point out, but Eve's was more informative. Sarah might have said *that's mommy's hairband*, a well-formed sentence five morphemes long, whereas Eve might have said, semigrammatically but with the same length, *that mommy broken hairband there*. Cazden (1967) concludes from this difference that Eve's intellectual development was greater than Sarah's. Such a difference may well exist. At any given length of utterance Eve included more information than Sarah did. But this comparison does not bear on the role of expansions, if this role is to facilitate the acquisition of transformations or the learning of restrictions on them. A child who receives more expansions has more opportunities to observe relations between underlying and well-formed surface structures. An appropriate base-line against which to measure this effect is chronological age. And on the scale of chronological age, Eve's linguistic development is far in advance of Sarah's.

The role or lack of role of expansion in linguistic development is thus open to dispute. The two experiments done on the phenomenon have contradictory outcomes. The evidence of recorded adult and child speech is interpretable in opposite ways, depending on the base-line of comparison.

'Prompting' is discussed by Brown *et al.* as another possible training situation, but its effectiveness is yet to be investigated.

One transformation in the derivation of English wh-questions is the preposing of Δ. *Dinosaurs can eat* Δ becomes Δ *dinosaurs can eat*. In a 'prompt' something very much like preposing is directly demonstrated to a child. A prompt begins with a wh-question from an adult—*What did you eat?* If the child does not answer, the adult might repeat the question in a different form—*You ate what?* The second version differs from the first in several respects, one being that preposing has not occurred. If a child understands the second question, and so has in mind the deep structure *you eat* Δ, he is in a position to observe the relation of this deep structure to the surface structure of *What did you eat?* For a child who has not formulated the preposing transformations, a prompt may provide the occasion to do so. Brown *et al.* note that children usually answer non-preposed questions, so prompting is at least potentially effective in revealing preposing to a child.

Brown *et al.* describe a third parent–child exchange, 'echoing', which also can be mentioned, although it does not correspond to any transformation and therefore cannot demonstrate one to a child. An echo begins with an utterance from a child that is in part unintelligible—for example, *I ate the gowish*. An adult may then echo the child but replace the unintelligible part with a wh-word—*You ate the what?* The form of the adult question is the same as in prompting. However, even if a child understands the adult question, he could not discover preposing. The only relations in an echo exist, on the one hand, between *you ate* Δ and the surface structure of *You ate the what?*, and on the other hand between *you ate* Δ and the answer *I ate the gowish*.

Echoing might therefore tell a child something about answering questions but not about preposing wh-words. It might also help him discover what in his own utterance belongs to a single sentence constituent (Brown *et al.* 1968); e.g., the *what* of *You ate what?* replaces an NP in the child's own sentence. It can, therefore, help in the learning of restrictions on rules.

For a child to discover a transformation (though not to discover the restrictions on transformations) a strange interpersonal contiguity must be brought about. Expansion, prompting, and imitation provide this contiguity, but echoing and modelling do not. The contiguity is this: To observe a transformational relation not yet known, an underlying structure that comes only from the child must be made contiguous with a surface structure that comes only from an adult. Diagrammatically,

TRANSFORMATIONAL

CHILD	RELATION	ADULT
Underlying structure	?	Surface structure

In other words, something in the child's mind must be brought together with something in the adult's speech. This contiguity must exist to understand a transformational relation as well as to produce one, so the gap between comprehension and production does not explain how it is overcome.

An expansion makes an adult surface structure contiguous with a child's underlying structure when the adult correctly infers the child's meaning. A prompt does so when a child understands the revised wh-question. Expansions and prompts therefore differ in who must do the comprehending. An imitation brings a surface structure together with the right underlying structure when a child repeats an adult sentence which he correctly understands on non-linguistic grounds. Echoing, however, never places an adult surface structure together with a child's correct underlying structure. And modelling, by definition, avoids meeting this condition. It is obvious that contiguity is not the only factor determining the acquisition of transformations. If it were, imitation would help and modelling would not.

There is a disappointing inconclusiveness to what can be said concerning the contribution of experience to language acquisition. Even the training situations described by Brown *et al.*, which are only four among what must be many, merely place linguistic information on display. The question of how a child notices and absorbs this information is not touched. Our state of knowledge is remote from anything envisioned in behaviourist theories of language learning (e.g., Osgood 1968). Not only is there nothing calling for behaviourist principles of language acquisition, but when situations favourable to response learning are examined, such as imitation or overt practice, one finds no effects that behaviourist principles can explain.

References

Allport, E. H. (1924) *Social Psychology*, Cambridge, Mass.: Houghton-Mifflin.

Brown, R., Cazden, C. and Bellugi, U. (1968) 'The Child's Grammar from I to III'. In J. P. Hill (ed.) *The 1967 Minnesota Symposium on Child Psychology*, University of Minnesota Press.

Cazden, C. (1965) 'Environmental Assistance to the Child's Acquisition of Grammar', Unpubl. Ph.D. Thesis, Harvard University.

— (1967) 'The acquisition of noun and verb inflections'. Paper given at Dept. of Social Relations, Harvard University.

Chomsky, C. S. (1969) *The Acquisition of Syntax in Children from 5 to 10*, Cambridge, Mass.: M.I.T Press.

Ervin, S. (1964) 'Imitation and structural change in children's language'. In E. H. Lenneberg (ed.) *New Directions in the Study of Language*, Cambridge, Mass.: M.I.T. Press.

Feldman, C. F. and Rodgon, M. (1970) 'The effects of various types of adult responses in the syntactic acquisition of two- to three-year-olds'. Unpubl. paper, Dept. of Psychology, University of Chicago.

Fraser, C., Bellugi, U. and Brown, R. (1963) 'Control of grammar in imitation, comprehension, and production' *J. Verb. Learning Verb. Behav.*, **2**, 121–35.

Lenneberg, E. H. (1967) *Biological Foundations of Language*, New York: Wiley.

McNeill, D. (1966a) 'Developmental Psycholinguistics'. In F. Smith and G. A. Miller (eds.) *The Genesis of Language*, Cambridge, Mass.: M.I.T. Press.

— (1966b) 'The creation of language by children'. In J. Lyons and R. Wales (eds.) *Psycholinguistic Papers*, Edinburgh University Press.

Osgood, C. E. (1968) 'Towards a wedding of insufficiencies'. In T. Dixon and D. Horton (eds.) *Verbal Behaviour and General Behaviour Theory*, Englewood Cliffs: Prentice-Hall.

Slobin, D. I. (1964) 'Imitation and the acquisition of syntax'. Paper presented at the Second Research Planning Conference of Project Literacy.

— and Welsh, C. A. (1967) 'Elicitated imitation as a research tool in developmental psycholinguistics'. Unpubl. paper, Dept. Psychol., Berkeley: University of California.

Weir, R. (1962) *Language in the Crib*, The Hague: Mouton.

3 LOIS BLOOM
Language in a Context

This article has been developed from her larger study (Bloom 1970) in which she specifically tries to relate the context and the meaning of children's utterances to their structure. Bloom's work has opened up the study of child language acquisition to include the concomitant development of certain underlying conceptual relations. These concepts are psychological, sociological, and emotional. Her discussion about the utterance 'Mommy sock' which was heard in two different contexts on the same day is justly famous.

Summary

Children's early attempts at syntax have been described in the recent language development literature in terms of 'pivot grammar.' The pivot-open class distinction is discussed in the light of the author's more recent research that inquired into the semantic intentions that underlie early sentences. When utterances were examined along with context and behaviour in the speech events in which they occurred, certain underlying conceptual relations could be identified. It is concluded that the 'pivot grammar' account is only a superficial characterization of the form and distribution of linguistic elements in early two-word utterances. It is suggested that a more productive model of early language development to use for evaluation and treatment of language pathology would need to specify the semantic relations among objects and events that are coded by syntax.

Recent studies of language development have focused attention on the early stages of emerging syntax—the use of two-word and three-word sentences sometime during the second half of the second year of life. A number of investigators have reported similar distributional phenomena in samples of early child speech. When children begin to use two words in juxtaposition there are often a small number of words that occur frequently, in relatively fixed position, in combination with a large number of other words,

Lois Bloom: Extract from 'Why not pivot grammar?', *Journal of Speech and Hearing Disorders*, XXXVI, 1, 1971, pp. 40–9.

each of which occurs less frequently. Braine (1963) named this first group of words 'pivots'; children's speech has since been described in the literature as 'pivotal', and an account of the systematic productivity of early utterances is often referred to in terms of 'pivot grammar'. The apparent convergence on this point in the literature (in particular, Bellugi and Brown 1964; McNeill 1966a) has led to its application to programmes for language disorders (see, for example, McNeill 1966b). However, more recent research (Bloom 1970) and a careful examination of earlier studies, such as the classic diary study of Leopold (1949), indicate that the time is at hand for a re-evaluation of the phenomenon. How real is pivot grammar?

This paper will begin with a review of the original evidence. Subsequently, several important questions will be raised concerning the adequacy of the notion of pivot grammar as an account of what children know about grammar as they begin to use syntax in their speech. Recent evidence of the underlying conceptual relations in children's early speech will be reported, and, finally, this information will be discussed as it relates to possible approaches to language disorders in children.

The Original Evidence

The studies of Braine (1963), Miller and Ervin (1964), and Brown and Fraser (1963) were essentially distributional studies. They viewed children's speech as evidence, potentially, of a distinctive language, and for this reason they were admirably motivated to avoid the classes and categories of adult speech in their accounts. As a linguist would approach an exotic language in order to describe its grammar, these investigators looked at large numbers of children's utterances, and described what they saw in terms of classes of words based on their privileges of occurrence. What they found was essentially an orderly arrangement of at least two, possibly three, classes of words. Certain words, such as 'no', 'no more', 'all gone', 'more', 'this', 'that', 'here', 'there', 'off', 'on', occurred frequently, in fixed position as either the first or second constituent in a two-word utterance, and shared contexts with a larger number of words that occurred relatively less frequently. Braine (1963) referred to the classes as 'pivots' and 'x-words', Brown and Fraser (1963) referred to 'functors' and 'contentives', and Miller and Ervin (1964) referred to 'operators' and 'non-operators'.

Only Braine (1963) was discussing a relatively complete corpus. His data consisted of (1) the records kept by the mothers of two boys of all of their first two-word utterances over a period of several months, and (2) tape-recorded samples of a third boy's speech during play sessions. Brown and Bellugi (1964) described only the constituents of noun phrases and the developmental differentiation of the initial position modifier class. Brown and Fraser (1963) and Miller and Ervin (1964) presented for discussion lists of two-word and three-word utterances that demonstrated the distributional phenomenon—for example, utterances with 'this' and 'that' or 'Mum' and 'Dad'.

McNeill (1966a), using some of Brown's data, presented an extended account of the 'pivotal' nature of children's speech. He viewed the original classes of pivots and x-words, or, as he named them, 'open' words (because of the apparent tendency of the class to admit new members freely), as the original generic classes from which all the category classes of the adult model ultimately develop, through some sort of differentiation. McNeill (1970) has since refined his distinction between pivot forms and other forms further, in terms of their syntactic features with respect to co-occurrence with noun forms. Essentially, his account specifies all noun forms as an unmarked class in the child's lexicon—the class of 'open' words. All other words are marked forms—marked, in the sense that they are identified as occurring only with nouns— the verbs, modifiers, and determiners which constitute the originally undifferentiated 'pivot' class.

At least two critical questions can be raised about the adequacy of the pivot grammar notion as an account of children's early speech. First, how does pivot grammar relate to the grammar of the adult, model language? Large enough samples of adult speech would undoubtedly reveal similar kinds of distributional evidence based on relative frequency of occurrence (see Zipf 1965). Certain words such as determiners, pronouns, and other function words or syntactic markers occur more frequently and in more varied linguistic environments in adult speech than do verbs, adjectives, and nouns. However, such rules of grammar as 'pivot+open', 'open+pivot', or 'open+open' have no real analogy among the syntactic structures of the adult model. How does the child progress from using pivotal utterances to using utterances that reflect the complex interrelation of rules that is the essence of adult phrase structure? McNeill, in both of the foregoing accounts, attempted to deal with this question. However, his conclusions are based upon certain assumptions—for example, that pivot forms do not occur in isolation, and that two nouns cannot occur together—that simply are not supported in the data.

The second question concerns the adequacy of the pivot grammar account for describing and explaining children's early speech. What does the notion of pivot grammar tell us about what children know about grammar when they begin to use syntax in their speech?

The Adequacy of a Pivot Grammar Account

The studies just discussed focused attention on the formal syntax of children's speech—on the arrangements of words in utterances. However, such descriptions of the form of speech provide minimal information about the child's intuitive knowledge of a linguistic code. Linguistic expression is intimately connected with cognitive-perceptual development and the child's interaction in a world of objects, events, and relations. The goal of the research discussed here (and reported at length in Bloom 1970) was to investigate the development of linguistic behaviour in relation to aspects of experience related to the speech children use.

The subjects of the study—Kathryn, Eric, and Gia—were the first-born children of white, college-educated, American English-speaking parents. They were each visited in their homes for approximately eight hours over a period of several days. Each sample of spoken language (at six-week intervals) was obtained during the child's (1) play with a selected group of toys, (2) eating, dressing, and toileting, and (3) play with a peer. The syntactic components of generative grammars were proposed for the earliest texts with mean length of utterance less than 1·5 morphemes. The syntactic and semantic development of negation was described until mean length of utterance was approximately 3·0 morphemes (in Bloom 1970). Kathryn was 21 months old when the study began; Eric and Gia were each 19 months, one week old.

Judgements were made of the semantic intent of utterances, based upon clues from the context and behaviour in the speech events in which utterances occurred. Using this kind of information an attempt was made to propose rules of grammar to account for the inherent semantic relations that underlie the juxtaposition of words in early sentences. The notion of sentence structure implies a pattern of organization—an arrangement of otherwise independent parts that is based on the relationship of the parts to each other—which is something more than simply a sequence of words. The semantic relations that were coded in the children's speech were essentially of two kinds: functional relations with invariable grammatical meaning, and grammatical relations with variable grammatical meaning between constituents in subject-predicate relationship.

Functional Relations: Semantics of Certain Pivot Forms

To begin with, the data from Kathryn, Eric, and Gia contained utterances that were similar to those reported in the earlier studies and described as pivotal: Kathryn's utterances with 'no', 'this', 'that', 'more', and 'hi'; Gia's utterances with 'more' and 'hi'; and Eric's utterances with 'no', 'another', 'there', and 'it'. The children's use of these forms, in terms of semantic intention, could be described with some confidence. 'No' most often signalled the non-existence of the referent named by the second constituent (as in 'no pocket'), where there was some expectation of its existence in the context of the speech event. 'More' or 'another' was used to comment on or to request the recurrence or another instance of an object or event (as in 'more raisin' and 'more read'). 'This' and 'that', and 'there' were not contrastive in proximal distal reference, and were used to point out an object or event in the environment (as in 'this book', or 'this cleaning'). 'Hi', which occurred less frequently, was used in a non-salutatory way as the child took notice of an object, person, or picture (as in 'Hi shadow', 'Hi spoon', 'Hi Jocelyn'). The forms occurred frequently, in fixed syntactic position, with a number of different words, and they shared contexts. All occurred as single-word utterances as well. However, they occurred with specific semantic intent, either in relation to the words with which they were juxtaposed or with inherent relation to something not specified, in the case of single-word utterances. Their use was motivated by their semantic function; they occurred in speech events that shared features of context and behaviour. This last point is of considerable importance; certain words occur often in children's speech apparently because of the nature of their referential function. Description of such utterances as pivotal is only a superficial description of relative frequency of occurrence and syntactic position.

Moreover, it turned out that the utterances described as pivotal, in the limited sense just indicated, proved to be a small percentage of the total number of utterances that were obtained from Gia and Kathryn. Only Eric's speech—during the period of time under discussion, when mean length of utterance was less than 1·5 morphemes—contained a preponderance of utterances such as have been so far described. The majority of the utterances of Kathryn and Gia presented certain critical problems for a pivot grammar account.

There were certain words in the children's speech that met all the distributional criteria for specification as pivots. The most frequent of these was either 'Mommy' or reference to self—either by first name or, in Kathryn's case, 'Baby' as well. However, not only did syntactic utterances with 'Mommy' occur frequently, but it was also the case that 'Mommy' occurred in relatively fixed position. For example, in 32 sentences with 'Mommy' in the first speech sample from Kathryn (when mean length of utterance was 1·32), 'Mommy' occurred in sentence-initial position 29 times. Moreover, 'Mommy' also shared contexts with other forms, for example 'Mommy sock' and 'no sock', 'Mommy haircurl' and 'more haircurl'.

One immediate objection to 'Mommy' as pivot is that 'Mommy' is a form having lexical status as a substantive or content word rather than a function word or syntactic marker. There is something intuitively wrong about classing 'Mommy' as a function word, and, indeed, there has been a general inclination to avoid such characterization in the literature (see, for example, the discussion in Smith and Miller 1966).

However, more important reasons for arguing against the distributional evidence that would class 'Mommy' as a pivot or function form had to do with the fact that different utterances with 'Mommy' meant different things. For example, in the first sample from Kathryn, the utterance 'Mommy sock' occurred twice in two separate contexts:

(1) Kathryn picking up her mother's sock
(2) Mommy putting Kathryn's sock on Kathryn

It appeared that the difference in semantic interpretation between the two utterances corresponded to a structural difference in grammatical relationship between the constituents 'Mommy' and 'sock'. In one instance the structure was a genitive relation and in the other the relation between subject and object.

Grammatical Relations

Constructions with two substantive forms (the 32 utterances with 'Mommy' and 24 utterances with 'Baby' or 'Kathryn', for example) were described by Braine (1963) and McNeill (1966a) as the juxtaposition of two x-words or open class words, respectively. But whether such utterances are classed together as 'pivot+open' or 'open+open', the two instances of 'Mommy sock' would have the same structural description in either case, because the surface form of each is the same. Rules that account for utterances in terms of the juxtaposition of pivots and open words cannot account for differences in semantic interpretation. And yet there was strong evidence in the data for ascribing different structural descriptions to utterances with similar surface form but different underlying relationship between constituents. The full argument regarding the correct structural representation of such utterances has already been presented (Bloom 1970). For the purpose of this paper, it will be pointed out that interpretation of the semantic intent of utterances with two substantive forms provided evidence that the children knew more about grammar at this early stage than merely rules for permitted juxtaposition of two different kinds of words.

There were a number of potential interpretations of the utterances that occurred with 'Mommy' in constructions with nouns.

The first possibility was that the child had simply named two aspects of a referent, or two referents, within the bounds of a single utterance—a conjunction (for example, 'Mommy' and 'sock'). If one interpreted children's use of single-word utterances (before and during the emergence of syntax) as labelling or naming behaviour, then this would be an intuitively appealing interpretation of the juxtaposition of two noun forms within an utterance. If such were the case, and the two noun forms were simply conjoined without connection or with any possible connection between them, one could reasonably expect the constituents to be named in variable order. If the child had simply named two referents, or two aspects of a referent, there would be no motivation for naming them in a particular order. But the occurrence of 'Mommy' in sentence-initial position 29 times in the 32 utterances that included 'Mommy' was impressive evidence that the motivation for the order of the constituents was strong.

In addition to the utterances with 'Mommy', there were 37 other noun+noun constructions in the first sample of Kathryn's speech and 66 utterances that juxtaposed two nouns in the second sample of Gia's speech (when mean length of utterance was less than 1·5 for each). Clearly, this utterance type was one of the most productive constructions in the speech of both children. Of the total of 135 noun+noun utterances, there were only seven that occurred with no other interpretable relationship between the forms than simple conjunction, for example, 'umbrella boot' from Kathryn as her mother walked into the room carrying her umbrella and boots, and 'Mommy Gia' from Gia as she looked at a photograph of Mommy and Gia. All of the remaining utterances appeared to present constituents with an inherent relationship between them, although in some instances the relationship was equivocal.

The utterances with two noun forms specified the following grammatical relations (given here in order of frequency): subject-object ('Mommy pig-tail'), the genitive relation ('Kathryn sock'), the attributive relation ('bread book'), subject-locative ('sweater chair'), and, marginally, conjunction ('umbrella boot'). However, it was not the case that any two words could occur with any possible relation between them. There were no instances of such other possible relations that could hold between two noun forms as identity ('Mommy lady'), disjunction (either-or relation), or direct-indirect object. If it could be assumed that the unobtained relations existed in the child's experience, for example, giving something to someone (direct-indirect object), then the children's utterances were not merely reflections of non-linguistic states of affairs. Such selectivity in expression and the impressive consistency of word order provided evidence for assuming that the children's utterances were motivated by an underlying cognitive-linguistic rule system.

The most frequently expressed relationship between two nouns was subject-object. All three children produced verb forms in predicate relation to noun forms in subject-verb and verb-object strings in the early two-word utterances, when subject-verb-object strings occurred only rarely. Utterances that have been described in the literature as simply the co-occurrence of two substantive words (x-word+x-word by Braine 1963, or two open-class words by McNeill 1966a) could thus be explained in terms of the inherent semantic relationship between the constituents. It was apparent that the children in the study were talking about the relations between actors or agents, actions, or states, and objects or goals, and that the order of constituents reflected the underlying order of basic sentence relations with remarkable consistency—subjects and verbs preceded objects or goals.

The possible grammatical relations were not equally represented in the data. Not only were certain relations more productive than others—that is, they occurred more often in different situations with different words—but the children differed in their use of each. For example, Eric used the verb-object relation first, and utterances expressing this relation were dominant in his speech before he began to use subject nouns in relation to verb forms. The most productive early relationship for Gia and Kathryn was subject-object; Eric never produced such utterances. I. M. Schlesinger (1971) reported the productivity of this structural relationship between two nouns in the early speech of two Hebrew-speaking Israeli children, and Leopold (1949) described its frequent occurrence in the speech of his daughter Hildegard. In the speech of Kathryn, Eric, and Gia, verb-object strings appeared earlier and were more productive than subject-verb strings.

Summary

The children's earliest sentences could thus be seen as expressing two kinds of conceptual relations. In grammatical relations, substantive words such as 'Mommy' and 'sock' enter into variable grammatical relationship with other words in sentences. Such words are not in themselves relational terms in the sense that they have independent lexical meaning. The children's earliest sentences also expressed functional relations, where inherently relational words such as 'more' and 'no' operate in linear structure with other (substantive) words to specify a particular relational aspect of such words (or their referents). Spoken alone as single-word utterances, such words manifestly imply such a semantic relationship to some unspecified aspect of experience.

It is not the case that the words the children used—for example, 'no' and 'more'—have only one meaning. All of the children used 'no' subsequently to signal rejection, as in 'no dirty soap' (I don't want to use the dirty soap) and, still later, denial, as in 'no truck' (that's not a truck, it's a car). In the adult model, 'more' is used to express the partitive notion (here is sand—and here is an addition to the quantity of sand, or 'more sand'), and the comparative notion as well. The partitive may be a derivative of recurrence, but it is clear that the notion of comparative 'more' is a relatively late development. Similarly, substantive forms with essentially constant semantic meaning vary in grammatical meaning in relation to other words in sentences, for example, '*Mommy* push', 'push *Mommy*', '*Mommy's* shoe', and 'my *Mommy*'. The function or use of certain forms is not implicit for the child in the word itself.

Given that children comment on the notions of existence, non-existence, and recurrence of objects and events, one might well wonder why they should talk about anything else—in the light of what we know to be the achievements of sensory-motor intelligence. Piaget (1960) has described a major achievement in the child's development of thought with the realization of the endurance of objects when removed in space and time. The child learns that objects and events exist, cease to exist, and recur, and so he talks about it. The important conclusion about the development of grammar appears to be that children do not simply use a relatively uncomplex syntactic frame (such as pivot+open); they talk about something, and syntax is learned by the child in his efforts to code certain conceptual relations.

There is a necessary distinction between a speaker-hearer's knowledge of grammar and the notion of grammar as a linguistic account of that knowledge. The nature of the underlying rules that the child uses to speak and understand utterances cannot be described directly. A generative grammar represents a formal linguistic account of how such rules specify the inherent relations in sentences. Such an account specifies the syntax of utterances (the arrangements of forms) that accounts for the semantic relations among the forms, and in this sense there is a crucial relationship between linguistic structure and underlying cognitive function. Indeed, it is difficult to distinguish between cognitive and linguistic categories when accounting for the expressed relations between actors or agents, actions or states, and objects or goals.

It appears that the notion of pivot grammar describes children's early speech in only the most superficial way. Although the notion of pivot speech describes certain distributional phenomena in early utterances, it is clear that children know more about grammar, that is, more about the inherent relationships between words in syntactic structure, than could possibly be accounted for in terms of pivot and open class analysis. If treatment for language disorders in children is ultimately to be derived from a model of normal language development, there is evidence to indicate that a pivot grammar is not the model of child speech to use.

Treatment of Language Disorders

Several conclusions from this discussion may be applicable to planning treatment of language disorders in children. There are necessary limitations in the extent to which the conclusions of this study pertain to all children learning language, and it would follow that similar limitations apply as well to using these results in evaluating and treating language pathology. Whether or not, and how, the normative data on language development in the literature can or should be directly applied to treating children with delayed language development are important questions (see Bloom 1967).

However, certain observations can be made at this time that should provide hypotheses for research directed towards evaluating procedures for treating language disorders.

First, the results of this study confirmed a conclusion that has been reached in every study of language development of children in the earliest stages of acquiring grammar. Children learn the syntax of language—the arrangements of words in sentences—before they learn inflections of noun, verb, and adjective forms. Although there may be alternation of certain forms from the beginning—'block', 'blocks', and 'sit', 'sits'—the different forms of a word do not occur in contrast. For example, in the early samples, '-s' did not signal a meaningful difference, such as marking reference to more than one block as opposed to reference to only one block without expression of '-s'. Thus, children learn word sequences (for example, 'throw block') before morphological contrasts (as between 'block', singular, and 'blocks', plural).

Second, Kathryn, Eric, and Gia did not produce constructions that were potentially analysable as noun phrases as their first (or most productive) syntactic structures. Rather, the most productive structures they produced (after utterances with initial /ə/ were those which, in the adult model, express the basic grammatical relations: subject-object, subject-verb, and verb-object strings. Although the grammars of Kathryn and Gia specified a noun phrase constituent (with attributive adjectives in Kathryn's lexicon only), this structure was far less productive than others which occurred, and Eric did not produce noun phrases at all. Based on these two observations, children appear to learn the expressions 'throw block' or 'Baby (subject) block (object)' before the expressions 'big block', 'red block', or 'blocks'.

Finally, the results of this study indicated that (1) the status of the referent in the context in which an utterance occurs, and (2) the child's relation to the referent in terms of behaviour are critically important as influences on language performance. There were four contextual variables which characterized the occurrence of early syntactic utterances: (1) existence of the referent within the context, (2) recurrence of the referent or addition to the referent after its previous existence, (3) action upon the referent, and (4) non-existence of the referent in the context where its existence was somehow expected.

The manifestation of the referent in the contexts of speech events was most significant. Utterances most often referred to objects or events which the child was able to see, and functioned as comments or directions, where the referent was manifest or imminent in the context of the speech event, as opposed to reports of distant past or future events. All of the children used a relational term, 'more' or 'another', to signal another instance of the referent or recurrence of the referent after previous occurrence. The productivity of verb-object and subject-object strings reflected the tendency for the children to talk about objects being acted upon. And, finally, as might be expected given the foregoing observations, their first negative sentences signalled the non-existence of the referent. On the simplest level, children appear to learn to perceive and to discriminate (and, ultimately, to communicate) (1) such aspects of a referent as its existence, recurrence, or non-existence, and (2) such relational aspects of events as between agent, action, and object before, among other things, such features of objects as relative size, colour, or other identifying attributes.

It might be said that children learn to identify particular syntactic structures with the behaviour and context with which they are perceived and then progress to reproducing structures in similar, recurring contexts. To use a structure in a new situation, the child needs to be able to perceive critical aspects of the context of the situation. Thus, the sequence in which the child learns syntactic structures may be influenced as much by his ability to differentiate aspects of situational context and to recognize recurrent contexts as by such factors as frequency of exposure to structures or their relative complexity.

Programmes for language therapy that present children with linguistic structure (for example, pivot grammar) without attention to content ignore the very nature of language. It appears that learning a linguistic code depends upon the child's learning to distinguish, understand, and express certain conceptual relations. It would follow that children with language disorders need to learn more than simply the permitted co-occurrence of different words in their efforts at the analysis and use of language.

References

Bellugi, U. and Brown, R. (eds.) (1964) *The Acquisition of Language*. Monograph No. 29, Chicago, Ill.: Society for Research in Child Development.

Bloom, L. (1967) 'A comment on Lee's developmental sentence types: A method for comparing normal and deviant syntactic development' *J. Speech Hearing Disorder*, **32**, 294–6.

— (1970) *Language Development: Form and Function in Emerging Grammars*, Cambridge, Mass.: M.I.T. Press.

Braine, M. D. S. (1963) 'The ontogeny of English phrase structure: The first phase' *Language*, **39**, 1–13.

Brown, R. and Bellugi, U. (1964), 'Three processes in the child's acquisition of syntax' *Harvard Educational Review*, **34**, 133–51.

Brown, R. and Fraser, C. (1963) 'The acquisition of syntax'. In Charles N. Cofer and Barbara S. Musgrave (eds.) *Verbal Behavior and Learning*, New York: McGraw-Hill.

Leopold, W. F. (1949) *Speech Development of a Bilingual Child* (Vol. III), Evanston, Ill.: Northwestern University.

McNeill, D. (1966a) 'Developmental psycholinguistics'. In Frank Smith and George A. Miller (eds.) *The Genesis of Language*, Cambridge, Mass.: M.I.T. Press, 15–84.

— (1966b) 'The capacity for language acquisition' *Volta Review*, reprint no. 852, 5–21.

— (1970) *The Acquisition of Language: The Study of Developmental Psycholinguistics*, New York: Harper & Row.

Miller, W. and Ervin, S. (1964) 'The development of grammar in child language'. In Ursula Bellugi and Roger Brown (eds.) *The Acquisition of Language*. Monograph No. 29, Chicago, Ill.: Society for Research in Child Development.

Piaget, J. (1960) *The Psychology of Intelligence*, Paterson, N. J.: Atherton.

Schlesinger, I. M. (1971) 'Learning grammar: From pivot to realization rule'. In Dan I. Slobin (ed.) *The Ontogenesis of Grammar*, New York: Academic Press.

Smith, F. and Miller, G. A. (eds.) (1966) *The Genesis of Language*, Cambridge, Mass.: M.I.T. Press.

Zipf, G. K. (1965) *The Psychobiology of Language: An Introduction to Dynamic Philology*, Cambridge, Mass.: M.I.T. Press.

The Functions of Language, in Understanding the Self, the World, and Society

Although the first reading in this section is not overtly dealing with language acquisition, it raises the fundamental issue of this collection. Language is not acquired by young children merely as a skilful trick to be exercised without meaning, but rather as an instrument for the simultaneous realization and communication of their personalities, understanding, feelings, and needs.

This view of the functional load carried by language forces us to review the acquisition process. Children can no longer be seen to be acquiring a transparently neutral medium, containing a phonological, syntactic and semantic component. They are acquiring *the uses* of language—uses of language which Halliday says are more complex than the externalized and consciously formulated ideas held by adults about language. Indeed, Halliday suggests that there is a reduction in the number of models of language generally available as the child grows into an adult.

4 M. A. K. HALLIDAY
Relevant Models of Language

The teacher of English who, when seeking an adequate definition of language to guide him in his work, meets with a cautious 'well, it depends on how you look at it' is likely to share the natural impatience felt by anyone who finds himself unable to elicit 'a straight answer to a straight question'. But the very frequency of this complaint may suggest that, perhaps, questions are seldom as straight as they seem. The question 'what is language?', in whatever guise it appears, is as diffuse and, at times, disingenuous as other formulations of its kind, for example 'what is literature?' Such questions, which are wisely excluded from examinations, demand the privilege of a qualified and perhaps circuitous answer.

In a sense the only satisfactory response is 'why do you want to know?', since unless we know what lies beneath the question we cannot hope to answer it in a way which will suit the questioner. Is he interested in language planning in multilingual communities? Or in aphasia and language disorders? Or in words and their histories? Or in dialects and those who speak them? Or in how one language differs from another? Or in the formal properties of language as a system? Or in the functions of language and the demands that we make on it? Or in language as an art medium? Or in the information and redundancy of writing systems? Each one of these and other such questions is a possible context for a definition of language. In each case language 'is' something different.

The criterion is one of relevance; we want to understand, and to highlight, those facets of language which bear on the investigation or the task in hand. In an educational context the problem for linguistics is to elaborate some account of language that is relevant to the work of the English teacher. What constitutes a relevant notion of language from his point of view, and by what criteria can this be decided? Much of what has recently been objected to, among the attitudes and approaches to language that are current in the profession, arouses criticism not so much because it is

M. A. K. Halliday: Extract from 'Relevant Models of Language', *Educationa Review*, Vol. 22, No. 1, 1969, pp. 26–37.

false as because it is irrelevant. When, for example, the authors of *The Linguistic Sciences and Language Teaching* suggested that teaching the do's and don'ts of grammar to a child who is linguistically unsuccessful is like teaching a starving man how to hold a knife and fork, they were not denying that there is a ritual element in our use of language, with rules of conduct to which everyone is expected to conform; they were simply asserting that the view of language as primarily good manners was of little relevance to educational needs. Probably very few people ever held this view explicitly; but it was implicit in a substantial body of teaching practices, and if it has now largely been discarded this is because its irrelevance became obvious in the course of some rather unhappy experience.

It is not necessary, however, to sacrifice a generation of children, or even one classroomful, in order to demonstrate that particular preconceptions of language are inadequate or irrelevant. In place of a negative and somewhat hit-and-miss approach, a more fruitful procedure is to seek to establish certain general, positive criteria of relevance. These will relate, ultimately, to the demands that we make of language in the course of our lives. We need therefore to have some idea of the nature of these demands; and we shall try to consider them here from the point of view of the child. We shall ask, in effect, about the child's image of language: what is the 'model' of language that he internalizes as a result of his own experience? This will help us to decide what is relevant to the teacher, since the teacher's own view of language must at the very least encompass all that the child knows language to be.

The child knows what language is because he knows what language does. The determining elements in the young child's experience are the successful demands on language that he himself has made, the particular needs that have been satisfied by language for him. He has used language in many ways—for the satisfaction of material and intellectual needs, for the mediation of personal relationships, the expression of feelings and so on. Language in all these uses has come within his own direct experience, and because of this he is subconsciously aware that language has many functions that affect him personally. Language is, for the child, a rich and adaptable instrument for the realization of his intentions; there is hardly any limit to what he can do with it.

As a result, the child's internal 'model' of language is a highly complex one; and most adult notions of language fail to match up to it. The adult's ideas about language may be externalized and consciously formulated, but they are nearly always much too simple. In fact it may be more helpful, in this connection, to speak of the child's 'models' of language, in the plural, in order to emphasize the many-sidedness of his linguistic experience. We shall try to identify the models of language with which the normal child is endowed by the time he comes to school at the age of five; the assumption being that if the teacher's own 'received' conception of language is in some ways less rich or less diversified it will be irrelevant to the educational task.

We tend to underestimate both the total extent and the functional diversity of the part played by language in the life of the child. His interaction with others, which begins at birth, is gradually given form by language, through the process whereby at a very early age language already begins to mediate in every aspect of his experience. It is not only as the child comes to act on and to learn about his environment that language comes in; it is there from the start in his achievement of intimacy and in the expression of his individuality. The rhythmic recitation of nursery rhymes and jingles is still language, as we can see from the fact that children's spells and chants differ from one language to another: English nonsense is quite distinct from French nonsense, because the one is English and the other French. All these contribute to the child's total picture of language 'at work'.

Through such experiences, the child builds up a very positive impression—one that cannot be verbalized, but is none the less real for that—of what language is and what it is for. Much of his difficulty with language in school arises because he is required to accept a stereotype of language that is contrary to the insights he has gained from his own experience. The traditional first 'reading and writing' tasks are a case in point, since they fail to coincide with his own convictions about the nature and uses of language.

Perhaps the simplest of the child's models of language, and one of the first to be evolved, is what we may call the INSTRUMENTAL model. The child becomes aware that language is used as a means of getting things done. About a generation ago, zoologists were finding out about the highly developed mental powers of chimpanzees; and one of the observations described was of the animal that constructed a long stick out of three short ones and used it to dislodge a bunch of bananas from the roof of its cage. The human child, faced with the same problem, constructs a sentence. He says 'I want a banana'; and the effect is the more impressive because it does not depend on the immediate presence of the bananas. Language is brought in to serve the function of 'I want', the satisfaction of material needs. Success in this use of language does not in any way depend on the production of well-formed adult sentences; a carefully contextualized yell may have substantially the same effect, and although this may not be language there is no very clear dividing line between, say, a noise made on a commanding tone and a full-dress imperative clause.

The old *See Spot run. Run, Spot, run!* type of first reader bore no relation whatsoever to this instrumental function of language. This by itself does not condemn it, since language has many other functions besides that of manipulating and controlling the environment. But it bore little apparent relation to any use of language, at least to any with which the young child is familiar. It is not recognizable as language in terms of the child's own intentions, of the meanings that he has reason to express and to understand. Children have a very broad concept of the meaningfulness of language, in addition to their immense tolerance of inexplicable tasks; but they are not accustomed to being faced with language which, in their own functional terms, has no meaning at all, and the old-style reader was not seen by them as language. It made no connection with language in use.

Language as an instrument of control has another side to it, since the child is well aware that language is also a means whereby others exercise control over him. Closely related to the instrumental model, therefore, is the REGULATORY model of language. This refers to the use of language to regulate the behaviour of others. Bernstein and his colleagues have studied different types of regulatory behaviour by parents in relation to the process of socialization of the child, and their work provides important clues concerning what the child may be expected to derive from this experience in constructing his own model of language. To adapt one of Bernstein's examples, as described by Turner, the mother who finds that her small child has carried out of the supermarket, unnoticed by herself or by the cashier, some object that was not paid for, may exploit the power of language in various ways, each of which will leave a slightly different trace or after-image of this role of language in the mind of the child. For example, she may say *you mustn't take things that don't belong to you* (control through conditional prohibition based on a categorization of objects in terms of a particular social institution, that of ownership); *that was very naughty* (control through categorization of behaviour in terms of opposition approved/disapproved); *if you do that again I'll smack you* (control through threat of reprisal linked to repetition of behaviour); *you'll make Mummy very unhappy if you do that* (control through emotional blackmail); *that's not allowed* (control through categorization of behaviour as governed by rule), and so on. A single incident of this type by itself has little significance; but such general types of regulatory behaviour, through repetition and reinforcement, determine the child's specific awareness of language as a means of behavioural control.

The child applies this awareness, in his own attempts to control his peers and siblings; and this in turn provides the basis for an essential component in his range of linguistic skills, the language of rules and instructions. Whereas at first he can make only simple unstructured demands, he learns as time goes on to give ordered sequences of instructions, and then progresses to the further stage where he can convert sets of instructions into rules, including conditional rules, as in explaining the principles of a game. Thus his regulatory model of language continues to be elaborated, and his experience of the potentialities of language in this use further increases the value of the model.

Closely related to the regulatory function of language is its function in social interaction, and the third of the models that we may postulate as forming part of the child's image of language is the INTERACTIONAL model. This refers to the use of language in the interaction between the self and others. Even the closest of the child's personal relationships, that with his mother, is partly and, in time, largely mediated through language; his interaction with other people, adults and children, is very obviously maintained linguistically. (Those who come nearest to achieving a personal relationship that is not linguistically mediated, apparently, are twins.)

Aside, however, from his experience of language in the maintenance of permanent relationships, the neighbourhood and the activities of the peer group provide the context for complex and rapidly changing interactional patterns which make extensive and subtle demands on the individual's linguistic resources. Language is used to define and consolidate the group, to include and to exclude, showing who is 'one of us' and who is not; to impose status, and to contest status that is imposed; and humour, ridicule, deception, persuasion, all the forensic and theatrical arts of language are brought into play. Moreover, the young child, still primarily a learner, can do what very few adults can do in such situations: he can be internalizing language while listening and talking. He can be, effectively, both a participant and an observer at the same time, so that his own critical involvement in this complex interaction does not prevent him from profiting linguistically from it.

Again there is a natural link here with another use of language, from which the child derives what we may call the PERSONAL model. This refers to his awareness of language as a form of his own individuality. In the process whereby the child becomes aware of himself, and in particular in the higher stages of that process, the development of his personality, language plays an essential role. We are not talking here merely of 'expressive' language—language used for the direct expression of feelings and attitudes—but also of the personal element in the interactional function of language, since the shaping of the self through interaction with others is very much a language-mediated process. The child is enabled to offer to someone else that which is unique to himself, to make public his own individuality; and this in turn reinforces and creates this individuality. With the normal child, his awareness of himself is closely bound up with speech: both with hearing himself speak, and with having at his disposal the range of behavioural options that constitute language. Within the concept of the self as an actor, having discretion, or freedom of choice, the 'self as a speaker' is an important component.

Thus for the child language is very much a part of himself, and the 'personal' model is his intuitive awareness of this, and of the way in which his individuality is identified and realized through language. The other side of the coin, in this process, is the child's growing understanding of his environment, since the environment is, first of all, the 'non-self', that which is separated out in the course of establishing where he himself begins and ends. So, fifthly, the child has a HEURISTIC model of language, derived from his knowledge of how language has enabled him to explore his environment.

The heuristic model refers to language as a means of investigating reality, a way of learning about things. This scarcely needs comment, since every child makes it quite obvious that this is what language is for by his habit of constantly asking questions. When he is questioning, he is seeking not merely facts but explanations of facts, the generalizations about reality that language makes it possible to explore. Again, Bernstein has shown the importance of the question-and-answer routine in the total setting of parent-child communication and the significance of the latter, in turn, in relation to the child's success in formal education: his research has demonstrated a significant correlation between the mother's linguistic attention to the child and the teacher's assessment of the child's success in the first year of school.

The young child is very well aware of how to use language to learn, and may be quite conscious of this aspect of language before he reaches school; many children already control a metalanguage for the heuristic function of language, in that they know what a 'question' is, what an 'answer' is, what 'knowing' and 'understanding' mean, and they can talk about these things without difficulty. Mackay and Thompson have shown the importance of helping the child who is learning to read and write to build up a language for talking about language; and it is the heuristic function which provides one of the foundations for this, since the child can readily conceptualize and verbalize the basic categories of the heuristic model. To put this more concretely, the normal five-year-old either already uses words such as *question, answer* in their correct meanings, or if he does not, is capable of learning to do so.

The other foundation for the child's 'language about language' is to be found in the imaginative function. This also relates the child to his environment, but in a rather different way. Here, the child is using language to create his own environment; not to learn about how things are but to make them as he feels inclined. From his ability to create, through language, a world of his own making he derives the IMAGINATIVE model of language; and this provides some further elements of the metalanguage, with words like *story*, *make up* and *pretend*.

Language in its imaginative function is not necessarily 'about' anything at all: the child's linguistically created environment does not have to be a make-believe copy of the world of experience, occupied by people and things and events. It may be a world of pure sound, made up of rhythmic sequences of rhyming or chiming syllables; or an edifice of words in which semantics has no part, like a house built of playing cards in which face values are irrelevant. Poems, rhymes, riddles and much of the child's own linguistic play reinforce this model of language, and here too the meaning of what is said is not primarily a matter of content. In stories and dramatic games, the imaginative function is, to a large extent, based on content; but the ability to express such content is still, for the child, only one of the interesting facets of language, one which for many purposes is no more than an optional extra.

So we come finally to the REPRESENTATIONAL model. Language is, in addition to all its other guises, a means of communicating about something, of expressing propositions. The child is aware that he can convey a message in language, a message which has specific reference to the processes, persons, objects, abstractions, qualities, states and relations of the real world around him.

This is the only model of language that many adults have; and a very inadequate model it is, from the point of view of the child. There is no need to go so far as to suggest that the transmission of content is, for the child, the least important function of language; we have no way of evaluating the various functions relatively to one another. It is certainly not, however, one of the earliest to come into prominence; and it does not become a dominant function until a much later stage in the development towards maturity. Perhaps it never becomes in any real sense the dominant function; but it does, in later years, tend to become the dominant *model*. It is very easy for the adult, when he attempts to formulate his ideas about the nature of language, to be simply unaware of most of what language means to the child; this is not because he no longer uses language in the same variety of different functions (one or two may have atrophied, but not all), but because only one of these functions, in general, is the subject of conscious attention, so that the corresponding model is the only one to be externalized. But this presents what is, for the child, a quite unrealistic picture of language, since it accounts for only a small fragment of his total awareness of what language is about.

The representational model at least does not conflict with the child's experience. It relates to one significant part of it; rather a small part, at first, but nevertheless real. In this it contrasts sharply with another view of language which we have not mentioned because it plays no part in the child's experience at all, but which might be called the 'ritual' model of language. This is the image of language internalized by those for whom language is a means of showing how well one was brought up; it downgrades language to the level of table-manners. The ritual element in the use of language is probably derived from the interactional, since language in its ritual function also serves to define and delimit a social group; but it has none of the positive aspects of linguistic interaction, those which impinge on the child, and is thus very partial and one-sided. The view of language as manners is a needless complication, in the present context, since this function of language has no counterpart in the child's experience.

Our conception of language, if it is to be adequate for meeting the needs of the child, will need to be exhaustive. It must incorporate all the child's own 'models', to take account of the varied demands on language that he himself makes. The child's understanding of what language is is derived from his own experience of language in situations of use. It thus embodies all of the images we have described: the instrumental, the regulatory, the interactional, the personal, the heuristic, the imaginative and the representational. Each of these is his interpretation of a function of language with which he is familiar. Doughty has shown, in a very suggestive paper, how different concepts of the role of the English teacher tend to incorporate and to emphasize different functions, or groups of functions, from among those here enumerated.

Let us summarize the models in terms of the child's intentions, since different uses of language may be seen as realizing different intentions. In its instrumental function, language is used for the satisfaction of material needs, this is the 'I want' function. The

regulatory is the 'do as I tell you' function, language in the control
of behaviour. The interactional function is that of getting along
with others, the 'me and him' function (including 'me and my
mummy'). The personal is related to this: it is the expression of
identity, of the self, which develops largely *through* linguistic
interaction; the 'here I come' function, perhaps. The heuristic is
the use of language to learn, to explore reality: the function of
'tell me why'. The imaginative is that of 'let's pretend', whereby
the reality is created, and what is being explored is the child's
own mind, including language itself. The representational is the
'I've got something to tell you' function, that of the communication of content.

What we have called 'models' are the images that we have of
language arising out of these functions. Language is 'defined' for
the child by its uses; it is something that serves this set of needs.
These are not models of language acquisition; they are not procedures whereby the child learns his language, nor do they define
the part played by different types of linguistic activity in the
learning process. Hence no mention has been made of the chanting
and repeating and rehearsing by which the child practises his
language. The techniques of mastering language do not constitute
a 'use', nor do they enter into the making of the image of language;
a child, at least, does not learn for the luxury of being a learner.
For the child, all language is doing something: in other words, it
has meaning. It has meaning in a very broad sense, including here
a range of functions which the adult does not normally think of as
meaningful, such as the personal and the interactional and probably most of those listed above—all except the last, in fact. But it
is precisely in relation to the child's conception of language that
it is most vital for us to redefine our notion of meaning; not
restricting it to the narrow limits of representational meaning
(that is, 'content') but including within it all the functions that
language has as purposive, non-random, contextualized activity.

Bernstein has shown that educational failure is often, in a very
general and rather deep sense, language failure. The child who
does not succeed in the school system is one who has not mastered
certain essential aspects of language ability. In its immediate
interpretation, this could refer to the simple fact that a child cannot read or write or express himself adequately in speech. But

these are as it were the externals of linguistic success, and it is likely that underlying the failure to master these skills is a deeper and more general failure of language, some fundamental gap in the child's linguistic capabilities.

This is not a lack of words; vocabulary seems to be learnt very easily in response to opportunity combined with motivation. Nor is it, by and large, an impoverishment of the grammar: there is no real evidence to show that the unsuccessful child uses or disposes of a narrower range of syntactic options. (I hope it is unnecessary to add that it has also nothing to do with dialect or accent.) Rather it would appear that the child who, in Bernstein's terms, has only a 'restricted code' is one who is deficient in respect of the set of linguistic models that we have outlined above, because some of the functions of language have not been accessible to him. The 'restriction' is a restriction on the range of uses of language. In particular, it is likely that he has not learnt to operate with language in the two functions which are crucial to his success in school: the personal function, and the heuristic function.

In order to be taught successfully, it is necessary to know how to use language to learn; and also, how to use language to participate *as an individual* in the learning situation. These requirements are probably not a feature of any particular school system, but rather are inherent in the very concept of education. The ability to operate effectively in the personal and heuristic modes is, however, something that has to be learnt; it does not follow automatically from the acquisition of the grammar and vocabulary of the mother tongue. It is not, that is to say, a question of which words and structures the child knows or uses, but of their functional significance and interpretation. In Bernstein's formulation, the child may not be oriented towards the meanings realized by the personal and heuristic functions of language. Restricted and elaborated code are in effect, as Ruqaiya Hasan suggests, varieties of language function, determining the meanings that the syntactic patterns and the lexical items have for the child who hears or uses them.

To say that educational failure is linguistic failure is merely to take the first step in explaining it: it means that the most immediately accessible cause of educational failure is to be sought in language. Beyond this, and underlying the linguistic failure, is a complex pattern of social and familial factors whose significance has been revealed by Bernstein's work. But while the limitations of a child's linguistic experience may ultimately be ascribed—though not in any simple or obvious way—to features of the social background, the problem as it faces the teacher is essentially a linguistic problem. It is a failure in the child's effective mastery of the use of language, in his adaptation of language to meet certain basic demands. Whether one calls it a failure in language or a failure in the use of language is immaterial; the distinction between knowing language and knowing how to use it is merely one of terminology. This situation is not easy even to diagnose; it is much more difficult to treat. We have tried here to shed some light on it by relating it to the total set of demands, in terms of the needs of the child, that language is called upon to serve.

The implication for a teacher is that his own model of language should at least not fall short of that of the child. If the teacher's image of language is narrower and less rich than that which is already present in the minds of those he is teaching (or which needs to be present, if they are to succeed), it will be irrelevant to him as a teacher. A minimum requirement for an educationally relevant approach to language is that it take account of the child's own linguistic experience, defining this experience in terms of its richest potential and noting where there may be gaps, with certain children, which could be educationally and developmentally harmful. This is one component. The other component of relevance is the relevance to the experiences that the child will have later on: to the linguistic demands that society will eventually make of him, and, in the intermediate stage, to the demands on language which the school is going to make and which he must meet if he is to succeed in the classroom.

We are still very ignorant of many aspects of the part language plays in our lives. But it is clear that language serves a wide range of human needs, and the richness and variety of its functions is reflected in the nature of language itself, in its organization as a system: within the grammatical structure of a language, certain areas are primarily associated with the heuristic and representational functions, others with the personal and interactional functions. Different bits of the system, as it were, do different jobs; and this in turn helps us to interpret and make more precise the notion of uses of language. What is common to every use of language is that it is meaningful, contextualized, and in the broadest sense social; this is brought home very clearly to the child, in the course of his day-to-day experience. The child is surrounded by language, but not in the form of grammars and dictionaries, or of randomly chosen words and sentences, of or undirected monologue. What he encounters is 'text', or language in use: sequences of language articulated each within itself and with the situation in which it occurs. Such sequences are purposive—though very varied in purpose—and have an evident social significance. The child's awareness of language cannot be isolated from his awareness of language function, and this conceptual unity offers a useful vantage point from which language may be seen in a perspective that is educationally relevant.

References

Bernstein, Basil (1970) 'A critique of the concept *compensatory education*'. In S. Williams (ed.), *Language and Poverty: Perspectives on a Theme*, Madison, Wisconsin: University of Wisconsin Press.

Doughty, P. S. (1969) 'Current Practice in English Teaching'. Paper presented to Conference of Teachers in Approved Schools, 'Language, Life and Learning'.

Halliday, M. A. K., McIntosh, Angus and Strevens, Peter (1964) *The Linguistic Sciences and Language Teaching*, London: Longman.

Hasan, Ruqaiya (1969) 'Code, Register and Social Dialect'. Paper presented to London School of Economics Seminar, 'Language and Society'.

Mackay, David and Thompson, Brian (1968) *The Initial Teaching of Reading and Writing*, Programme in Linguistics and English Teaching, Paper 3, London: Longman.

Turner, G. J. (1969) 'Social Class Differences in Regulatory Language'. Report prepared for Sociological Research Unit, University of London Institute of Education.

5 CHARLES F. HOCKETT
Linguistic Continuity

At the same time as they listen to their parents, children internalize a language which is slightly different from that of the parents. These differences can be apparent on each level of linguistic description—phonological, semantic and syntactic. This reading concentrates on the phonological level, but the general point can be made that all these slight differences help foster a different childhood culture from generation to generation in so far as it is coded by language. Hockett suggests that these changes are continuous and entirely regular. They form yet another element in the communicative process as children gradually realize that even though their language may differ from that of their parents, they still have to communicate with them.

Regrettably there has been little work which has looked at the other two levels of possible change—the semantic and the syntactic. Read's article later on in this section shows an associated problem concerning the meanings of words but does not cover the ground prepared by Hockett.

The origin and development of speech habits in individuals, through their life cycles from birth to death, can appropriately be termed LINGUISTIC ONTOGENY. In contrast to this, the subject matter of historical linguistics—changes through decades and centuries in the speech patterns of communities—is of course linguistic PHYLOGENY. The present paper deals with certain relations between these two: specifically, with the mechanisms whereby continuity of linguistic tradition is maintained in a community in the face of the constant turnover of population through birth and death, immigration and emigration. Jespersen had discussed this problem, and has connected it with historical linguistics by asking what relation there may be between these mechanisms and the fact that languages change in the course of time. But Jespersen, as is well known, did not accept the assumption that phonetic

Charles F. Hockett: Extract from 'Age-grading and Linguistic Continuity' *Language*, **26**, Linguistic Society of America 1950, pp. 449–57.

change is regular. Because we do accept this, we can investigate a more specific problem: what is the relation between the mechanisms of continuity and the regularity of phonetic change?

Our remarks will be organized about the following four propositions:

1. The fundamental speech habits of an individual are in most cases firmly established by the age of puberty.

2. The most important environmental force shaping the emerging dialect of a child is the speech of other children.

3. In any community, there is a continuity of linguistic tradition through successive generations of children.

4. It is within this childhood continuity of tradition that phonetic change, the kind of linguistic change characterizable as 'regular', takes place.

These four propositions are not all equally certain; the last one, as a matter of fact, is no more than a reasonable hypothesis requiring investigation. Such investigation is important, however; for if the proposition is true or partly true, it may be necessary for us to modify in some minor ways our customary assumption of regularity in phonetic change, before the latter can be accepted as a generalization of cross-cultural validity. In this paper, we will present what evidence is available for the first three propositions, and outline a set of possible tests for the fourth.

1. The first proposition may be sharpened as follows: By the age of puberty, the individual has normally acquired (1) his complete phonemic inventory; (2) his allophonic inventory and the distribution of allophones both in phonemes and in positions; (3) most of the shorter sequences of phonemes (e.g. consonant clusters) which he will ever use with ease; (4) all, or almost all, the grammatical patterns ('constructions') destined to occur in his later speech. If this is true, it implies that later modifications of pattern, in the normal and most frequent case, will be confined to (a) substitution, in a given lexical item, of one already occurrent phoneme or phoneme sequence for another, and (b) addition of new lexical items, each involving old phonemes and phoneme sequences and each falling into patterns of grammatical usage already present. An example of the first is the Middle-Westerner who comes to live in the East and takes to saying *water* with his

vowel of *sought* instead of with his vowel of *cot*, which has formerly been his habit. Examples of the second hardly need be given.

For the validity of our first proposition there is a good deal of evidence.

(1) Countless numbers of individuals, at some point in their lives, have faced the task of accommodating to a totally alien linguistic environment. We know that when this task is confronted during childhood it is usually accomplished more thoroughly than when it comes in later years.

(2) Specialists in American dialectology are often able to detect, in the speech of an adult, a childhood core of speech habits even when it is overlaid with several later periods of influence from other dialects.

(3) Interesting support comes from Haugen's investigation of the process whereby Wisconsin communities, monolingually Norwegian half a century ago, have slowly become more and more infused with English. At any given time, the adult members of such a community fall into four classes: the monolingual Norwegian, the monolingual English, the preferential Norwegian-speaker who can use some English when necessary, and the preferential English-speaker with Norwegian when necessary. Through the years, English replaces Norwegian because more and more of those entering the adult community, either by migration or by passing through childhood in the community, fall into the monolingual or preferential English class, while the older generations of monolingual or preferential Norwegians die off. This is not to say, of course, that there is not some learning of each language by adult speakers of the other language. But it does imply that this process, among the adults, is relatively unimportant in its long-term results. In general, by the time of puberty a given individual has come to fall into one of the four classes, and thereafter he remains in that class throughout his life. By the time of puberty, his linguistic fate has been determined.

The term 'puberty' appears in our proposition partly, but not entirely, as a short way of referring to the early teens. As Joos has pointed out, this is the age at which a child's moral sensibilities become fixed: before this age, a child can be persuaded fairly easily to reclassify types of possible behaviour as 'right' and 'wrong', but after this age his evaluations along such lines are far less flexible. This is part of what we mean by the term 'puberty', and it is not unrelated to the concomitant loss of linguistic flexibility: the sounds and forms of one's own language are, after that age, in some real sense 'right', and the sounds and forms of other languages are 'wrong'. The resemblance between this importance of the pre-puberty formative years for linguistic ontogeny and the similar importance of childhood experience for personality formation, so much stressed by modern psychiatrists and genetic psychologists, is hardly an accident; indeed, this is a matter which should receive detailed investigation.

There seems to be no reason to believe that our first proposition is valid only for our own modern western society. Some recasting of the proposition may in time be necessary, but it seems to be of cross-cultural validity, and to have been true for an indefinitely large period of man's past history.

2. Our second proposition asserts the outstanding importance of other children among the environmental forces which condition the emerging dialect of a child.

Language, like any other facet of culture, has to be acquired from those with whom one comes in contact. For any child there is, of course, an initial 'cradle stage' during which the mother and father, or other adult parent-surrogates, are of primary importance. But in most societies—the exceptions will occupy us later—this interval is relatively short compared to the remainder of the pre-puberty period, during which the child is continually playing or working with other children. Thus the six-year-olds teach the five-year-olds, the huskier children lead the punier, those with more prestige are imitated by those with less. Childhood culture is not necessarily a microcosmic image of the adult culture of the same community. Prestige-bestowing characteristics can be quite different among children and among adults. This is another field which would bear investigation from the linguistic point of view.

Evidence for this second proposition is also easily mustered.

(1) When a family with young children moves from one part of English-speaking North America to another, the speech of the children becomes adapted to the patterns of the new community, regardless of the extent to which the parents make such adaptation

or fail to make it. Parental authority can countermand some superficial aspects of this influence. If Johnny, born in Michigan but currently living in Texas, comes home from the schoolyard saying *greasy* with /z/, and his mother beats him, with instructions to pronounce the word with /s/, the influence of the new community is being countermanded. But note that it is apt to require genuine disciplinary measures to accomplish this, and that the mother who succeeds in replacing the /z/ by the /s/ in this one word has not even heard the vast majority of the adaptations her child is making.

(2) Fieldworkers for the dialect atlas find that the speech patterns of the oldest generation of native-bred inhabitants of a community, and those of adolescents who have spent their childhood in the area, are more apt to resemble each other than either set of patterns resembles that of non-native-bred inhabitants of the middle generation.

(3) Whoever has heard the English of someone raised by English-speaking parents in a foreign country, where his childhood companions were not speakers of English and where, in consequence, he was obliged to acquire his English exclusively from adults, can vouch for the peculiar flavour of the resulting speech. Such a speaker may have the same phonemes in the same distribution, and may hit his phonemic targets just as accurately; but the targets themselves seem to be placed a little differently in the acoustic and articulatory range. Sometimes there are clear similarities between the pronunciation of such a speaker and the phonological pattern of the foreign language spoken in the country where he grew up. One person of this kind, raised in China, speaks a brand of English whose peculiar cast is plainly noticeable and yet highly elusive; on close observation, it turns out that he uses Chinese-style stop consonants in his English. On the other hand, the peculiarities of such English cannot always be ascribed to the pattern of the other language involved. Unusual features of pronunciation, of vocabulary, of grammatical structure, or of style level in various situations, may stem rather from the inappropriateness of adult speech for many childhood situations, or, sometimes, from fallacious adult theories as to how the language 'should' be spoken. A child born and raised in the Philippines spoke once, in a play situation, of taking *many little papers* instead of *lots of little*

pieces of paper. The use of *paper* (in this sense) as a countable noun may have stemmed from the Spanish or French in his home background; but the stylistically inappropriate use of *many* for *lots of* was a transfer of adult speech into a situation where it did not fit. The reason that peculiarities of this kind survive in such a person's speech, is that he does not pass through the fires of childhood competition and conflict which forge the native-bred speaker's idiolect.

Our first proposition is tantamount to saying that for linguistic ontogeny the old saw 'as the twig is bent' is valid. Our second suggests an addition: 'as the twig is bent—and it is bent by other twigs'.

3. Our third proposition asserts that, as a consequence of the first and second, there is a continuity of tradition in a community through successive generations of children. This is valid to the extent that the first two propositions are found to hold true. A diagram will help to clarify the situation, and will be useful in further discussion. In this diagram, the abscissa (horizontal axis) is time, and the ordinate (vertical axis) is years-of-age. Each diagonal line represents a single life-history: an individual born in a given

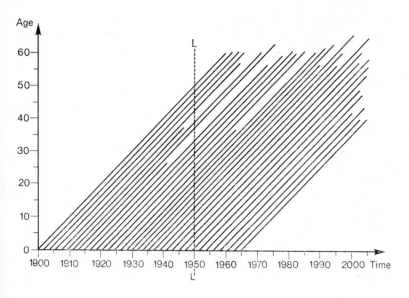

year is zero years old at birth, and each year is one year older, so
that the slope of each such life-line is unity—every line slants at
forty-five degrees. At any moment, there are individuals of roughly
every age in the community; this is seen by taking a vertical cross-
section such as line LL, here drawn through the year 1950.

On this diagram we can now superimpose, in imagination,
Bloomfield's chart of density of communication, by drawing an
arrow from each individual's line, each time he speaks, to the line
of each individual who hears him. The continuity of linguistic
tradition through successive generations of children, of concern to
us here, would then be represented visually by a particularly dense
massing of arrows in the lower regions of the diagram.

Now this particular continuity is never the only one found in a
given society. Anthropologists tell us that the tendency for the
members of a community to fall into various subgroups on the
basis of similar age, with differentiation of economic function,
ceremonial activity, and so on, is a universal phenomenon; this
phenomenon is termed AGE-GRADING. We can therefore expect to
find, in any society whatsoever, various post-childhood continuities
too. On the other hand, these continuities are not hermetically
insulated one from another, even where age-grading reaches its
peak of formal development. There is always plenty of inter-
individual activity, including talking, between persons of widely
disparate ages. The relation between the childhood continuity
and any given post-childhood continuity thus takes two forms:
(1) talking, of one kind or another, between children and older
people; (2) the influence, inside the skin of a given individual, of
the habits acquired early in life on his later behaviour. The first
of these is an interrelation, but the second is a one-way process.

It is instructive to see what this picture reveals about that
particular post-childhood continuity which in our own society we
call the literary tradition. If an individual, in his adult life, comes
to participate in the literary tradition, he is going to be influenced
by the habits of his adult predecessors in that tradition. But he is
also going to be influenced continually and profoundly by his
own childhood acquisitions. These will constantly shape the way
in which he turns and twists the literary devices to which, as an
adult, he has fallen heir, in the determination of his own individual
'style'. On the other hand, even if he is one of the great literary

masters, what he does to the literary continuity is *not* going to affect in any major way the *everyday* speaking habits of later generations, for those habits will be acquired, as were his own, during childhood from other children. Thus it is that the study of language is relevant for the study of literature, but the latter—though of great importance in its own right—has little to contribute to the study of language.

In our third proposition (and likewise in the second), we must allow for the existence of exceptions and marginal cases. In some communities, the population is broken into such small local groups, so relatively isolated from each other, that children have relatively little opportunity to be together; where this is the case, linguistic (and, indeed, general cultural) continuity necessarily assumes a different guise. The Tarahumara of northwestern Mexico afford an example. These people live in separate family groups—not, of course, wholly without contact between families, but with such contact at a minimum and for very short periods. We have no figures of the number of children per family, but the evidence suggests that it cannot be very high. Now one can learn a new dance step, or a new carving technique, or even a new song or word, at an occasional festival; but one cannot learn a language that way. It is obvious that the Tarahumara child must learn his language mainly from adults. There are doubtless other communities in which this is the case, and probably there were many more in earlier times than now. Wherever such a fashion of living persists over any great length of time, the linguistic continuity must necessarily be a sort of stair-step affair: adults teach their children, who grow up and teach their children, and so on.

4. Our fourth proposition is the hypothesis that the kind of linguistic change which has been characterized as 'regular' takes place within the childhood continuity.

The only way to prove this is by a contrapositive method. If there are episodes in which the childhood continuity is broken, and if in such cases the familiar pattern of regular phonetic change does not appear, then the assertion may be accepted as valid. Or if there are communities (like the Tarahumara) where childhood continuity is impossible and where at the same time we fail to find the familiar pattern of phonetic change, then again the assertion is reasonable. On the other hand, if under such conditions phonetic change is still as we usually expect to find it, then the hypothesis requires modification rather than outright rejection: it would follow that a childhood continuity is not *necessary* for regularity; but it might still be true that where and when a childhood continuity does exist, it is indeed the carrier of this type of linguistic change.

It is easy to show that ontogenetic developments later than the 'cradle stage' are essential if phonetic change is to be regular. In his earliest speech, a child manifests a phonemic system far less fully differentiated than that of the adult speech about him. This phonemic system develops by splits, by the development of new contrasts where before there were none, until eventually a reasonable facsimile of the surrounding adult phonemic system is attained. In the earlier stages, the child may go through a period in which, say, adult words beginning with /p/ and /b/ are all mapped into child words with an undifferentiated bilabial stop phoneme /p/. Then a period may ensue in which NEW adoption of adult words beginning with /b/ are mapped into the child's bilabial voiced (and, incidentally, nasal) phoneme /m/. The older vocabulary layer, with initial /p/ for adult /b/, and the newer, with /m/ for /b/, now exist side by side, and there is thus double representation of a single adult phoneme. Unless such double representations are eliminated by relearning the words involved, either in the later cradle stage or in the long childhood stage, the results after a century or so will not be such as to lead anyone to postulate 'regularity of phonetic change'. Indeed, survival in adult language (or reborrowing into adult language) of such infant words is doubtless one of the sources of the vast load of words of indeterminable origin found in every language (e.g. English *boy, girl, put, pull*).

This proves the importance of childhood as against infancy. Our remaining discussion outlines possible lines of investigation for the proof (or disproof) of the importance of childhood as against adulthood. There are three main lines for such investigation: (1) different conditions for the borrowing of words; (2) pidgins and creolized languages; (3) communities where childhood continuity does not exist.

(1) The learned words of the Romance languages, which 'come

from' Latin without being simple descendants of Latin words, have entered the Romance languages through the activity of adults. It is an adult who reads a Latin book or manuscript and adapts a word he finds there to the pattern of the language that he himself speaks. On the other hand, when Scandinavian words entered English, the conditions of borrowing were quite different: English- and Scandinavian-speaking families lived side by side, and children probably played just as important a role as adults in the borrowing process. It would be instructive, therefore, to perform the following experiment: compare the structure of learned loanwords in French with the structure of their Latin prototypes, and see to what extent the French shapes can be accounted for on the assumption of any set of 'regular sound shifts'; then do the same for the Scandinavian loanwords of English in terms of their old Scandinavian prototypes. It might turn out that the Scandinavian load in English, thus examined, would bear a greater resemblance to the result of continuous tradition than would the learned load of French. If so, there would be some evidence for the importance of children. If not, no conclusion could be drawn either way.

(2) The formation of a pidgin dialect is the nearest approach to a 'revolution' in linguistic history. If our accounts are correct, furthermore, it is a process in which children play little or no part. Between the history of English, say, prior to the formation of Melanesian Pidgin English, and the history of the latter after its formation, we therefore have an episode in which childhood continuity is broken. From this we can derive several possible tests of our fourth proposition, not all of them, unfortunately, equally workable:

(a) We could compare the vocabulary of some English-based pidgin with English itself—preferably, of course, with the particular variety of English which underlies the pidgin—to see whether we find regularity of phonetic correspondence or not.

(b) A further step would be to compare several pidginized English dialects and attempt the reconstruction from them, by the comparative method, of a common ancestor; this could then be compared with our knowledge of English of a few centuries ago. For this test and the preceding, it would be necessary to have data from speakers of the pidgins who were not also native speakers of English; for the native speaker of English who learns a pidgin is constantly reshaping the pidgin words on the basis of the English words that he thinks are 'the same'. Unfortunately, most of the reliable records of pidgin so far available have been based on the use of informants who also spoke standard English.

(c) Third, we could compare successive stages of development of some pidgin which has existed over several centuries without becoming creolized (i.e. without becoming the only language of a community) to see whether the familiar patterns of regular phonetic change manifest themselves or not. This will not be possible until more centuries have passed, for the only adequately reliable records of pidgin so far available are based on current habits.

(d) An inversion is possible. Hall assures us that Haitian Creole is a Romance language, specifically a form, even though highly aberrant, of North French, and that between Old French and current Haitian Creole one finds the usual patterns of phonetic change. Given this, the problem is to determine, so far as historical records allow, the extent to which children participated in the original pidginization of French in Haiti several centuries ago. It might be that in this case childhood continuity was not effectively broken. But if it was, then our hypothesis must immediately be rejected.

(3) Finally, there is the study of communities where childhood continuity is minimal or lacking because of the isolation of small groups from each other. In most known cases of real isolation, such as the Tarahumara, the linguistic picture has not yet been adequately investigated, so that the test has to be deferred. But here, also, a sort of inversion is possible. We may search the records of those communities where the historical linguistic situation is already known to be normal, in order to find the worst possible conditions for childhood continuity. This will in a sense set a lower limit: if childhood continuity is indeed essential, then the minimum *amount* of such childhood continuity will be, at most, not greater than the amount found under these worst conditions.

So far the worst conditions that I have been able to discover are those among certain subgroups of the Cree Indians—where, in Bloomfield's Algonquian studies, we are assured of a normal historical linguistic picture. The Cree Indians spend the fall and winter hunting season in small hunting groups, several of which come together for the spring and summer. Among the Grand Lake Victoria Cree, the hunting group consists, on the average, of five or six persons, of whom one or two are active hunters—and hence relatively mature males. Since the remainder of the hunting group cannot consist entirely of children, we have an average figure of one to three children per group. At worst, a child during the hunting season will be in contact with no other children at all; at best, he will have contact with a handful only. In the spring and summer, more children will be thrown together. This yearly cycle of relative isolation and relatively greater contact, then, is at least enough to guarantee regularity of phonetic change; the actual necessary minimum may be smaller.

In concluding, we must emphasize the nature and purpose of the line of study proposed here. The assumption of regular phonetic change has been demonstrated to hold for every group of languages which has been seriously studied. It is our best working hypothesis in studying a new family of possibly related languages; it has never yet failed us, and without it we would not know what to do. But we must reserve judgement on whether regularity of phonetic change is a human universal, a generalization of genuine cross-cultural validity, until such matters as have been discussed here are more thoroughly investigated. If it is indeed a valid cross-cultural generalization, then the feather in the cap of nineteenth-century linguistic science grows to gigantic proportions, for 'regularity of phonetic change' then becomes a NATURAL LAW in the sphere of human behaviour—one of the few such natural laws, if not the only one, so far established by social science. But if there are certain limitations on its validity, this is also important for us to know—and certainly no honour is lost to the masters of the nineteenth century.

6 KINGSLEY DAVIS
Severe Social Isolation

These two extracts cover the important area of literature on children isolated for a variety of reasons from all or most human contact. The myths and realities of the so-called 'wolf-children' extend back into history—Romulus and Remus, Caspar Hauser, Kamala and Amala. R. Brown (1958) gives many references and an interesting summary of the evidence.

The children when found had adapted themselves to whatever had been their environment. Kamala and Amala who had evidently lived with wolves in India went on all fours, having large callouses on their hands, knees and feet. They barked and could kill and devour a live chicken; their teeth were evidently fang-like.

Generally these wolf children cannot speak and indeed have no clear understanding of the need to communicate. If they are found early enough in life they have been able to be taught to say a few words; but none of them seems to have lived long after being found.

The descriptions of these poor children can show us clearly how much of cultural aspects of behaviour are transferred to children when they are young and that there appears to be little human behaviour which is not learned including communicating, talking, walking upright, playing with toys.

R. Brown (1958) *Words and Things*, New York: The Free Press. See pp. 186-92 for a discussion of wolf children.

Abstract

A girl of more than five years was discovered incarcerated in an upstairs room. She had apparently been there since babyhood and was physically malnourished and apathetic as well as mentally blank. Taken first to a county home, then to a foster-home, and finally to a school for defective children, she improved very slowly. She is still a virtually unsocialized creature, manifesting many parallels with other cases of

Kingsley Davis: Extract from 'Extreme social isolation of a child' *American Journal of Sociology*, Vol. 52, No. 4, University of Chicago Press 1940, pp. 554–565.

isolated children and bearing out the Cooley-Mead-Dewey-Faris theory of socialization.

The present paper, dealing with an incarcerated child, is of the nature of a progress report. The girl it describes is still under observation and is likely to remain so for many years. Hence the present results are necessarily inconclusive.

According to the *New York Times* for February 6, 1938, a girl of more than five years had been found 'tied to an old chair in a storage room on the second floor' of a farm home seventeen miles from a small Pennsylvania city. The child, said the report,

> was wedged into the chair which was tilted backwards to rest on a coal bucket, her spindly arms tied above her head. She was unable to talk or move. . . . 'The child was dressed in a dirty shirt and napkin', the officer said. 'Her hands, arms and legs were just bones, with skin drawn over them, so frail she couldn't use them. She never had enough nourishment. She never grew normally, and the chair on which she lay, half reclining and half sitting, was so small the child had to double her legs partly under her.'

The reason for this situation was that the child, Anna, was illegitimate. She was the second illegitimate child the mother had borne, and since the mother resided with her father and other relatives in the paternal homestead, she found her father so angry that he was averse even to seeing this second child. Hence she kept it in an out-of-the-way room.

Upon reading this report the writer and a student assistant went to see the child. Later, subsequent trips were made, and between visits reports from various persons connected with the child were received by mail. Our records now seem reasonably complete and confirm the salient facts in the *Times* account.[1]

By the time we arrived on the scene, February 7, Anna had been in her new abode, the county home,[2] for only three days. But she

---

[1] It is doubtful that the child's hands at the time of discovery were tied. It is more likely that she was confined to her crib in the first period of life and at all times kept locked in her room to keep her from falling down the steep stairs leading immediately from the door and to keep the grandfather from seeing her. It is doubtful if the child was ever kept in the attic, as the report also stated.

[2] She remained in the home more than nine months, being removed on

was already beginning to change. When first brought to the county home she had been completely apathetic—had lain in a limp, supine position, immobile, expressionless, indifferent to everything. Her flaccid feet had fallen forward, making almost a straight line with the skeleton-like legs, indicating that the child had long lain on her back to the point of exhaustion and atrophy of her foot muscles. She was believed to be deaf and possibly blind. Her urine, according to the nurse, had been extremely concentrated and her stomach exceedingly bloated. It was thought that she had suffered at one time from rickets, though later medical opinion changed the diagnosis to simple malnutrition. Her blood count had been very low in haemoglobin. No sign of disease had been discovered.

Upon our arrival, three days after she was brought to the county home, most of these conditions still prevailed. But her stomach had retracted a little and she had become fairly active, being able to sit up (if placed in a sitting position) and to move her hands, arms, head, eyes, and mouth quite freely. These changes had resulted from a high vitamin diet, massage, and attention. In spite of her physical condition she had an attractive facial appearance, with no discernible stigmata. Her complexion, features, large blue eyes, and even teeth (in good shape though not quite normal in size) gave her a favourable appearance.

Since Anna turned her head slowly towards a loud-ticking clock held near her, we concluded that she could hear. Other attempts to make her notice sounds, such as clapping hands or speaking to her, elicited no response; yet when the door was opened suddenly she tended to look in that direction. Her feet were sensitive to touch. She exhibited the plantar, patellar, and pupillary reflexes. When sitting up she bounced rhythmically up and down on the bed—a recent habit of which she was very fond. Though her eyes surveyed the room, especially the ceiling, it was difficult to tell if she was looking at anything in particular. She neither smiled nor cried in our presence, and the only sound she made—a slight sucking intake of breath with the lips—occurred rarely. She did frown or scowl occasionally in response to no observable stimulus; otherwise she remained expressionless.

November 11 to a foster-home. The institution is primarily for the aged and infirm in the county where Anna lived, but contains cases of nearly all types

Next morning the child seemed more alert. She liked food and lay on her back to take it. She could not chew or drink from a cup but had to be fed from a bottle or spoon—this in spite of the fact that she could grasp and manipulate objects with her hands. Towards numerous toys given her by well-wishers all over the country she showed no reaction. They were simply objects to be handled in a distracted manner; there was no element of play. She liked having her hair combed. When physically restrained she exhibited considerable temper. She did not smile except when coaxed and did not cry.

She had thus made some progress during her three days in the county home. Subsequently her progress in the home was slower. But before dealing with her later history, let us first review more completely the background facts in the case.

Anna was born March 6, 1932, in a private nurse's home. Shortly thereafter she was taken to a children's home. For a time she was boarded with a practical nurse. To those who saw and cared for her, she seemed an entirely normal baby—indeed, a beautiful child, as more than one witness has asserted. At the age of six to ten months she was taken back to her mother's home because no outside agency wished the financial responsibility of caring for her. In her mother's home she was perpetually confined in one room, and here she soon began to suffer from malnutrition, living solely on a diet of milk and getting no sunshine. She developed impetigo. The doctor, according to the mother, prescribed some external medicine which made the child 'look like a nigger', and which the mother ceased to use for that reason. The mother,[1] a large woman of twenty-seven, alleges that she tried to get the child welfare agency to take Anna, but that she was refused for financial reasons. The mother, resenting the trouble which Anna's presence caused her and wanting to get rid of the girl, paid little attention to her. She apparently did nothing but

---

[1] The mother was reported to have the mentality of a child of ten. We did not interview the persons who gave the intelligence test but did interview the mother herself. She seems probably subnormal, and this is the opinion of most people who know her. But it is doubtful if her status is any lower than that of a high-grade moron, and she may be merely a dull normal.

Anna's father, according to one story, is a wealthy farmer living in the same rural section as the mother, distantly kin to her. Another story has it, however, that a syphilitic married man in the near-by town is the father.

feed the child, not taking the trouble to bathe, train, supervise, or caress her. Though she denies tying the child at any time, it is perhaps true that the child was restrained in some way (by tying, confining in a crib, or otherwise) and gradually, as her physical condition became worse, due to confinement and poor diet, became so apathetic that she could be safely left unrestrained without danger of moving from her chair. Anna's brother, the first illegitimate child, seems to have ignored her except to mistreat her occasionally.

The bedroom in which Anna was confined was reported to have been extraordinarily dirty and contained a double bed on which the mother and son slept while Anna reclined in a broken chair. The mother carried up and fed to Anna huge quantities of milk. Towards Anna's fifth birthday the mother, apparently on advice, began feeding her thin oatmeal with a spoon, but Anna never learned to eat solid food.

Anna's social contacts with others were then at a minimum. What few she did have were of a perfunctory or openly antagonistic kind, allowing no opportunity for *Gemeinschaft* to develop. She affords therefore an excellent subject for studying the effects of extreme social isolation.

Ten days after our first visit Anna showed some improvement. She was more alert, had more ability to fix her attention, had more expression, handled herself better, looked healthier. Moreover, she had found her tongue—in a physical sense. Whereas it had formerly lain inactive back in her mouth, she now stuck it out frequently and with enjoyment. She showed taste discrimination, for she now resisted taking cod-liver oil, which she had previously not distinguished from milk. She was beginning, in fact, to dislike any new type of food. Visual discrimination was attested by the fact that she apparently preferred a green pencil to a yellow one. She smiled more often, regularly followed with her eye the movements of the two other small children temporarily quartered in her room, and handled her toys in a more definite fashion. She could sit up better and, while lying down, could raise her head from the pillow. She liked now to sit on the edge of the bed and dangle her feet. The doctor claimed that she had a new trick every day.

She had not, however, learned any way to seek attention, to

manifest wants, to chew, or to control her elimination. Only one sociable stunt had she begun to learn—rubbing foreheads with the nurse, a sport of which she later became very fond. On the other hand, her ritualistic hand play, a noticeable trait at this time, was entirely asocial.[1]

On this second visit we took along a clinical psychologist, Edward Carr. He began by checking the reflexes, finding none that were defective. He then gave Anna a three-figure form board test used in the Form L Revision of the Stanford-Binet. Anna was unable to place the blocks in the appropriately shaped holes, though apparently by chance she did once place the round piece satisfactorily. She more readily removed the blocks from the board and played with them idly for a time. When Mr. Carr first attempted by pantomine to get her to place the blocks, she seemed to concentrate, but only momentarily; and this concentration, so limited in results, apparently tired her too greatly for further efforts.[2]

The next visit, on March 22, revealed little change, except for slight physical improvement. She could lift her hips from the bed; the nurse had induced her to laugh outright by tickling her and laughing uproariously herself; and the nurse believed that Anna recognized her. The doctor had changed his early optimistic opinion; he now believed the child was congenitally deficient.

After another month Anna was five pounds heavier, more energetic, given to laughing a good deal, and credited with having made a sound like 'da'. But that was all.

On June 9, another month later, she had scarcely improved in

[1] She would hold one hand in front of her with the little finger pressed against the palm, the other three fingers close together and straight out, and would then manipulate the hand shaped in this way close to her eyes. Often when doing this she would hold a finger of her other hand in her ear. These actions gave her an idiotic appearance. She showed more skill in bending the fingers than any of us could exhibit.

[2] Mr. Carr, who represented the Psycho-educational Clinic at Pennsylvania State College, found that Anna showed accommodation for both light and distance, that she winked when a pencil was suddenly shoved towards her eyes and when a tumbler was struck with a spoon just behind her ear, and that the patellar and plantar reflexes were present. It being impossible to administer any standardized tests involving language, he examined her with reference to the motor-behaviour items in Gesell's developmental scale. The items passed included the following: resisting head pressure (appears normally at four months), lifting head while in prone position (six months), sitting up (nine months), clasping cubes (six months), picking up cube (six months), scribbling (eighteen months—but this 'scribbling' appeared to us to be an accident).

any respect. When tested by the writer according to the items of the Gesell schedule, she seemed to rank with a one-year-old or better in motor activities involving hands and eyes. But with regard to linguistic and purposive behaviour, she lagged behind. If any estimate were made, it could be said that she definitely ranked below the one-year-old child.

By August 12 she was still improving physically. Her legs had calves in them, and she liked to exhibit her strength in rough-housing. She would laugh heartily, often make a 'tsha-tsha-tsha' sound with her lips, once or twice making a verbal type of sound, though meaningless. When held by someone, she could 'walk' by putting one foot in front of the other in ostentatious steps. Her interest in other persons had become more obvious, her responses more definite and discriminating.[1]

Until removed from the county home on November 11, there were few additional changes. By this time she could barely stand while holding to something. When put on a carpet she could scoot but not crawl. She visibly liked people, as manifested by smiling, rough-housing, and hair-pulling. But she was still an unsocialized individual, for she had learned practically nothing.

If we ask why she had learned so little—not even to chew or drink from a glass—in nine months, the answer probably lies in the long previous isolation and in the conditions at the county home. At the latter institution she was early deprived of her two little room-mates and was left alone. In the entire establishment there

[1] Anna had for weeks been without any playmates in her room. As a test a little boy (age five) was brought in. We all left the room and peered back. Anna took a definite interest in him. She tried her trick of looking hard into his eyes and moving her head near his to rub foreheads. She clapped her hands, manifesting more interest in him than he in her.

The nurse said that Anna had played with kittens a few days previously by swinging them by their tails. We secured two kittens and put them on her bed. This time she became paralysed with fright. She made little noise, except a stifled yell once or twice, and she made no effort to get away or push the kittens off.

This paralysed type of reaction was characteristic. Initiative seemed virtually impossible for her. A temper tantrum previously exhibited had this character. She waved her head from side to side and flipped her hands up and down—a nervous, futile sort of tantrum behaviour. It was as if she had no channels of expression or action, no mode of dealing with the environment.

As soon as the kittens were out of sight she forgot about them, but the fright returned whenever they were placed in her presence. During her fright she broke into the first crying spell the writer had witnessed. It was a real child's cry.

was only one nurse, who had three hundred and twenty-four other inmates to look after. Most of Anna's care was turned over to adult inmates, many of whom were mentally deficient and scarcely able to speak themselves. Part of the time Anna's door was shut. In addition to this continued isolation, Anna was given no stimulus to learning. She was fed, clothed, and cleaned without having to turn a hand in her own behalf. She was never disciplined or rewarded, because nobody had the time for the tedious task. All benefits were for her in the nature of things and therefore not rewards. Thus she remained in much the same animal-like stage, except that she did not have the animal's inherently organized structure, and hence remained in a more passive, inadequate state.

On our visit of December 6 a surprise awaited us, for Anna had undergone what was for her a remarkable transformation—she had begun to learn. Not that she could speak, but she could do several things formerly considered impossible. She could descend the stairs (by sitting successively on each one), could hold a doughnut in her hand and eat it (munching like a normal child), could grasp a glass of tomato juice and drink it by herself, could take a step or two while holding to something, and could feed herself with a spoon. These accomplishments, small indeed for a child of seven, represented a transformation explainable, no doubt, by her transference from the county home to a private family where she was the sole object of one woman's assiduous care.

Anna had been in the foster-home less than a month, but the results were plain to see. Her new guardian was using the same common-sense methods by which mothers from time immemorial have socialized their infants—unremitting attention, repetitive correction, and countless small rewards and punishments, mixed always with sympathetic interest and hovering physical presence. These Anna was getting for the first time in her life.

One thing seemed noticeable. Anna was more like a one-year-old baby than she had been before. She was responsive in the untutored, random, energetic way of a baby. When one beckoned and called her, she would make an effort to come, smiling and going through excited extra motions.

A month later more improvement along the same lines was noted. Though grave limitations remained, Anna was definitely becoming more of a human being.

Still later, on March 19, 1939, her accomplishments were the following: she was able to walk alone for a few steps without falling; she was responsive to the verbal commands of her foster-mother, seeming to understand in a vague sort of way what the latter wanted her to do; she definitely recognized the social worker who took her weekly to the doctor and who therefore symbolized to her the pleasure of an automobile ride; she expressed by anxious bodily movements her desire to go out for a ride; she seemed unmistakably to seek and to like attention, though she did not sulk when left alone; she was able to push a doll carriage in front of her and to show some skill in manipulating it. She was, furthermore, much improved physically, being almost fat, with chubby arms and legs and having more energy and alertness. On the visit prior to this one she had shown that she could quickly find and eat candy which she saw placed behind a pillow, could perform a knee-bending exercise, could use ordinary utensils in eating (e.g., could convey liquid to her mouth in a spoon), could manifest a sense of neatness (by putting bread back on a plate after taking a bite from it). Limitations still remaining, however, were as follows: she said nothing—could not even be taught to say 'bye-bye'; she had to be watched to tell when elimination was imminent; she hardly played when alone; she had little curiosity, little initiative; it seemed still impossible to establish any communicative contact with her.

On August 30, 1939, Anna was taken from the foster-home and moved to a small school for defective children. Observations made at this time showed her to have become a fat girl twenty pounds overweight for her age. Yet she could walk better and could almost run. Her toilet habits showed that she understood the whole procedure. She manifested an obvious comprehension of many verbal instructions, though she could not speak.

Comparison of Anna with other cases of isolated children reveals several interesting parallels, both in their histories and in the interpretation of them. First of all, we note the almost universal failure to learn to talk with any facility, and hence the failure to master much of the cultural heritage. Second, we note the nearly universal presence of sensory abnormalities. Finally, we note, and also question, the usual interpretation of these recurrent facts—namely, that they are due to congenital feeble-mindedness.

Though Anna at present cannot speak, she is not an unusual member of her peculiar class. The feral child, Kamala, found at the age of eight, was able to utter only forty words after six years of tutoring,[1] and somewhat similar slowness is encountered in other cases.[2] Inability to walk or run and pronounced peculiarities of gait are also exceedingly characteristic; and some sort of abnorf mality of the senses, either as acuteness or dullness, appears in nearly every instance.[3]

In view of these similarities it is not surprising that a standard interpretation has been applied to practically every case—namely, that the child was innately feeble-minded. Pinel declared the Wild Boy of Aveyron to be a fake as to wildness and an incurable idiot as to mentality, and Itard, after five years of exasperating effort,

[1] P. C. Squires, 'Wolf Children of India' *American Journal of Psychology*, XXXVIII, 1927, 313–15.

[2] Sanichar, found at about the age of seven, could not speak even as a grown man. He merely uttered incomprehensible sounds (G. C. Ferris, *Sanichar, the Wolf-Boy of India* [New York: Published by the Author, 1902], pp. 31–3). The girl of Songi, discovered at about ten years of age, learned after several years to speak, but apparently not very well (Madam Hecquet, *The History of a Savage Girl* [London: Dursley, Davison, Mauson, Bland, & Jones], pp. 23, 34–5, and 61–3). Caspar Hauser, who might seem an exception to the rule, actually remained, to the last, awkward in language (Anselm von Feuerbach, *Caspar Hauser*, trans. from German [2nd ed.; Boston: Allen & Ticknor, 1833], I, 54). His case is not clear, however, for it appears he could pronounce some words when first discovered (ibid., pp. 4–5). Other instances of speech difficulties seem as numerous as the cases of isolated children, though the evidence is scanty and dubious.

[3] Kamala possessed extremely acute hearing when discovered and an animal-like sense of smell. She could smell meat at a great distance. After six years in civilization she could still see better at night than in the daytime (Squires, op. cit.). Sanichar's sense of hearing seemed practically destroyed (Ferris, op. cit., p. 28). The senses of the boy of Aveyron 'were extraordinarily apathetic. His nostrils were filled with snuff without making him sneeze. He picked up potatoes from boiling water. A pistol fired near him provoked hardly any response though the sound of cracking a walnut caused him to turn round' (J. M. G. Itard, *The Wild Boy of Aveyron*, trans. with Introd. by George Humphrey [New York and London, 1932]). The resemblance to Anna is obvious. Months after Anna had been in the county home we blew up a paper bag, exploded it suddenly behind her head, and found that she winced a bit, but did not really mind a loud sound next to her ear. This in spite of the fact that nothing seemed wrong with her hearing apparatus. Like many isolated children, she was fond of music. The conclusion seems inescapable that her deafness was functional, not organic, just as that of the boy of Aveyron. Caspar Hauser's senses 'appeared at first to be in a state of torpor, and only gradually to open to the perception of external objects'. Yet he had an extraordinary ability to see in the dark (Feuerbach, op. cit., pp. 26 and 166–7).

ultimately admitted that the boy may have been mentally deficient from the start, though he still attributed great importance to his long isolation. Popular interest in feeble-mindedness and in biological determinism led to general agreement with Pinel's verdict. But recently scientific opinion has been changing. F. S. Freeman, an authority on individual differences, believes that the Aveyron boy's stupidity was due to his long period of social isolation.

Even if it is granted that the boy was quite dull to begin with, it should have been possible to achieve much more with him than was the case, unless one allows for the peculiar conditions under which he lived, and for the 'fixing' process resulting from these conditions. . . . Itard's reports present the case of an individual whose early life so shaped his behaviour and fixed his abilities that even five years of painstaking, devoted, and intelligent instruction were inadequate to produce the mental manifestations of even a low-grade moron.

Similarly, W. N. Kellog argues for the innate normality of this and other feral children. He assumes that they probably possessed an entirely normal equipment—otherwise survival in a harsh environment would have been impossible. They developed responses suitable to their surroundings. Hence their subsequent inability to learn is attributable to the difficulty of uprooting fundamental, basically intrenched habits formed by earlier experience.[1]

There is one actual case in which the hypothesis was disproved. This was the case of Edith Riley, who, after incarceration in a closet for some years, was said at twelve to be feeble-minded. She recovered complete normality within two years.[2]

[1] This agrees with the general opinion concerning the importance of the early years in development. 'A large percentage of children previously diagnosed as feeble-minded have been proved to be sound in all respects except in . . . acquired reactions. If discovered at an early age the 'inherited' deficiencies of these individuals have been satisfactorily corrected through specialized education, although this has not been possible if they have persisted too long in their original habits' ('Humanizing the Ape' *Psychological Review*, XXXVIII, 1931, 160–76). Similar arguments are contained in Humphrey's Introduction to Itard's work, op. cit., pp. x–xi.

[2] *New York Times*, November 17, 1931, sec. 4, p. 6, and December 24, 1931, sec. 12, p. 1; *New York Daily Mirror*, magazine section, March 27, 1938, p. 6. This is an interesting case. differing from most of the others in that the child was

Conclusions

1. Comparing Anna with other isolated children, bearing in mind that she seemed normal in infancy, and noting her progress to date, one can maintain that though she is still at the idiot level in mentality this fact is largely the result of social isolation.

2. But if the striking parallel with other known cases diminishes the probability of congenital deficiency, it also diminishes the chance of a favourable outcome, for it seems almost impossible for any child to learn to speak, think, and act like a normal person after a long period of early isolation. Yet Anna is in one respect a marginal case: she was discovered before she had reached six years of age. This is young enough to allow for some plasticity. In fact, she has made a good many adjustments.

3. The comparative facts seem to indicate that the stages of socialization are to some extent necessarily related to the stages of organic development. If the delicate, complex, and logically prior stages of socialization are not acquired when the organism is plastic, they will never be acquired and the later stages never achieved (except crudely).

4. Anna's history, like others, seems to demonstrate the Cooley-Mead-Dewey-Faris theory of personality—namely, that human nature is determined by the child's communicative social contacts as much as by his organic equipment and that the system of communicative symbols is a highly complex business acquired early in life as the result of long and intimate training. It is not enough that other persons be merely present; these others must have an intimate, primary-group relationship with the child.

5. Other than this, however, the theories of socialization are generally neither wrong nor right with respect to Anna, but simply inapplicable. The psychoanalytic theory, in so far as it assumes certain wishes as given inherently in the organism and responsible for a series of subsequent developmental states, seems wrong; but in so far as it talks in terms of dynamic mechanisms, such as conflict and anxiety, it simply does not apply—because such

---

incarcerated at the late age of eight. She lost the capacity for speech and vision. But since she had once acquired these abilities, she recovered them again fairly rapidly.

mechanisms assume that socialization has already begun; that the initial stages have been traversed. The latter characteristic seems indeed true of most theories of socialization. The central problem of how the organism first acquires a self, first begins the communicative process, is skipped and taken for granted, the theory going on from this point.

A Final Note on a Case of Extreme Isolation

Abstract

Anna, an extremely isolated girl described in 1940, died in 1942. By the time of her death she had made considerable progress, but she never achieved normality. Her slowness is probably explained by long isolation, poor training, and mental deficiency. Comparison with another case, a girl found in Ohio at the same age and under similar circumstances, suggests that Anna was deficient, and that, at least for some individuals, extreme isolation up to age six does not permanently impair socialization.

Early in 1940 there appeared an account of a girl called Anna. She had been deprived of normal contact and had received a minimum of human care for almost the whole of her first six years of life. At that time observations were not complete and the report had a tentative character. Now, however, the girl is dead, and, with more information available, it is possible to give a fuller and more definitive description of the case from a sociological point of view.

Anna's death, caused by hemorrhagic jaundice, occurred on August 6, 1942. Having been born on March 1 or 6, 1932, she was approximately ten and a half years of age when she died. The previous report covered her development up to the age of almost eight years; the present one recapitulates the earlier period on the

[1] Kingsley Davis: Extract from 'Final note on a case of extreme isolation' *American Journal of Sociology*, Vol. 52, No. 5, University of Chicago Press 1947, pp. 432–7.

basis of new evidence and then covers the last two and a half years of her life.

Early History

The first few days and weeks of Anna's life were complicated by frequent changes of domicile. It will be recalled that she was an illegitimate child, the second such child born to her mother, and that her grandfather, a widowed farmer in whose house her mother lived, strongly disapproved of this new evidence of the mother's indiscretion. This fact led to the baby's being shifted about.

Two weeks after being born in a nurse's private home, Anna was brought to the family farm, but the grandfather's antagonism was so great that she was shortly taken to the house of one of her mother's friends. At this time a local minister became interested in her and took her to his house with an idea of possible adoption. He decided against adoption, however, when he discovered that she had vaginitis. The infant was then taken to a children's home in the nearest large city. This agency found that at the age of only three weeks she was already in a miserable condition, being 'terribly galled and otherwise in very bad shape'. It did not regard her as a likely subject for adoption but took her in for a while anyway, hoping to benefit her. After Anna had spent nearly eight weeks in this place, the agency notified her mother to come to get her. The mother responded by sending a man and his wife to the children's home with a view to their adopting Anna, but they made such a poor impression on the agency that permission was refused. Later the mother came herself and took the child out of the home and then gave her to this couple. It was in the home of this pair that a social worker found the girl a short time thereafter. The social worker went to the mother's home and pleaded with Anna's grandfather to allow the mother to bring the child home. In spite of threats, he refused. The child, by then more than four months old, was next taken to another children's home in a near-by town. A medical examination at this time revealed that she had impetigo, vaginitis, umbilical hernia, and a skin rash.

Anna remained in this second children's home for nearly three weeks, at the end of which time she was transferred to a private foster-home. Since, however, the grandfather would not, and the mother could not, pay for the child's care, she was finally taken back as a last resort to the grandfather's house (at the age of five and a half months). There she remained, kept on the second floor in an attic-like room because her mother hesitated to incur the grandfather's wrath by bringing her downstairs.

The mother, a sturdy woman weighing about 180 pounds, did a man's work on the farm. She engaged in heavy work such as milking cows and tending hogs and had little time for her children. Sometimes she went out at night, in which case Anna was left entirely without attention. Ordinarily, it seems, Anna received only enough care to keep her barely alive. She appears to have been seldom moved from one position to another. Her clothing and bedding were filthy. She apparently had no instruction, no friendly attention.

It is little wonder that, when finally found and removed from the room in the grandfather's house at the age of nearly six years, the child could not talk, walk, or do anything that showed intelligence. She was in an extremely emaciated and undernourished condition, with skeleton-like legs and a bloated abdomen. She had been fed on virtually nothing except cow's milk during the years under her mother's care.

Anna's condition when found, and her subsequent improvement, have been described in the previous report. It now remains to say what happened to her after that.

Later History

In 1939, nearly two years after being discovered, Anna had progressed, as previously reported, to the point where she could walk, understand simple commands, feed herself, achieve some neatness, remember people, etc. But she still did not speak, and, though she was much more like a normal infant of something over one year of age in mentality, she was far from normal for her age.

On August 30, 1939, she was taken to a private home for retarded children, leaving the county home where she had been for more than a year and a half. In her new setting she made some further progress, but not a great deal. In a report of an examination made November 6 of the same year, the head of the institution pictured the child as follows:

> Anna walks about aimlessly, makes periodic rhythmic motions of her hands, and, at intervals, makes gutteral and sucking noises. She regards her hands as if she had seen them for the first time. It was impossible to hold her attention for more than a few seconds at a time—not because of distraction due to external stimuli but because of her inability to concentrate. She ignored the task in hand to gaze vacantly about the toom. Speech is entirely lacking. Numerous unsuccessful attempts have been made with her in the hope of developing initial sounds. I do not believe that this failure is due to negativism or deafness but that she is not sufficiently developed to accept speech at this time. . . . The prognosis is not favourable. . . .

More than five months later, on April 25, 1940, a clinical psychologist, the late Professor Francis N. Maxfield, examined Anna and reported the following: large for her age; hearing 'entirely normal'; vision apparently normal; able to climb stairs; speech in the 'babbling stage' and 'promise for developing intelligible speech later seems to be good'. He said further that 'on the Merrill-Palmer scale she made a mental score of 19 months. On the Vineland social maturity scale she made a score of 23 months.'

Professor Maxfield very sensibly pointed out that prognosis is difficult in such cases of isolation. 'It is very difficult to take scores on tests standardized under average conditions of environment and experience,' he wrote, 'and interpret them in a case where environment and experience have been so unusual'. With this warning he gave it as his opinion at that time that Anna would eventually 'attain an adult mental level of six or seven years'.

The school for retarded children, on July 1, 1941, reported that Anna had reached 46 inches in height and weighed 60 pounds. She could bounce and catch a ball and was said to conform to group socialization, though as a follower rather than a leader. Toilet habits were firmly established. Food habits were normal, except that she still used a spoon as her sole implement. She could dress herself except for fastening her clothes. Most remarkable of all, she had finally begun to develop speech. She was characterized as being at about the two-year level in this regard. She could call attendants by name and bring in one when she was asked to. She had a few complete sentences to express her wants. The report concluded that there was nothing peculiar about her, except that she was feeble-minded—'probably congenital in type'.

A final report from the school, made on June 22, 1942, and evidently the last report before the girl's death, pictured only a slight advance over that given above. It said that Anna could follow directions, string beads, identify a few colours, build with blocks, and differentiate between attractive and unattractive pictures. She had a good sense of rhythm and loved a doll. She talked mainly in phrases but would repeat words and try to carry on a conversation. She was clean about clothing. She habitually washed her hands and brushed her teeth. She would try to help other children. She walked well and could run fairly well, though clumsily. Although easily excited, she had a pleasant disposition.

Interpretation

Such was Anna's condition just before her death. It may seem as if she had not made much progress, but one must remember the condition in which she had been found. One must recall that she had no glimmering of speech, absolutely no ability to walk, no sense of gesture, not the least capacity to feed herself even when the food was put in front of her, and no comprehension of cleanliness. She was so apathetic that it was hard to tell whether or not she could hear. And all this at the age of nearly six years. Compared with this condition, her capacities at the time of her death seem striking indeed, though they do not amount to much more than a two-and-a-half-year mental level. One conclusion therefore seems safe, namely, that her isolation prevented a considerable amount of mental development that was undoubtedly part of her capacity. Just what her original capacity was, of course, is hard to say; but her development after her period of confinement (including the ability to walk and run, to play, dress, fit into a social situation, and, above all, to speak) shows that she had at least this much capacity—capacity that never could have been realized in her original condition of isolation.

A further question is this: What would she have been like if she had received a normal upbringing from the moment of birth? A definitive answer would have been impossible in any case, but even an approximate answer is made difficult by her early death. If one assumes, as was tentatively surmised in the previous report, that it is 'almost impossible for any child to learn to speak, think, and act like a normal person after a long period of early isolation', it seems likely that Anna might have had a normal or near-normal capacity, genetically speaking. On the other hand, it was pointed out that Anna represented 'a marginal case, [because] she was discovered before she had reached six years of age', an age 'young enough to allow for some plasticity'. While admitting, then, that Anna's isolation *may* have been the major cause (and was certainly a minor cause) of her lack of rapid mental progress during the four and a half years following her rescue from neglect, it is necessary to entertain the hypothesis that she was congenitally deficient.

In connection with this hypothesis, one suggestive though by no means conclusive circumstance needs consideration, namely, the mentality of Anna's forebears. Information on this subject is easier to obtain, as one might guess, on the mother's than on the father's side. Anna's maternal grandmother, for example, is said to have been college educated and wished to have her children receive a good education, but her husband, Anna's stern grandfather, apparently a shrewd, hard-driving, calculating farmowner, was so penurious that her ambitions in this direction were thwarted. Under the circumstances her daughter (Anna's mother) managed, despite having to do hard work on the farm, to complete the eighth grade in a country school. Even so, however, the daughter was evidently not very smart. 'A schoolmate of [Anna's mother] stated that she was retarded in school work; was very gullible at this age; and that her morals even at this time were discussed by other students.' Two tests administered to her on March 4, 1938, when she was thirty-two years of age, showed that she was mentally deficient. On the Stanford Revision of the Binet-Simon Scale her performance was equivalent to that of a child of eight years, giving her an I.Q. of 50 and indicating mental deficiency of 'middle-grade moron type'.

As to the identity of Anna's father, the most persistent theory holds that he was an old man about seventy-four years of age at the time of the girl's birth. If he was the one, there is no indication of mental or other biological deficiency, whatever one may think of his morals. However, someone else may actually have been the father.

To sum up, Anna's heredity is of the kind that *might* have given rise to innate mental deficiency, though not necessarily.

Comparison with Another Case

Perhaps more to the point than speculations about Anna's ancestry would be a case for comparison. If a child could be discovered who had been isolated about the same length of time as Anna but had achieved a much quicker recovery and a greater mental development, it would be a stronger indication that Anna was deficient to start with.

Such a case does exist. It is the case of a girl found at about the same time as Anna and under strikingly similar circumstances. A full description of the details of this case has not been published, but, in addition to newspaper reports, an excellent preliminary account by a speech specialist, Dr. Marie K. Mason, who played an important role in the handling of the child, has appeared.[1] Also the late Dr. Francis N. Maxfield, clinical psychologist at Ohio State University, as was Dr Mason, has written an unpublished but penetrating analysis of the case. Some of his observations have been included in Professor Zingg's book on feral man.[2] The following discussion is drawn mainly from these enlightening materials. The writer, through the kindness of Professors Mason and Maxfield, did have a chance to observe the girl in April, 1940, and to discuss the features of her case with them.

Born apparently one month later than Anna, the girl in question, who has been given the pseudonym Isabelle, was discovered in November, 1938, nine months after the discovery of Anna. At the time she was found she was approximately six and a half years of age. Like Anna, she was an illegitimate child and had been kept

[1] Marie K. Mason, 'Learning To Speak after Six and One-Half Years of Silence' *Journal of Speech Disorders*, VII, 1942, 295–304.
[2] J. A. L. Singh and Robert M. Zingg, *Wolf-Children and Feral Man* (New York: Harper & Bros., 1941), pp. 248–51.

in seclusion for that reason. Her mother was a deaf-mute, having become so at the age of two, and it appears that she and Isabelle had spent most of their time together in a dark room shut off from the rest of the mother's family. As a result Isabelle had no chance to develop speech; when she communicated with her mother, it was by means of gestures. Lack of sunshine and inadequacy of diet had caused Isabelle to become rachitic. Her legs in particular were affected; they 'were so bowed that as she stood erect the soles of her shoes came nearly flat together, and she got about with a skittering gait'. Her behaviour towards strangers, especially men, was almost that of a wild animal, manifesting much fear and hostility. In lieu of speech she made only a strange croaking sound. In many ways she acted like an infant. 'She was apparently utterly unaware of relationships of any kind. When presented with a ball for the first time, she held it in the palm of her hand, then reached out and stroked my face with it. Such behaviour is comparable to that of a child of six months.' At first it was even hard to tell whether or not she could hear, so unused were her senses. Many of her actions resembled those of deaf children.

It is small wonder that, once it was established that she could hear, specialists working with her believed her to be feeble-minded. Even on non-verbal tests her performance was so low as to promise little for the future. Her first score on the Stanford-Binet was 19 months, practically at the zero point of the scale. On the Vineland social maturity scale her first score was 39, representing an age level of two and a half years. 'The general impression was that she was wholly uneducable and that any attempt to teach her to speak, after so long a period of silence, would meet with failure.'

In spite of this interpretation, the individuals in charge of Isabelle launched a systematic and skilful programme of training. It seemed hopeless at first. The approach had to be through pantomime and dramatization, suitable to an infant. It required one week of intensive effort before she even made her first attempt at vocalization. Gradually she began to respond, however, and, after the first hurdles had at last been overcome, a curious thing happened. She went through the usual stages of learning characteristic of the years from one to six not only in proper succession but far more rapidly than normal. In a little over two months after her first vocalization she was putting sentences together. Nine months after that she could identify words and sentences on the printed page, could write well, could add to ten, and could retell a story after hearing it. Seven months beyond this point she had a vocabulary of 1,500–2,000 words and was asking complicated questions. Starting from an educational level of between one and three years (depending on what aspect one considers), she had reached a normal level by the time she was eight and a half years old. In short, she covered in two years the stages of learning that ordinarily require six. Or, to put it another way, her I.Q. trebled in a year and a half. The speed with which she reached the normal level of mental development seems analogous to the recovery of body weight in a growing child after an illness, the recovery being achieved by an extra fast rate of growth for a period after the illness until normal weight for the given age is again attained.

When the writer saw Isabelle a year and a half after her discovery, she gave him the impression of being a very bright, cheerful, energetic little girl. She spoke well, walked and ran without trouble, and sang with gusto and accuracy. Today she is over fourteen years old and has passed the sixth grade in a public school. Her teachers say that she participates in all school activities as normally as other children. Though older than her classmates, she has fortunately not physically matured too far beyond their level.

Clearly the history of Isabelle's development is different from that of Anna's. In both cases there was an exceedingly low, or rather blank, intellectual level to begin with. In both cases it seemed that the girl might be congenitally feeble-minded. In both a considerably higher level was reached later on. But the Ohio girl achieved a normal mentality within two years, whereas Anna was still marked inadequate at the end of four and a half years. This difference in achievement may suggest that Anna had less initial capacity. But an alternative hypothesis is possible.

One should remember that Anna never received the prolonged and expert attention that Isabelle received. The result of such attention, in the case of the Ohio girl, was to give her speech at an early stage, and her subsequent rapid development seems to have been a consequence of that. 'Until Isabelle's speech and language development, she had all the characteristics of a feeble-minded child.' Had Anna, who, from the standpoint of psychometric tests and early history, closely resembled this girl at the start, been given a mastery of speech at an earlier point by intensive training, her subsequent development might have been much more rapid.

The hypothesis that Anna began with a sharply inferior mental capacity is therefore not established. Even if she were deficient to start with, we have no way of knowing how much so. Under ordinary conditions she might have been a dull normal or, like her mother, a moron. Even after the blight of her isolation, if she had lived to maturity, she might have finally reached virtually the full level of her capacity, whatever it may have been. That her isolation did have a profound effect upon her mentality, there can be no doubt. This is proved by the substantial degree of change during the four and a half years following her rescue.

Consideration of Isabelle's case serves to show, as Anna's case does not clearly show, that isolation up to the age of six, with failure to acquire any form of speech and hence failure to grasp nearly the whole world of cultural meaning, does not preclude the subsequent acquisition of these. Indeed, there seems to be a process of accelerated recovery in which the child goes through the mental stages at a more rapid rate than would be the case in normal development. Just what would be the maximum age at which a person could remain isolated and still retain the capacity for full cultural acquisition is hard to say. Almost certainly it would not be as high as age fifteen; it might possibly be as low as age ten. Undoubtedly various individuals would differ considerably as to the exact age.

Anna's is not an ideal case for showing the effects of extreme isolation, partly because she was possibly deficient to begin with, partly because she did not receive the best training available, and partly because she did not live long enough. Nevertheless, her case is instructive when placed in the record with numerous other cases of extreme isolation. This and the previous article about her are meant to place her in the record. It is to be hoped that other cases will be described in the scientific literature as they are discovered (as unfortunately they will be), for only in these rare cases of extreme isolation is it possible 'to observe *concretely separated* two factors in the development of human personality which are always otherwise only analytically separated, the biogenic and the sociogenic factors'.

7 B. L. WHORF
The Organization of Reality

In this reading and the one following, the significance of language in the transmission and development of social and cultural structure is discussed. Whorf concentrates on how the particular language that we acquire as our maternal language 'dissects nature' and thus gives us our particular 'world view'. Whorf, although not a professional linguist, spent many years examining the languages and cultures of Amerindians. In this he was following a distinguished group of Americans, including Edward Sapir, who found it unhelpful to describe the language of these Amerindian tribes in conventional, i.e. Standard Average European (SAE), terms.

Whorf's work on 'linguistic relativity' shows us that ways of structuring the experiences of the world and the ways of thinking are linked to the language which is spoken, for as a child acquires his language he also acquires a 'shaper of ideas', or what Carroll has called a 'lattice'.

Every normal person in the world, past infancy in years, can and does talk. By virtue of that fact, every person—civilized or uncivilized—carries through life certain naïve but deeply rooted ideas about talking and its relation to thinking. Because of their firm connection with speech habits that have become unconscious and automatic, these notions tend to be rather intolerant of opposition. They are by no means entirely personal and haphazard; their basis is definitely systematic, so that we are justified in calling them a system of natural logic—a term that seems to me preferable to the term common sense, often used for the same thing.

According to natural logic, the fact that every person has talked fluently since infancy makes every man his own authority on the process by which he formulates and communicates. He has merely to consult a common substratum of logic or reason which he and everyone else are supposed to possess. Natural logic says that

B. L. Whorf: Extract from 'Science and Linguistics'. In J. B. Carroll (ed.) *Language, Thought, and Reality*, M.I.T. Press, 1956, pp. 207–19.

talking is merely an incidental process concerned strictly with communication, not with formulation of ideas. Talking, or the use of language, is supposed only to 'express' what is essentially already formulated non-linguistically. Formulation is an independent process, called thought or thinking, and is supposed to be largely indifferent to the nature of particular languages. Languages have grammars, which are assumed to be merely norms of conventional and social correctness, but the use of language is supposed to be guided not so much by them as by correct, rational, or intelligent *thinking*.

Thought, in this view, does not depend on grammar but on laws of logic or reason which are supposed to be the same for all observers of the universe—to represent a rationale in the universe that can be 'found' independently by all intelligent observers, whether they speak Chinese or Choctaw. In our own culture, the formulations of mathematics and of formal logic have acquired the reputation of dealing with this order of things: i.e., with the realm and laws of pure thought. Natural logic holds that different

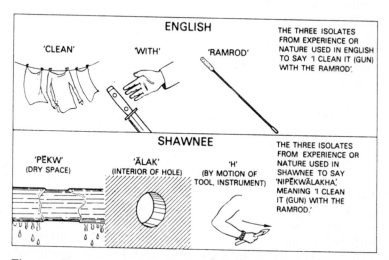

Figure 1. Languages dissect nature differently. The different isolates of meaning (thoughts) used by English and Shawnee in reporting the same experience, that of cleaning a gun by running the ramrod through it. The pronouns 'I' and 'it' are not shown by symbols, as they have the same meaning in each language. In Shawnee ni- equals 'I'; -a equals 'it'.

languages are essentially parallel methods for expressing this one-and-the-same rationale of thought and, hence, differ really in but minor ways which may seem important only because they are seen at close range. It holds that mathematics, symbolic logic, philosophy, and so on are systems contrasted with language which deal directly with this realm of thought, not that they are themselves specialized extensions of language. The attitude of natural logic is well shown in an old quip about a German grammarian who devoted his whole life to the study of the dative case. From the point of view of natural logic, the dative case and grammar in general are an extremely minor issue. A different attitude is said to have been held by the ancient Arabians: Two princes, so the story goes, quarrelled over the honour of putting on the shoes of the most learned grammarian of the realm; whereupon their father, the caliph, is said to have remarked that it was the glory of his kingdom that great grammarians were honoured even above kings.

The familiar saying that the exception proves the rule contains a good deal of wisdom, though from the standpoint of formal logic it became an absurdity as soon as 'prove' no longer meant 'put on trial'. The old saw began to be profound psychology from the time it ceased to have standing in logic. What it might well suggest to us today is that, if a rule has absolutely no exceptions, it is not recognized as a rule or as anything else; it is then part of the background of experience of which we tend to remain unconscious. Never having experienced anything in contrast to it, we cannot isolate it and formulate it as a rule until we so enlarge our experience and expand our base of reference that we encounter an interruption of its regularity. The situation is somewhat analogous to that of not missing the water till the well runs dry, or not realizing that we need air till we are choking.

For instance, if a race of people had the physiological defect of being able to see only the colour blue, they would hardly be able to formulate the rule that they saw only blue. The term blue would convey no meaning to them, their language would lack colour terms, and their words denoting their various sensations of blue would answer to, and translate, our words 'light, dark, white, black', and so on, not our word 'blue'. In order to formulate the rule or norm of seeing only blue, they would need exceptional moments in which they saw other colours. The phenomenon of gravitation forms a rule without exceptions; needless to say, the untutored person is utterly unaware of any law of gravitation, for it would never enter his head to conceive of a universe in which bodies behaved otherwise than they do at the earth's surface. Like the colour blue with our hypothetical race, the law of gravitation is a part of the untutored individual's background, not something he isolates from that background. The law could not be formulated until bodies that always fell were seen in terms of a wider astronomical world in which bodies moved in orbits or went this way and that.

Similarly, whenever we turn our heads, the image of the scene passes across our retinas exactly as it would if the scene turned around us. But this effect is background, and we do not recognize it; we do not see a room turn around us but are conscious only of having turned our heads in a stationary room. If we observe critically while turning the head or eyes quickly, we shall see, no motion it is true, yet a blurring of the scene between two clear views. Normally we are quite unconscious of this continual blurring but seem to be looking about in an unblurred world. Whenever we walk past a tree or house, its image on the retina changes just as if the tree or house were turning on an axis; yet we do not see trees or houses turn as we travel about at ordinary speeds. Sometimes ill-fitting glasses will reveal queer movements in the scene as we look about, but normally we do not see the relative motion of the environment when we move, our psychic makeup is somehow adjusted to disregard whole realms of phenomena that are so all-pervasive as to be irrelevant to our daily lives and needs.

Natural logic contains two fallacies: First, it does not see that the phenomena of a language are to its own speakers largely of a background character and so are outside the critical consciousness and control of the speaker who is expounding natural logic. Hence, when anyone, as a natural logician, is talking about reason, logic, and the laws of correct thinking, he is apt to be simply marching in step with purely grammatical facts that have somewhat of a background character in his own language or family of languages but are by no means universal in all languages and in no sense a common substratum of reason. Second, natural logic confuses agreement about subject matter, attained through use of language, with knowledge of the linguistic process by which agreement is attained: i.e., with the province of the despised (and to its notion superfluous) grammarian. Two fluent speakers, of English let us say, quickly reach a point of assent about the subject matter of their speech; they agree about what their language refers to. One of them, *A*, can give directions that will be carried out by the other, *B*, to *A*'s complete satisfaction. Because they thus understand each other so perfectly, *A* and *B*, as natural logicians, suppose they must of course know how it is all done. They think, e.g., that it is simply a matter of choosing words to express thoughts. If you ask *A* to explain how he got *B*'s agreement so readily, he will simply repeat to you, with more or less elaboration or abbreviation, what he said to *B*. He has no notion of the process involved. The amazingly complex system of linguistic patterns and classifications, which *A* and *B* must have in common before they can adjust to each other at all, is all background to *A* and *B*.

These background phenomena are the province of the grammarian—or of the linguist, to give him his more modern name as a scientist. The word linguist in common, and especially newspaper, parlance means something entirely different, namely, a person who can quickly attain agreement about subject matter with different people speaking a number of different languages. Such a person is better termed a polyglot or a multilingual. Scientific linguists have long understood that ability to speak a language fluently does not necessarily confer a linguistic knowledge of it, i.e., understanding of its background phenomena and its systematic processes and structure, any more than ability to play a good game of billiards confers or requires any knowledge of the laws of mechanics that operate upon the billiard table.

The situation here is not unlike that in any other field of science. All real scientists have their eyes primarily on background phenomena that cut very little ice, as such, in our daily lives; and yet their studies have a way of bringing out a close relation between these unsuspected realms of fact and such decidedly foreground activities as transporting goods, preparing food, treating the sick, or growing potatoes, which in time may become very much modified, simply because of pure scientific investigation in no way concerned with these brute matters themselves. Linguistics presents a quite similar case; the background phenomena with which it deals are involved in all our foreground activities of talking and of reaching agreement, in all reasoning and arguing of cases, in all law, arbitration, conciliation, contracts, treaties, public opinion, weighing of scientific theories, formulation of scientific results. Whenever agreement or assent is arrived at in human affairs, and whether or not mathematics or other specialized symbolisms are made part of the procedure, *this agreement is reached by linguistic processes, or else it is not reached.*

As we have seen, an overt knowledge of the linguistic processes by which agreement is attained is not necessary to reaching some sort of agreement, but it is certainly no bar thereto; the more complicated and difficult the matter, the more such knowledge is a distinct aid, till the point may be reached—I suspect the modern world has about arrived at it—when the knowledge becomes not only an aid but a necessity. The situation may be likened to that of navigation. Every boat that sails is in the lap of planetary forces; yet a boy can pilot his small craft around a harbour without benefit of geography, astronomy, mathematics, or international politics. To the captain of an ocean liner, however, some knowledge of all these subjects is essential.

When linguists became able to examine critically and scientifically a large number of languages of widely different patterns, their base of reference was expanded; they experienced an interruption of phenomena hitherto held universal, and a whole new order of significances came into their ken. It was found that the background linguistic system (in other words, the grammar) of each language is not merely a reproducing instrument for voicing ideas but rather is itself the shaper of ideas, the programme and guide for the individual's mental activity, for his analysis of impressions, for his synthesis of his mental stock in trade. Formulation of ideas is not an independent process, strictly rational in the old sense, but is part of a particular grammar, and differs, from slightly to greatly, between different grammars. We dissect nature along lines laid down by our native languages. The categories and types that we isolate from the world of phenomena we do not find there because they stare every observer in the face; on the contrary, the world is presented in a kaleidoscopic flux of impressions which has to be organized by our minds—and this means largely by the linguistic systems in our minds. We cut nature up, organize it into concepts, and ascribe significances as we do, largely because we are parties to an agreement to organize it in this way—an agreement that holds throughout our speech community and is codified in the patterns of our language. The agreement is of course an implicit and unstated one, *but its terms are absolutely obligatory*; we cannot talk at all except by subscribing to the organization and classification of data which the agreement decrees.

This fact is very significant for modern science, for it means that no individual is free to describe nature with absolute impartiality but is constrained to certain modes of interpretation even while he thinks himself most free. The person most nearly free in such respects would be a linguist familiar with very many widely different linguistic systems. As yet no linguist is in any such position. We are thus introduced to a new principle of relativity, which holds that all observers are not led by the same physical evidence to the same picture of the universe, unless their linguistic backgrounds are similar, or can in some way be calibrated.

This rather startling conclusion is not so apparent if we compare only our modern European languages, with perhaps Latin and Greek thrown in for good measure. Among these tongues there is a unanimity of major pattern which at first seems to bear out natural logic. But this unanimity exists only because these tongues are all Indo-European dialects cut to the same basic plan, being historically transmitted from what was long ago one speech community; because the modern dialects have long shared in building up a common culture; and because much of this culture, on the more intellectual side, is derived from the linguistic backgrounds of Latin and Greek. Thus this group of languages satisfies the special case of the clause beginning 'unless' in the statement of the linguistic relativity principle at the end of the preceding paragraph. From this condition follows the unanimity of description of the world in the community of modern scientists. But it must be emphasized that 'all modern Indo-European-speaking observers' is not the same thing as 'all observers'. That modern Chinese or Turkish scientists describe the world in the same terms as Western scientists means, of course, only that they have taken over bodily the entire Western system of rationalizations, not that they have corroborated that system from their native posts of observation.

When Semitic, Chinese, Tibetan, or African languages are contrasted with our own, the divergence in analysis of the world becomes more apparent; and, when we bring in the native languages of the Americas, where speech communities for many millenniums have gone their ways independently of each other and of the Old World, the fact that languages dissect nature in many different ways becomes patent. The relativity of all conceptual systems, ours included, and their dependence upon language stand revealed. That American Indians speaking only their native tongues are never called upon to act as scientific observers is in no wise to the point. To exclude the evidence which their languages offer as to what the human mind can do is like expecting botanists to study nothing but food plants and hothouse roses and then tell us what the plant world is like!

Let us consider a few examples. In English we divide most of our words into two classes, which have different grammatical and logical properties. Class 1 we call nouns, e.g., 'house, man'; class 2, verbs, e.g., 'hit, run'. Many words of one class can act secondarily as of the other class, e.g., 'a hit, a run', or 'to man (the boat)', but, on the primary level, the division between the classes is absolute. Our language thus gives us a bipolar division of nature. But nature herself is not thus polarized. If it be said that 'strike, turn, run,' are verbs because they denote temporary or short-lasting events, i.e., actions, why then is 'fist' a noun? It also is a temporary event. Why are 'lightning, spark, wave, eddy, pulsation, flame, storm, phase, cycle, spasm, noise, emotion' nouns? They are temporary events. If 'man' and 'house' are nouns because they are long-lasting and stable events, i.e., things, what then are 'keep, adhere, extend, project, continue, persist, grow, dwell,' and so on doing among the verbs? If it be objected that 'possess, adhere' are verbs because they are stable relationships rather than stable percepts, why then should 'equilibrium, pressure, current, peace, group, nation, society, tribe, sister', or any kinship term be among the nouns? It will be found that an 'event' to us means 'what our language classes as a verb' or something analogized therefrom. And it will be found that it is not possible to define 'event, thing, object, relationship', and so on, from nature, but that to define them always involves a circuitous return to the grammatical categories of the definer's language.

In the Hopi language, 'lightning, wave, flame, meteor, puff of smoke, pulsation' are verbs—events of necessarily brief duration cannot be anything but verbs. 'Cloud' and 'storm' are at about the lower limit of duration for nouns. Hopi, you see, actually has a classification of events (or linguistic isolates) by duration type, something strange to our modes of thought. On the other hand, in Nootka, a language of Vancouver Island, all words seem to us to be verbs, but really there are no classes 1 and 2; we have, as it were, a monistic view of nature that gives us only one class of word for all kinds of events. 'A house occurs' or 'it houses' is the way of saying 'house', exactly like 'a flame occurs' or 'it burns'. These terms seem to us like verbs because they are inflected for durational and temporal nuances, so that the suffixes of the word for house event make it mean long-lasting house, temporary

Figure 2. Languages classify items of experience differently. The class corresponding to one word and one thought in language A may be regarded by language B as two or more classes corresponding to two or more words and thoughts.

house, future house, house that used to be, what started out to be a house, and so on.

Hopi has one noun that covers every thing or being that flies, with the exception of birds, which class is denoted by another noun. The former noun may be said to denote the class (*FC–B*)— flying class minus bird. The Hopi actually call insect, aeroplane, and aviator all by the same word, and feel no difficulty about it. The situation, of course, decides any possible confusion among very disparate members of a broad linguistic class, such as this class (*FC–B*). This class seems to us too large and inclusive, but so would our class 'snow' to an Eskimo. We have the same word for falling snow, snow on the ground, snow packed hard like ice, slushy snow, wind-driven flying snow—whatever the situation may be. To an Eskimo, this all-inclusive word would be almost unthinkable; he would say that falling snow, slushy snow, and so on, are sensuously and operationally different, different things to contend with; he uses different words for them and for other kinds of snow. The Aztecs go even farther than we in the opposite direction, with 'cold', 'ice', and 'snow' all represented by the same basic word with different terminations; 'ice' is the noun form; 'cold', the adjectival form; and for 'snow', 'ice mist'.

What surprises most is to find that various grand generalizations of the Western world, such as time, velocity, and matter, are not essential to the construction of a consistent picture of the universe. The psychic experiences that we class under these headings are, of course, not destroyed; rather, categories derived from other kinds of experiences take over the rulership of the cosmology and seem to function just as well. Hopi may be called a timeless language. It recognizes psychological time, which is much like Bergson's 'duration', but this 'time' is quite unlike the mathematical time, T, used by our physicists. Among the peculiar properties of Hopi time are that it varies with each observer, does not permit of simultaneity, and has zero dimensions; i.e., it cannot be given a number greater than one. The Hopi do not say, 'I stayed five days', but 'I left on the fifth day'. A word referring to this kind of time, like the word 'day', can have no plural. The puzzle picture (Fig. 3) will give mental exercise to anyone who would like to figure out how the Hopi verb gets along without tenses. Actually, the only practical use of our tenses, in one-verb sentences, is to distinguish among five typical situations, which are symbolized in the picture. The timeless Hopi verb does not distinguish between the present, past, and future of the event itself but must always indicate what type of validity the *speaker* intends the statement to have: (a) report of an event (situations

OBJECTIVE FIELD	SPEAKER (SENDER)	HEARER (RECEIVER)	HANDLING OF TOPIC RUNNING OF THIRD PERSON
SITUATION 1 a.			ENGLISH..'HE IS RUNNING' HOPI........'WARI' (RUNNING, STATEMENT OF FACT)
SITUATION 1 b. OBJECTIVE FIELD BLANK DEVOID OF RUNNING			ENGLISH..'HE RAN' HOPI........'WARI' (RUNNING, STATEMENT OF FACT)
SITUATION 2			ENGLISH..'HE IS RUNNING' HOPI........'WARI' (RUNNING, STATEMENT OF FACT)
SITUATION 3 OBJECTIVE FIELD BLANK			ENGLISH..'HE RAN' HOPI........'ERA WARI' (RUNNING, STATEMENT OF FACT FROM MEMORY)
SITUATION 4 OBJECTIVE FIELD BLANK			ENGLISH..'HE WILL RUN' HOPI........'WARIKNI' (RUNNING, STATEMENT OF EXPECTATION)
SITUATION 5 OBJECTIVE FIELD BLANK			ENGLISH..'HE RUNS' (E.G. ON THE TRACK TEAM) HOPI ....'WARIKNGWE' (RUNNING, STATEMENT OF LAW)

Figure 3. Contrast between a 'temporal' language (English) and a 'timeless' language (Hopi). What are to English differences of time are to Hopi differences in the kind of validity.

1, 2, 3 in the picture); (b) expectation of an event (situation 4); (c) generalization or law about events (situation 5). Situation 1, where the speaker and listener are in contact with the same objective field, is divided by our language into the two conditions, 1*a* and 1*b*, which it calls present and past, respectively. This division is unnecessary for a language which assures one that the statement is a report.

Hopi grammar, by means of its forms called aspects and modes, also makes it easy to distinguish among momentary, continued, and repeated occurrences, and to indicate the actual sequence of reported events. Thus the universe can be described without recourse to a concept of dimensional time. How would a physics constructed along these lines work, with no T (time) in its equations? Perfectly, as far as I can see, though of course it would require different ideology and perhaps different mathematics. Of course V (velocity) would have to go too. The Hopi language has no word really equivalent to our 'speed' or 'rapid'. What translates these terms is usually a word meaning 'intense' or 'very', accompanying any verb of motion. Here is a clue to the nature of our new physics. We may have to introduce a new term I, intensity. Every thing and event will have an I, whether we regard the thing or event as moving or as just enduring or being. Perhaps the I of an electric charge will turn out to be its voltage, or potential. We shall use clocks to measure some intensities, or, rather, some *relative* intensities, for the absolute intensity of anything will be meaningless. Our old friend acceleration will still be there but doubtless under a new name. We shall perhaps call it V, meaning not velocity but variation. Perhaps all growths and accumulations will be regarded as V's. We should not have the concept of rate in the temporal sense, since, like velocity, rate introduces a mathematical and linguistic time. Of course we know that all measurements are ratios, but the measurements of intensities made by comparison with the standard intensity of a clock or a planet we do not treat as ratios, any more than we so treat a distance made by comparison with a yardstick.

A scientist from another culture that used time and velocity would have great difficulty in getting us to understand these concepts. We should talk about the intensity of a chemical reaction; he would speak of its velocity or its rate, which words we should at first think were simply words for intensity in his language. Likewise, he at first would think that intensity was simply our own word for velocity. At first we should agree, later we should begin to disagree, and it might dawn upon both sides that different systems of rationalization were being used. He would find it very hard to make us understand what he really meant by velocity of a chemical reaction. We should have no words that would fit. He would try to explain it by likening it to a running horse, to the difference between a good horse and a lazy horse. We should try to show him, with a superior laugh, that his analogy also was a matter of different intensities, aside from which there was little similarity between a horse and a chemical reaction in a beaker. We should point out that a running horse is moving relative to the ground, whereas the material in the beaker is at rest.

One significant contribution to science from the linguistic point of view may be the greater development of our sense of perspective. We shall no longer be able to see a few recent dialects of the Indo-European family, and the rationalizing techniques elaborated from their patterns, as the apex of the evolution of the human mind, nor their present wide spread as due to any survival from fitness or to anything but a few events of history—events that could be called fortunate only from the parochial point of view of the favoured parties. They, and our own thought processes with them, can no longer be envisioned as spanning the gamut of reason and knowledge but only as one constellation in a galactic expanse. A fair realization of the incredible degree of diversity of linguistic system that ranges over the globe leaves one with an inescapable feeling that the human spirit is inconceivably old; that the few thousand years of history covered by our written records are no more than the thickness of a pencil mark on the scale that measures our past experience on this planet; that the events of these recent millenniums spell nothing in any evolutionary wise, that the race has taken no sudden spurt, achieved no commanding synthesis during recent millenniums, but has only played a little with a few of the linguistic formulations and views of nature bequeathed from an inexpressibly longer past. Yet neither this feeling nor the sense of precarious dependence of all we know upon linguistic tools which themselves are largely unknown need be discouraging to science but should, rather, foster that humility which accompanies the true scientific spirit, and thus forbid that arrogance of the mind which hinders real scientific curiosity and detachment.

D. L. GOYVAERTS
8 The Acquisition of Social Roles

The focus of attention changes in this article away from the system of dissecting nature shared by whole speech communities to a consideration of how an *individual* in society acquires a use and understanding of the different roles he has to play in that society. Goyvaerts relates role behaviour and its acquisition to language functions. It is possible to see the relationship between the last reading and this one if we quote from the conclusion of Reading 8 (p. 124): 'language is a process by which the individual internalizes the social structure'. But at the same time it is possible to see how disparate are the two views: Goyvaerts does not discuss the place of language in determining what the social structure shall be. He sees the latter as merely something which has to be internalized with the aid of language. Whorf, on the other hand, assigns to language a major role in actually determining what our 'world view', including social structure, is to be. This debate, separated by decades, is a critical one, but neither Whorf's nor Goyvaerts' position completely excludes the other.

1. R. Brown (1965) defines roles as norms that apply to categories of persons. To enter a category one needs particular characteristics which are essential to the category. Male and female, mother and son, child and adult are roles which are ascribed on biological grounds. Occupational roles like lawyer and milkman have their membership defined by procedures of certification, contract, etc. When the essential characteristic applies to someone, then the norms of the role apply to him. In the course of this paper we will try to elaborate the notion 'social role' and we will also raise some suggestions with regard to roles in general, i.e. making a distinction between 'social role' which is especially relevant in terms of the *society* as a whole and 'role' being a synonym for (a separate) 'pattern of behaviour' which has relevance for the *individual* in

D. L. Goyvaerts: Extract from 'Linguistic behaviour and acquisition of social roles: one aspect of linguistic performance' *Studia Linguistica*, XXVI, 1972, pp. 1–13.

the society. These ideas seem to be implied in the writings of
M. A. K. Halliday (1966), J. Firth (1964), B. Bernstein (1964)
and R. Brown (1965). Both aspects are to be discussed because of
the importance they have in the socialization process of the
individual and because they are mainly responsible for the
equilibrium of the relationship between society on the one hand
and the individual on the other. We will also try to find out the
part that language plays with regard to these 'roles'. In essence
we will consider the co-variation between linguistic and social
phenomena. This co-variation is important when we consider the
function of language in establishing and maintaining value systems and in defining the roles which for the individual living in
society make up the total role set that constitutes his identity
which he himself takes into consideration (Halliday 1966). In
this paper we will mainly concern ourselves with sociolinguistics,
i.e. the study of the relations between (i) linguistic structure and
(ii) social structure.

2. When R. Brown speaks of categories of persons he actually
means social categories. Although Jews, Negroes etc. are categories, it seems hard to talk about the social role of Jews, the
social role of Negroes etc. This emphasizes the primary importance
of the society with regard to a discussion on 'roles'. Indeed, if
we want to answer the question 'Who holds the expectations or
prescriptions that constitute a role (i.e. social role)' the answer
is 'everyone in society'. This gives us the first possibility of conflict *within* the notion 'role'. This can be illustrated by means of a
rather extreme example, viz. the place of a hermit in the social
system. We may believe that the hermit himself regards his role
to be that of a 'religious person'. The members of a society have
particular expectations which can be said to set up the boundary
of a role. If someone consciously or unconsciously crosses this
boundary, others will look upon him as a 'character'. We reach
a strange, though by all means valid, conclusion that the hermit
has become a 'perceptible personality by violating minor role
norms. A similar procedure is reflected in language where the
use of the adverb 'too' often indicates that one has gone outside
the boundaries of an aspect (be it a role or a semantic field). The
phrase 'too good' reflects the existence of a value system within the

community and it will always have a pejorative flavour (Fig. 1). A person who is 'too good' is similar to the hermit, in that he probably does not realize the impact of the idea which the members of a society have formed about him. In order to restore the equilibrium in social interaction we refer to him as 'a character', 'an individual' or even 'an exception'. To a certain extent the use of language conditions the behaviour of any child in the society

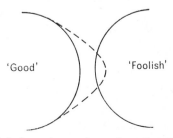

'Good'   'Foolish'

Figure 1. Violating minor rules or 'crossing the boundary'

in that it helps him to find his identity within social reality in terms of 'what should be done' and 'what should not be done'. This is one aspect of language playing a part in the acquisition of roles; these roles are mainly social because they have relevance by virtue of the society which governs the behaviour of its members; they are also partly 'patterns of behaviour' in that they are equally relevant with regard to the individual in the middle of the socialization process. Language is related to this process in the following ways: (i) the acquisition of a mastery of speech constitutes a prerequisite to full participation in one's society, (ii) language is the principal channel through which social beliefs and attitudes are communicated to the growing child, (iii) language provides a feeling of belonging to a particular community or any special subdivision of it, and (iv) the members of the community use language to *describe* the roles which the child is expected to identify (Bram 1963).

3. Roles are sets of norms and norms are prescriptions for behaviour. A person may have more than one role. We get an inter-role conflict if the expectations of other people clash with regard to the particular role. Language may play a part in this conflict if e.g. we assume, among other things, that particular styles of language are expected from an individual by his father on the one hand and his teacher on the other. A similar conflict might arise with respect to the use of a particular dialect on one occasion and the use of RP on another. This sort of conflict may eventually have a negative effect on the individual. Generally speaking, however, social roles are set against the background of sociological organization as a whole. Therefore we must take into account (i) interpersonal relationships and (ii) the classes that constitute the society. We believe that especially by virtue of these two aspects the child comes to find his identity within the social system. It can be argued that language plays an important part in this process because it is a means to make someone conscious of his position. The choice of address forms depends on the relation between speaker and addressee i.e. it depends on the particular group they belong to or on the particular role they have in society. It is important to realize that forms of address usually follow rules that are understood by an entire society. If someone uses a particular form of address, this could mean that he wants to assign you a particular role (e.g. he may regard you as a stranger, a superior, a subordinate / cf. also: formality, intimacy, belonging to the 'same' group, etc.). Similar observations can be made with regard to social classes. When certain interactions occur within a set of persons but not between sets, there is evidence of stratification. Language may be one particular aspect of interaction. Linguistic differences between status groups are most marked where the gap between the groups is very great. These differences are revealed almost from the beginnings of speech. It may be suggested that the inter-status linguistic differences between the lower working class and the middle class result from entirely different modes of speech which are dominant within these strata. It should be realized at this point that different social groups place their stress on different possibilities inherent in language use; once this stress is placed, then the resulting linguistic form is one of the most important means of eliciting and strengthening ways of feeling and thinking which are related to the social group. Uniformity and discontinuity in the form of language may be evidence of stratification. If classes are real then their boundaries will be detectable (Brown 1965). In many communities, language is a possible factor to detect such boundaries, i.e. forms of language (style, vocabulary, 'accent', etc.) will be strikingly uniform within a stratum on the one hand and there will be clear contrasts between strata on the other. The concept of stratification is closely linked with the concept of 'status'. Let us quickly discuss the notion 'status'. There seem to be normative definitions in all phases of our social lives, as we have seen before. Whether we are aware of it or not, the norms subtly guide our conversation. Those norms are often built around a recurrent identity in a social system and come to form a new reality of their own. The concept that refers to a distinctive set of rights, duties, expectations, etc. is identified as 'a social status' (arranged on a scale of prestige). A status represents a unit of a social structure; it is a set of potentials for interaction. The character of the interaction is established by the distinctive normative imperatives which give the status its unique form. Role on the other hand is the dynamic integration of the potentials of a social status by an actor who puts the status into play. Status is the *positional* unit located within the social system, while role consists of the *process* dimension of status (i.e. the behaviour that goes along with a particular position). Having said this, we must realize that interaction is more frequent within a social class than across classes. We may therefore put forward the hypothesis that in many societies the forms of language and the *frequency* with which these forms occur, offer another way of defining both primary and secondary groups (see Fig. 2). Groups

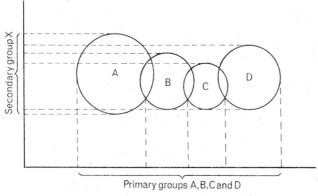

Figure 2

are marked out in terms of differential social intercourse; language is one aspect whereby the group members become conscious of their membership. To conclude with a statement made by Sprott (1969). 'It is in fact in the primary group that the general standards are learnt, practised and reinforced, but in addition pressure is brought to conform to the special standards which characterize the particular group in which a person may be.'

4. 'The infant has no idea of himself as a separate individual, it is a bundle of needs arising out of inner tensions, and capacities to respond to stimulation. It is not an "I"' (Sprott 1969). For a full sense of 'I' social interaction is required first. A main aspect of social interaction is of course language. Any human being makes use of speech to elicit certain responses. According to Mead (Sprott 1969) this comes about because the individual using speech takes on the *role* (in the second sense) of the other with whom he is interacting, i.e. how he expects the other to behave. Similarly, if someone addresses other persons in a particular way, then this means that he expects those persons to behave in a particular way; he assigns them a certain role (in the first sense). In order to guide his action, the individual must take into himself a general complicated reflection of the responses (attitudes) of the others (society) who are involved in the same process. Once again we need to take into account the two parts that constitute any 'social role' or 'role' in general. This dichotomy is reflected in a discussion on 'I' and 'me' by G. Mead and quoted by Sprott (1969). Mead stresses the importance of social intercourse (language?) in developing not only the idea of ourselves as separate beings but also as beings with standards of conduct incorporated from the people with whom we have had to deal. 'I' is so to speak the 'personality' while 'me' is built out of the attitude of others. The latter has the status of 'object' and is the product of social contact; it is the real role content of the actual role (cf. aspects of overlap). Group pressure (in the direction of conformity) and social control are especially directed towards this 'real content' of the role. In making evaluations the members of the society use language which being itself a form of social contact helps in shaping the behaviour of the child. We may even go one step further and consider the importance of language *as a system* without paying attention to the particular way in which people talk, or the particular lexicon they use. The language system as such may help the child to find out his own identity at the intersection of a network of social relationships. We must realize that the forms of the language predetermine the framework within which interaction takes place, i.e. we must understand the linguistic system as a range of possible choices within which the speakers are operating (Halliday 1966). A child learns to say 'father' and 'my father', but not '*my Robert'. We see that there is a grammatical distinction (common noun v. proper noun) between elder kin and others. Halliday (1966) argues that 'all the various distinctions that the child learns to associate with nouns, such as common or proper, general or specific, count or mass, concrete or abstract, definite or indefinite, as well as the various roles occupied by nouns in clause structure, provide a part of the conceptual framework for his mental development, and thus for the formation of his ideas about himself and about society'.

5. Especially with regard to the notion of 'social roles', it is clear that we must concentrate chiefly on the functions of language and on the relationships between these functions and the nature of language as a system of signs, rather than as the human faculty of language as such. This means that we must consider the relationship between the form of linguistic patterns and the uses to which language is put in society. This relationship is basic to the works of J. Firth. In referring to Firth we must mention his views on linguistics and especially his ideas about meaning. We all agree that the notion 'meaning' is rather difficult to account for (meaning is something more than the 'object' which a word comes to 'represent' in the language). Any aspect of meaning is always strongly influenced by contextual features whatever these may be. In view of the complexity and vagueness which surrounds the notion 'meaning', Firth considered the context of situation to be the central concept of semantics. This context mainly consists of the human participant(s), what is said and what is going on; it is the province of sociolinguistics. According to Firth we need more accurately to determine linguistic categories for the principal types of usage we employ in our various social roles. Though these categories might often not be found after a

dictionary entry, we believe that several members of a community will label a particular utterance as colloquial, literary,
dialectal etc. In communities where attention is paid to what is
generally called RP, language may be the main factor in terms of
which people are put in a hierarchy of social classes. This seems
to be the case in England, Germany, Belgium etc. This is, however, not true for the USA, where every person can speak his own
dialect provided he can be understood by his fellow-men. Could
this be one of the reasons why Brown (1965) argues that life in the
USA is not stratified? We do of course believe in the primary
importance of socio-economic status (which in the US happens
to be organized as a continuum of positions rather than a set of
classes); but on the other hand, the existence of language norms
cannot simply be ruled out. Notice in passing that in the case of
the three nations mentioned above, many persons still talk in
terms of U and Non-Un. Could it not be that language helps to
retain a certain class-consciousness? If so, how does it come about?
From the time that we begin to be socially active we gradually
accumulate social roles, i.e. we are born as more or less 'individuals'
(from the point of view of society), but to satisfy our needs we have
to become social persons and every social person is a bundle of
'roles'. We are all incorporated into our social organization by
means of learning to say what the other person expects us to say
under the given circumstances; i.e. once someone speaks to us,
we are in a relatively determined context and we are not free just
to do what we please: essentially speaking we get our roles through
speech.[1] How does language mould people to a role? In many
cases it provides the vocabulary for a particular role. A child has
got the linguistic apparatus for his role of child; parents may use
a particular language because they do not want the child to get
out of his role. When someone addresses us by saying 'Ladies and
Gentlemen . . .' then this means that we are in for the 'role' of
captive audience. If someone uses the phrase 'dear sir' instead of
saying 'dear John', then the distinction between both phrases is a
matter of difference in the role one assigns to the particular per-

[1] Consider the following statement made by Luria (mentioned by Bernstein,
1964): 'Language marks out what is relevant cognitively and socially, and
experience is transformed by that which is made relevant; as a result the child
gets to the social organization through the acquisition of language.'

son. Similar examples may be found with regard to the vocabulary of register. To summarize: as the child grows up, he finds small significant clues as to the sort of assignment other people expect from him. Firth goes even further to say that for each stage of childhood of each type of child, there are a relevant environment and relevant forms of language. If this is true—and we believe it is—then we may say that language helps a great deal in the acquisition of roles and that social reality is then defined in terms of the amount of overlap within the context (Fig. 3). This also sheds light on the general statement from which any linguistic investigation should start, viz. that linguistic systems have only existence in the minds of the individuals. The many (social) roles we have to play involve a certain degree of linguistic specialization.

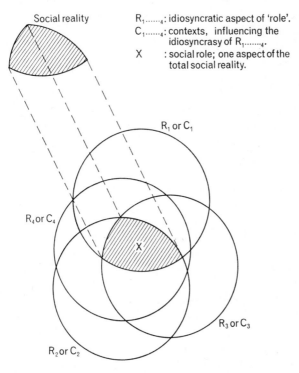

Figure 3. Definition of social role 'X'

The 'same' word may be used in different roles but until a specific context occurs, it is the 'neutral' meaning that counts. Here again we find an illustration of overlap.

6. In the preceding paragraphs we have mentioned the term 'types of language' and the impact they had on the individual with respect to his role set (actual and potential). Most people have mastery of a range of types. Indeed, we speak differently when we speak to different people (child, friend, superior). We even speak differently to the same person in different circumstances. Apart from the contents of the utterance we assess people from the language they use and often our actions and attitudes are determined by such assessments. As to the varieties of language we must mention the dialect of the speaker (cf. regional, social), the 'correctness' of the vocabulary and grammar, the level of the vocabulary and grammar (cf. slang, colloquial) and the choice he makes of his vocabulary with respect to what he is saying. Variations within language are as often a question of register as of specific dialectal variations. Social judgements often have a flavour of what is thought to be the linguistic idea of 'correctness'. Though linguists are inclined to reject the idea of correctness, it remains true that there are certain forms which are considered more appropriate than others on particular occasions. Although particular utterances may convey the same meaning (information) the different relations of the speaker to the eventual hearer may cause him to express the information in rather different language forms. When this happens we say that the speaker has moved from one register to another. Every time we hesitate whether to say 'dear sir' or 'dear Henry' or wonder 'how best to put it', we are trying to select the appropriate register. When one thinks of a particular role, one is undoubtedly setting up central processes— and perhaps even peripheral ones—that have been associated with that particular role in the past. The past experience of any person (through language for example) builds up a choosing and rejecting system. The ultimate explanation of this system may be in terms of principles like those of conditioning, but at the descriptive level it has quite different laws. Though no comprehensive categorization of registers is yet available (Gregory 1967), we may assume that any human being in the course of (and because of!) the socialization process uses the ideas behind any such potential categorization. If a particular register is used we know our 'role' because we happen to be able to detect what the speaker expects of us, i.e. what role he expects us to play. It is important to realize that the regional or social variety of language used by a speaker may affect the social judgement passed upon him by others. Even if the linguist does not use terms such as e.g. 'correct grammar', it must be realized that society itself decides upon the 'appropriate' grammar. The choice of e.g. 'appropriate register' has in fact been 'learned' one way or another. There are a number of 'fashions of speaking' and Bernstein (1965) argues that the particular 'fashion' a speaker adopts is likely to be decided by his social experiences, but in turn his 'fashion of speaking' determines his social relationship to other speakers. His social behaviour is constrained within the limits set by his linguistic behaviour, which is in turn constrained by his social experience. A child who has access to many different 'fashions of speaking' will therefore be able to operate in many more contexts than the child who has access to only a limited number of such speech fashions. To put it another way, a person with a large number of linguistic codes at his disposal can switch from one social role to another with greater ease and can adapt with greater flexibility to the varying demands of different situations. Bernstein (1964) also considers the question as to the means through which the social process is 'learned'. He claims that an approach to this question can be made by examining an intervening variable (language?) which is shaped by a given type of social organization and which conditions the form of a basic learning process. He continues to say that forms of spoken language, in the process of their learning, initiate and reinforce special types of relationship with the environment and as such create particular dimensions of significance.

Conclusion

7. Having looked at social reality (and reality in general) we have observed that particular social contexts are dominated by the use of a certain type of language. We have also argued that language is an important factor in preserving the boundaries between classes and that it plays an important part with regard to social roles and role conflicts. We may therefore suggest that 'language' is a process by which the individual internalizes the social structure. Different social structures will emphasize different aspects (types, varieties) of language and this in turn will create for the individual particular dimensions of relevance. To put it another way: speech will influence the child with respect to the norms of the group to which it belongs. Actual speech, then, may reinforce the internalization of the social structure but may also be responsible for certain conflicts arising from (i) the position of the individual in society and (ii) his role set. It has also become clear that 'language' is essentially a phenomenon operating within the field of both psychology and sociology. We may even modify de Saussure's statement about language (*langue*) and speech (*parole*) in saying that (as we have seen in the previous paragraphs) speech is a social phenomenon while language (*langue*) is a mere psychological phenomenon.

References

Bernstein, B. (1964) 'Aspects of Language and Learning in the Genesis of the Social Process'. In D. Hymes (ed.), *Language in Culture and Society*, New York: Harper & Row.
— (1965) 'A Socio-Linguistic Approach to Social Learning'. In *Penguin Survey of the Social Sciences 1965*, Penguin Books.
Bram, J. (1963) *Language and Society*, New York: Random House.
Brown, R. (1965) *Social Psychology*, New York: Collier-Macmillan.
Firth, J. (1964) 'On Sociological Linguistics'. In D. Hymes 1964.
—(1966) *The Tongues of Men & Speech*, London: Oxford University Press.
Gregory, M. (1967) 'Aspects of Varieties Differentiation', *Journal of Linguistics*, **3**, 2.
Halliday, M. A. K., McIntosh, Angus and Strevens, Peter (1964) *The Linguistic Sciences and Language Teaching*, London: Longman.
Halliday, M. A. K. (1966) 'Grammar, Society and the Noun'. Inaugural lecture.
Sprott, W. (1969) *Human Groups*, Penguin Books.

9

ALLEN WALKER READ
Family Language

The child has not only to learn about the wider world and its social structure, he also learns about that smaller world around him—his home. The previous sentence probably puts things in the wrong order, for *after* the child has learned the particulars of his home he learns about the wider world. His parents, his family, his home act as agents in showing and explaining the outside world to the child. In this reading, Read takes issue with Hockett in Reading 5. Hockett says

> The most important environment factor shaping the emerging dialect of a child is the speech of other children. (p. 67)

Read stresses the whole family situation from 'Grannie down to little Dick from over the way' as being an important factor in what language the child actually learns.

Students of language have long been aware that every speaker participates in a number of overlapping speech communities. The broadest speech community is that using 'the language' itself. In the case of English, this is the body of speakers not only in the home area of the British Isles but in the far-flung regions where English has been carried. Then there are speech communities of descending size, on the basis of geography, social class, education, occupation, ceremonial activities, recreational interests, and so on, until one reaches the fundamental speech community, the family.

The linguistic importance of the family has been somewhat obscured by the practice of linguists of referring to 'child language' or 'nursery words' as if the young age group were an entity. Truly enough, there is a remarkable homogeneity in the language of the nursery and of young children, and its terms are widespread over the entire English-speaking world. The family group, however, comprises not only the children but several generations in

Allen Walker Read: Extract from 'Family words in English' *American Speech*, 37, No. 1, Columbia University Press 1962, pp. 5–12.

communion with one another. As Jespersen has wisely acknowledged, 'the truth of the matter is that a child is normally surrounded by people of all ages and learns its language more or less
from all of them, from Grannie down to little Dick from over the
way. . . .'

A number of observers have pointed out the importance of the
family as a unit for linguistic purposes. The earliest of these
statements is from the mid-seventeenth century, by the Duchess
of Newcastle, who wrote in 1653: 'And not onely every *Shire* hath
a severall *Language,* but every *Family,* giving *Marks* for things
according to their *Fancy.*' In 1913 George Philip Krapp commented: 'Certain forms of speech will be used only among the
members of the family in their family relations, and these will
often be the very forms which give the group its deepest sense of
intimacy and unity.' Eric Partridge in 1933 supported this point
of view, saying:

> All families, if they are more than a mere collocation of related
> individuals, if they often meet together, and especially if they
> prefer their own company to that of others, have their own
> private slang; some few an extensive vocabulary, most a score
> or a dozen or even fewer words and phrases. Occasionally a
> stranger will hear a complete sentence that obviously means
> something quite different.

In 1937 R. A. Stewart Macalister expressed his agreement, as
follows.

> Probably every family, even of moderate size, has a more or
> less extensive vocabulary of current words and phrases, the
> sources of which may have been forgotten—may even never
> have been known to the junior members—but which are quite
> comprehensible in the household, though totally unintelligible
> outside.

In 1945 Logan Pearsall Smith made a 'collection of words privately
invented by some groups and families', and he proposed to put
it into print, but I have not heard that this was done.

In this article I present examples of words that have had their
currency within family limits. Here we can see to good advantage
the effervescing of language creation. My material is drawn from

a variety of sources: oral reports from friends and students, auto-
biographies and reminiscences, and in some cases fictional accounts
that report family situations with an attempt at verisimilitude.

Let us first take up some expressions that involve figurative
speech, chiefly metaphorical leaps in the naming of things. In a
New York family, according to a student, parsnips are known as
'white carrots' and pepper as 'black salt'. The English novelist
G. B. Stern reminisced from her youth concerning *squashed flies*:
'What biscuits did you have at your nursery tea-table? We had
"squashed flies". Garibaldis was their statelier name.' In the
family of Henry Beckett, a New York journalist, an aeroplane was
called a 'bird-bus', from the coinage of his daughter Martha, and
the American Museum of Natural History was 'the bone house'.
William Holt, an English broadcaster, has reported an animal
known as a 'Yukon', invented by his daughter:

> She had invented fanciful animals which were suggested to her
> by new words and names which she had heard or had come
> across when reading. Animals such as 'Yukons'. She really
> believed at one time that there was such an animal. The word
> 'fetlock' provided her with a useful collective noun for associat-
> ing with Yukons—'a fetlock of Yukons'. When I probed her
> with questions as to where her idea of a 'Yukon' had come
> from she told me she had seen a book being loaded on to one
> of my motor libraries, called *The Call of Yukon*, and I have no
> doubt that she distinctly heard its peculiar cry.

Jessica Mitford has reported: 'It was easy to make her huge
blue eyes brim with tears—known as "welling" in family circles.'
The family of the poet A. E. Housman used the coinages that he
invented in childhood play. As his brother Laurence Housman
described them:

> Alfred, the eldest of us, and always our leader, invented three
> new instruments of war—the Bath Bridge, the Martin Luther,
> and the Flying Torpedo; outwardly quite homely objects of
> garden use, but imaginatively endowed with terrific powers of
> destruction. The Bath Bridge, a mere drainpipe to look at, was
> designed to swallow lighted tallow candles at one end, and send
> them rushing out in fire at the other. We got some candle-ends,

and tried the experiment; but only a melting mess and no fire came of it. The Martin Luther was a species of gatling gun which never gatled, being nothing more than a semicircle of wood with a ground-stake, for the running of bird-lines; the Flying Torpedo was a stump of wood which he threw. But if they failed to do much execution, the names made us happy; for Alfred was always able to make us believe that his word-inventions had a meaning, and that the meaning was good.

Let us turn next to instances in which devices of word coinage are illustrated. The verb *to gramp*, a back formation meaning 'to blow like a grampus', can be given. W. E. Collinson has said of it: 'This is a good instance of an individual's creation becoming a family word.' The process of analogy accounts for *drinkative*. As a writer of 1942 has recounted: 'A family I know has invented a word (I think) which always pleases me—"drinkative"—less objectionable than "drunken". It is probably based upon "talkative".'

The change from one part of speech to another was reported by a New Englander in 1908:

> There is hardly a family but has some expressive improvised word. In my own family 'humbly' reigns supreme. This is not the adverb of current usage, but an adjective, and a cross between 'humble' and 'homely'; and it was first used to describe our washwoman, who takes such pride in her humbleness, and is of such a superlative weatherbeaten homeliness, that she needed something special to express her personality. . . . 'Humbly' she is, and as 'humbly Mrs. Wheeler' she will be known in our family, while the brother who invented the word quite puffs himself up about it.

Folk etymology is illustrated by the formation *suppertash* in place of *succotash*, used by a child and carried on by the family.

Blending, or the formation of portmanteau words, is found in other families. Louise Pound has recorded the following: 'The mind, hesitating between *swindle* and *wheedle*, compromises on *sweedle*. When the result pleases the coiners, it sometimes continues in family use, as *sweedle* in the case of a Nebraska family.' Herbert Quick, the Iowa novelist, in *Vandemark's Folly* of 1922, put into the fictional narration of an old Iowa pioneer the following sentence: 'I remembered, though, how she had skithered back to the carriage.' Then he added a footnote to *skithered*, attributed to an educated granddaughter of the pioneer:

> A family word, to the study of which one would like to direct the attention of the philologists, since traces of it are found in the conversation of folk of unsophisticated vocabulary outside the Clan van de Marck. Doubtless it is of Yankee origin, and hence old English. It may, of course, be derived according to Alice-in-Wonderland principles from 'skip' and 'hither' or 'thither' or all three; but the claim is here made that it comes, like monkeys and men, from a common linguistic ancestor.

Compton Mackenzie, in a novel of 1926, *Fairy Gold*, portrayed an isolated family on a small island off the coast of Cornwall in which three children used a number of blends in talking with one another, for example: 'We can't go on being glumpy about it', where *glumpy* combines *gloomy* and *grumpy*; or 'I'm sorry if I was uffish', where *uffish* combines *uppish* and *selfish*; or 'You are a silly sloach', where *sloach* combines *slow* plus *coach*.

The cleverest of all the family words that have come to my attention is one from Scotland: a celebration of Burns's birthday, at which haggis was served, was known by the 'sandwich' formation *Walp-haggis-nicht!*

Other family words represent distortions that are hard to analyse. One of these, *squiblums*, was described by Lois I. Woodville, of Oswestry, Shropshire, as follows:

> One of our household words is 'squiblums'. This was first heard at a pantomime when the ugly sisters of Cinderella sought to gain entry to Prince Charming's ball. The footmen at the door asked to see their 'tickets, credentials or the equivalents'. The word 'equivalents' degenerated into 'squiblums', and I am sure it must have been the only part of the pantomime we clearly remembered. From then on, before one could expect to gain entry, one or another member of the family would demand, 'Where's your squiblums?' And, before opening the door to another member of the family it's common practice to ask for 'Squiblums, squiblums, please?'

Angela Thirkell, in a novel of 1954, recorded the following:

'When Laurence—my eldest brother—was a little boy he used to get his words muddled and he called gold-beaters' skin Peter Goatskin, so the whole family called it that.' And a Sussex family employed *sittybah* for 'good-bye', derived from the local dialectal way of saying *see yer ter-morrah*. In one American family the word *pumpernickel* was habitually altered to [knʌŋknknʌŋkl] and *whistle* became [hwɔrsl]. In another family string beans are always 'strim bims', and the name *alligator* for 'elevator' has been adopted by all members.

Fairly mysterious is the word *hoosh-mi*, from the royal family of England. As the Queen's former nanny, Marion Crawford, has chronicled:

The pram . . . remained in purdah for some years together with . . . the hoosh-mi dish. 'Hoosh-mi' is a pleasant word made up by [Princess] Margaret for the nursery mixture of chopped meat, potato and gravy, all 'hoosh-mied' up together and spoon-fed to its victim. Later the word was to become part of the schoolroom vocabulary, and a mix of any kind was always known as a hoosh-mi.

Its use is illustrated in a later passage by the nanny: 'Margaret . . . has a large round table on which can always be found a lavish clutter. Letters, invitations, dance programmes, greeting tele-grams—in short, a hoosh-mi.' Thus this manifestation of 'family words' reaches even into the English royal family.

Many types of word formation are illustrated in a family vocabulary of about a dozen items provided by Meredith Starr, the English author and philosopher. These are as follows:

Cobs, tea (the meal); *Don Johns*, onions; *droomers*, bedroom slippers, by way of *bedroomers*: *expud*, not nice, rejected, un-comfortable (but usually of food); *flimmick*, to throw away; *jimkins*, jam; *miffy*, stale (of food gone mouldy); *Samuel Widgeons*, sandwiches; *woozles!*, an exclamation when anything goes wrong; *yarrup!*, when it goes still more wrong; *Ye cods and cuttle fishes!*, from *Ye gods and little fishes!*

Another favourite type of family expression is the alphabetica abbreviation or acronym. One immediately thinks of *F.H.B.*, for

'Family Hold Back' as a warning when an article of food is low but guests are not supposed to know it. Quite probably this arose as a family expression, but it broke into general usage many generations ago. I remember it from my boyhood as a subject of joking, and Partridge has marked it as from the mid-nineteenth century. It may well be, however, that the companion expression *M.I.T.K.*, meaning 'More in the Kitchen', has been limited. The English publisher Ernest Benn told of it in reminiscences of 1949: when unexpected guests were brought home to tea or dinner, the signal *F.H.O.* for 'Family Hold Off' sometimes had to be passed, but this would bring the prompt response from an irresponsible junior, 'M.I.T.K.' Another acronym was recorded by Christopher Morley in 1942—*T.E.T.* As he wrote: 'Aunt Bee cautioned Jeff with an esoteric allusion. "Geoffrey, remember T.E.T." . . . Jeff remembered: T.E.T. was a private mnemonic for Temper, Excitement and Tongue.' Compton Mackenzie's family on the island off Cornwall used *N.A.N.P.*, as follows: ' "Just tell him to bart out of it for good and all, because he's an N.A.N.P." "A what?" "A Not-a-Nice person." '

Let us turn now to expressions that have their origin in chance incidents that have taken place in a family. Thus *You ought to see my aunt* had currency in an American family, as recorded in 1924 by Harry G. Paul:

> In another home a dull servant once said, 'If you think I am foolish, you ought to see my aunt'; from this grew a custom of the various members of the family censuring themselves for any unwise act by repeating, 'You ought to see my aunt', an expression which sometimes astonished and puzzled any stranger who happened to hear it.

When Eleanor Roosevelt was travelling in England with her family in 1929, a family term for a disease arose. As she described it: 'In London, Franklin, junior, developed for the third time that year a curious illness which we came to call "Franklin pox", but the doctor insisted that it was German measles. It was over in two days and did not interfere very much with our sightseeing.'

From an Irish family is recorded the idiomatic phrase, *to sing the hundredth psalm*. As Macalister explained it in 1937:

How could any non-initiate guess that 'to sing the hundredth psalm' meant to 'fetch a glass of water'—as it does in a family known to me? If he be admitted to the domestic arcana so far as to learn the phrase and its meaning, how could he guess the nexus between the two ideas—a chance remark made upon a midsummer day, that to allow the heated water to run off from the cold-water tap took about as long a time as it would take to perform the act of piety specified?

Again from the Housman family comes another term. In Laurence Housman's reminiscences of his youth in the Midlands, he recorded *Yorkshire-pudding bell*:

At one o'clock on Sundays a bell was again rung—why, I cannot imagine; but to that ringing we gave a domestic name and meaning of our own—'the Yorkshire-pudding bell' we called it; Yorkshire pudding being, on three Sundays out of five, or thereabouts, the most popular feature of the midday meal.

Sometimes a family phrase results from exposure to a foreign language. When William Dean Howells and his family were travelling in Germany, they were much amused by the description of a variety show in Würzburg as a *decentes Familienprogramm*. The daughter, Mildred Howells, stated that this then 'had become a family phrase'. When Howells later described a village fair in Cornwall, he wrote: 'A small fair, with swings and games . . . was going on in a pasture next the house. Very *"decentes familienprogramm"*.' The same family adapted the German *Hoheit* into *high-hote*, as Mildred Howells explained: ' "High-hotes" was a reversal of the German *Hoheit* that Howells had invented at Carlsbad, and which had become a family word for the nobility.' As Howells wrote in a letter of April 12, 1904, from London, to his wife, on visiting the National Portrait Gallery: 'It is prodigious, and full of high-hotes of every age and degree.'

Another fruitful source of family words is the naming of various rooms of a house. Robert Haven Schauffler in 1925 recorded the following: 'Children, too, have a sure instinct at times for word coining. I know some who christened their play-room "The Squealery".' In a family in Essex, the water closet was called 'the Euphemism'. This arose from the time when a party of visitors came and one delicate-minded lady asked in a whisper, 'May we, to use a euphemism, wash our hands?' Thereafter the lavatory was always referred to as 'the Euphemism'. In the Mitford family, Lord Redesdale's study was known as the 'Closing Room'. His daughter Jessica explained how this arose:

My father's study had once been known by the more usual terms for such rooms—library, business room, smoking room—but I pointed out to Farve that since he spent virtually his entire life within its walls, one day, inevitably, his old eyes would close there, never to open again. Thus it came to be called the Closing Room, even by the servants.

The term *glory hole* has been recorded as the name of a catch-all closet, a development from the sailor's term; but this apparently has spread to many families. In the William Dean Howells family the library, which was housed in a barn, was known as the 'barnbury'.

The terms such as I have been citing are of small use to the lexicographer. He would not wish to include them in his inventory, unless they could be shown to have broken into wider currency. Nevertheless, such material should be watched by the lexicologist for its value in showing tendencies in the language. The family is the matrix in which we see the bubbling up of linguistic experimentation.

Jespersen has pointed out that there are dangers in the indulgence that a family may show to the experiments of a child. As he said,

It would not do, however, for the child's 'little language' and its dreadful mistakes to become fixed. This might easily happen, if the child were never out of the narrow circle of its own family, which knows and recognizes its 'little language'. But this is stopped because it comes more and more into contact with others—. . . as the child becomes a member of a social group larger than that of his own little home.

Nevertheless, it surely is desirable for the child to have an opportunity for free linguistic play, to try out analogies in a sympathetic atmosphere. The family serves as this experimental arena. One of the greatest gifts that can come to a speaker of a language is the sense of freedom to move about among the possible patterns that the language provides for him. This feeling of 'at-home-ness' develops and flowers in the family circle.

10

IONA and PETER OPIE
Language in Children's Culture

In their book, *The Lore and Language of Schoolchildren*, the Opies have traced the extent and the ramifications of the culture which can properly be said to be of childhood. They show that such a childhood culture is known to most children and has an enduring history going back to our origins. Much of the childhood culture is contained in oral traditions as this culture is passed on orally. Their book and the work of other people is not intended as a primer for children learning the culture. As an orally transmitted culture, language, and games with language, play a supremely important role. Some of the highly complex language games are included in the following extracts. Of a different kind is the folklore which has grown up connected with bus tickets. For some children of today's world, bus tickets replace the reading of the auguries of the classical world. There is as much lore and faith in the proper reading of bus tickets as there appears to be in the reading of the Zodiac by contemporary adults.

The language used by children attending publicly provided schools is not merely the least recorded of all the varieties of speech spoken in Britain, it is also, some will say, the least recordable. Tongue-tied though a child may be when made to use adult words, his vocabulary can be extensive when speaking his own language. For instance a pair of Hertfordshire 14-year-olds, of not notably high I.Q., when asked about their classmates and invited to set down their epithets for them, promptly came to life and wrote:

'Phumph, lumber bontts [bonce], lush, Gables, square head, pugh, Jimpy, Hepsiba, lofty, big head, Rudolth, hog, scoffer, flippin kid, titty, rocker box, chubby cheaks, chink, coaca, Cowson, screawy, nuts, bolts, Tweedle, woolly wog, Kedah Wong, gilly, ruby nose, Bullet Head, nutty and cominist.'

Iona and Peter Opie: Extracts from *The Lore and Language of School Children*, Oxford University Press 1959. 'Obtaining respite', pp. 141–4; 'Nicknames and epithets', pp. 154–9; 'Bus tickets', pp. 329–34. © Iona and Peter Opie, 1959.

Nor is the rare child who speaks the argot of the refined adult necessarily unilingual. In a debate in the House of Commons (11 March 1949) the ex-schoolmaster member for Southampton, Ralph Morley, told how, near the school where he was once teaching, there was a girls' school with a teacher who was a very highly trained and enthusiastic elocutionist. 'One day she brought one of her girls into our assembly. The girl recited some poetry and although she was a working-class girl she pronounced "how" as if she had spent some considerable time at Eton and Harrow. When the assembly was over I said to my boys: "I wish you would talk as nicely as that girl whom you have just heard talk." The boys replied at once, and almost in chorus: "You ought to hear her talk in the street".'

Characteristics of Schoolchild Language

Two apparently conflicting emotions are active in schoolchild language: respect for tradition and desire for fun. Respect for tradition shows itself in their words of honour, as we have seen, and in the retention of many dialect words, for instance names for birds and animals: blackie (blackbird), barker or growler (dog), moggy (cat), drummer (snipe), horse-stinger (dragonfly), Joey (owl), Scribbly Jack (yellowhammer), spuggy (sparrow), and stiggy (starling). Their love of fun, on the other hand, is shown in the constant welcome given to slang and innovation. Money, for instance, is variously referred to as: brass, lolly, tin, dough, mazuma, moolah, dosh (common), sploosh, bees and honey, and champagne coupons. A pound is a 'quid', a 'smacker', or a 'nicker'; ten shillings is 'half a nicker' or 'half a bar'; five shillings is a 'dollar'; one shilling is a 'bob', 'dienner', or 'thumber'; sixpence is a 'kick', 'sprat', or 'tanner'; a threepenny piece is a 'bit' or 'tiddler'; and twopence is 'deuce'. Coppers are referred to as 'mouldies'. A penny is a 'clod' or a 'dee' (usually spoken of as 'one dee'), a halfpenny is a 'meg' or 'rusty meg', a farthing is a 'mite', and to have nothing is to be 'skint' or 'boko'.

Occasionally children's names for things are expressive, almost amounting to poetic speech: a postman, in Aberdeen, is 'Slottie Johnnie', a tramp, very generally, is a 'milestone inspector', the floor is the 'dog's shelf', a boy's mouth is his 'cake hole', his stomach is his 'breadbasket' or 'porridge bag', and large feet are 'beetle crushers'.

Chiefly, however, children go in for short sharp words, as in their more usual names for parts of the body: 'nob', 'nut', 'loaf', 'bonce', 'block', and 'dome' for head; 'mug', 'dial', and 'phiz' for face; 'conk', 'beak', 'snitch', 'snout', 'snot-box', 'snorer', 'snozzle', and 'boko' for nose; 'gob' for mouth; 'flaps' or 'lugs' for ears; 'mitts', 'dukes', or 'paws' for hands. Sometimes they have the most breath-saving past tenses: 'tug' for tigged (i.e. touched), 'scum' for skimmed, 'thunk' for thought, and 'knat' for knitted.

But perhaps the most distinctive feature of juvenile parlance is the use of the standard endings, *-ass*, *-bug*, *-cat*, *-dick*, *-gog*, *-guts*, *-pot*, *-puss*, *-sides*, and, most of all, *-ies* or *-sy*, endings which are regularly affixed to certain words. These syllables are used either to replace the second half of a word, as: newbug, rasbug, straw-bug, goosegog, and wellygogs (Wellington boots); or to turn a verb or adjective into a descriptive noun, as: creep-ass, squall-ass, copycat, stare-cat, tease-cat, funny-dick, clever-dick, greedy-guts, grizzle-guts, lazy-guts, scabby-guts, fuss-pot, stink-pot, swank-pot, blubber-puss, sleepy-puss, sour-puss, sobersides, solemnsides, and—in games terminology—onesies, twosies, commonies, shot-ties, farsy, nearsy, plainsy, and dumbsy. In fact the addition of 'ies' is so common it is sometimes added where not absolutely necessary, for instance in the school chant: 'Easties are beasties, Northies are horsies, Westies are besties.' Sometimes, indeed, the addition is a matter of conscious preference; thus a Dulwich girl, giving the rhyme,

> Good night, sweet repose,
> Mind the mosquitoes don't bite your toes,

added, 'That's how I was told it, but I always say "reposes" and "toeses" because I like it better'.

Their Own Name

Children attach an almost primitive significance to people's names, always wanting to find out a stranger's name, yet being correspondingly reluctant to reveal their own. They have ways of avoiding telling their name. They answer, 'Haven't got a name, only got a number'. They say, 'Same name as me Dad'.

'What's your Dad's then?'

'Same as mine.'

And there is the recurrent set-piece: 'What's your name?' 'Sarah Jane.' 'Where do you live?' 'Down the lane.' 'What's your number?' 'Cucumber.' 'What's your shop?' 'Lollipop.' 'What's your town?' 'Dressing-gown.' It can be a blessing to a new child to know a formula like this. Girls circle round a new girl, crying 'What's your name? What's your name?' and the circle will disperse only if the untrue ritual answer is forthcoming. Sometimes a game can be joined only if the correct response is made to 'What's your number?' 'Cucumber.' Real Sarah Janes, Mary Janes, and Elizabeth Janes are teased with the pointless questions. And sometimes children recite the curious catechism, or catechize each other, for no reason except that children have been doing so since time long ago.

What's your name?
Mary Jane.
Where do you live?
Down the grid.
What number?
Cucumber.
What street?
Pig street.
                    Lancaster.

What's your name?
Baldy Bain.
What's your ither?
Ask ma mither.
                    Glasgow.

What's your name?
Elecampane (or 'elegant pain').
What's your number?
Cucumber.

What's your road?
Big black toad.
                    Nottingham.

What's your name?
Lady Jane.
Where do you live?
Cabbage Lane.
What's your number?
Bread and cucumber.
What's your address?
Bread and watercress.
                    Market Rasen.

What's your name?
Mary Jane.
Where do you live?
Down the lane.
What do you keep?
A little shop.
What do you sell?

Ginger pop.	Twenty-four, now go away.
How many bottles do you sell in a day?	*Swansea, for skipping.*

In Alton, Hampshire, the very clever have lately learned to say:

My name is:
Addi, addi, chickeri, chickeri,
Ooney, pooney, om pom alari,
Alla balla whisky,
Chinese salt!

In the United States:

What's your name?	What's your name?
Puddin Tame.	John Brown.
Ask me again	Ask me again
And I'll tell you the same.	And I'll knock you down.
Maryland.	*New Jersey.*

Other People's Names

Needless to say children are not respecters of names once they have learnt them, and have a fondness, in particular, for giving a familiar sound to those names which are unfamiliar to them. Thus Edwin Schiff becomes 'Bedouin Chief', Clara Dace becomes 'Clear-a-space', and Fred Maddox becomes 'Fresh Haddocks'. (Baden-Powell, at Charterhouse, was known as 'Bathing Towel'.) Puns or abridgements are introduced whenever possible. A boy with the surname Wood will be called 'Splinter', a boy surnamed Bell will be 'Dinger'. Sedgewick will be reduced to 'Sedge', and Nixon to 'Nick'; Poulton will be turned to 'Polly', and June become 'Spoon'.

Children like names which fall into patterns, and for more than a hundred years they have been fitting people's names into peculiar spell-like mocking chants.

Maggy, my baggy,	Belly bug,
My rick stick staggy,	Bandy-legged Maggy.
Hum bug,	*Aberdeen.*

Jenny, my benny,
My rick stick stenny,
Hum bug,
Belly bug,
Bandy-legged Jenny.
*Same formula, applied to
Jenny.*

Similar is:

    Joan the roan,
    The rix stix stoan,
    The iron-nosed,

The copper-nosed,
The bandy-legged Joan.
          London.

Joan Hassall, when a girl, was called:
    Joan to oan,
    Pepp-in-tus scoan,
    Frastockadilla moan,
    Fring frang froan.
          Surrey.

Sometimes this play on names is known as 'new spelling' and goes:

    Shirley-wirley,
    Nick and nirley,
    Pam birley,
    Bobby rirley,
    That's the way to spell Shirley.
          Cambridge.

    John-won,
    Nick and non,
    Pam bon,
    Bobby ron,
    That's the way to spell
    John.
          London.

Secret Keeping

When wishing a person to keep a thing quiet children ordinarily enjoin 'Keep it dark', 'Don't spread it', 'Mum's the word', 'Don't split'; but if they require a vow of silence there are, in some places, special formulas. In Penrith a child swears: 'I vow never to tell as long as the sun and the moon shall endure.' In Swansea: 'Take my oath and take my little finger' (linking little fingers). In Welshpool:

    Cut my throat and wipe it dry,
    If I tell I'll surely die.

In Lydney, according to an 11-year-old girl:

    Prick of the finger, prick of the thumb,
    I won't tell what you've done.

'We prick our fingers with a pin and write it on paper in blood like *"Me and J. B. swears to keep mum"*.' Often, of course, the formulas are ordinary imprecations: 'God strike me dead if I split', 'God cut my throat if I tell of you', 'If I let the secret out I'll drop down dead on this spot'.

In and around Market Rasen, in Lincolnshire, children use an old and charming poetic formula (of which they sent ten versions) for testing a friend's ability to keep a secret. They take the person's hand and run their finger round the palm, repeating:

Can you keep a secret?
I don't suppose you can,
You mustn't laugh or giggle
While I tickle your hand.
    Girl, 11, Market Rasen.

Can you keep a secret?
Tell me if you can
If you laugh or show your teeth
You can't keep one.
    Girl, 12, Binbrook, Lincs.

Can you keep a secret?
If you can you must not
  laugh,
You must not smile,
And you must not cry.
  Girl, 12, Normanby-by-Spital,
      Lincs.

Can you keep a secret?
If you can, tell me your name.
  Jean Holland.
No, you can't then!
    Girl, 11, Market Rasen.

In Ohio children bind themselves to silence by saying: 'Cross my heart and hope to die, lock my lips and throw away the key', and they make the gesture of turning a key in their lips and throwing it away.

Obtaining Respite

Perhaps the most important word in the schoolchild's vocabulary is his truce term. Certainly to the adult observer it is his most interesting word, for when a child seeks respite he uses a term to which there is now no exact equivalent in adult speech. If, when engaged in some boisterous activity with his fellows, a child is exhausted or out of breath, or cuts himself, or has a shoelace undone, or fears his clothes are getting torn, or wants to know if it is time to go home, he makes a sign with his hands, and calls out a word which brings him immediate but temporary relief from the strife. Thus a 12-year-old Cleethorpes girl writes:

> 'If one gets a stitch while playing chase, one crosses one's fingers and says "Kings" and the person who is "he" does not chase one until one is ready.'

Similarly an 11-year-old Headington girl:

> 'If you don't want to be tug when you play tig you keep your fingers crossed and call out "cruses".'

A 10-year-old Bishop Auckland boy:

> 'Scinch—you cross your fingers and walk to the other gang to tell them something.'

A 9-year-old Ipswich girl describing 'Kiss Chase':

> 'Boys chase girls and if they catch them kiss them. If you don't want to be kissed say "exsie".'

'Sometimes', remarks a boy at Shoreham-by-Sea (where the truce term is 'fains' or 'vains'), 'when people have been saying "vains" too much we say "No vains in the game" before we play a game which contains running about.'

It will be appreciated that uttering a truce term does not of itself imply that a child has given in or surrendered, although it may sometimes be used preparatory to surrendering. A London urchin when fighting may cry 'faynights', whereupon his opponent, on ceasing to belabour him, may inquire 'Wanna give in?' and the boy will perhaps do so ('Okay, you win, leave me alone'). But more often, if a boy says 'faynights' or 'faynights—hang on a sec' in the middle of a struggle, he does so because he wants to take off his jacket or his glasses before continuing the combat. And before we ourselves appreciated that children were sensitive to the difference between making a truce and surrendering, we were puzzled by the number of boys who declared stoutly (and correctly) that they had no term for giving in.

In England and Wales the usual way a child shows that he wants to drop out of a game is by crossing fingers. Usually it is considered enough if he crosses the first and second fingers of one hand; but sometimes he must cross the fingers of both hands, and hold them up, and he may have to keep his fingers crossed all the time he wants to be immune—even when tying a shoelace. Occasionally feet are crossed as well, or instead; and at Headington, in an extreme situation, the child sits on the ground cross-legged. At Lydney, although the majority cross their fingers and say 'cruce', some say 'cree' and raise their right hand, palm forwards. At Bradford-on-Avon children hold their hand up and extend three fingers. In Ipswich when saying 'exsie', 'exes', or 'scrucies' children hold up only their right hand with crossed fingers: to hold up the left hand or both hands is reputed to be unlucky.

In Scotland, instead of crossing fingers, it is customary to put thumbs up, sometimes licking them first. In Lancashire, although the usual practice is to cross fingers, in a few places, for instance Radcliffe and Nelson, some children raise their thumbs as in Scotland, and in South Elmsall, in Yorkshire, some children declare their immunity by crying 'I've got my thumbs up'.

As will have been noticed, the word a child uses varies according to the part of Britain where he lives. In some places more than one term is current, and occasionally the pupils at a school will between them know four or five terms so that, at the outset, the words appear to be of purely arbitrary adoption. Children at Kirkcaldy High School, for instance, when first questioned, produced the terms: barleys, barrels, bees, tibs, tubs, dubs, or dubbies, thumbs, checks, peas, pearls, and parleys.

A class at the Southern Grammar School for Girls, Portsmouth, knew: creams, creamos, creamy-olivers, ollyoxalls, olly-olly-ee, double queenie, cross kings, fingers, pax, and also said that they shouted 'breather'.

Further investigation, however, showed more uniformity. At Kirkcaldy, when each child wrote down the terms he or she used, 'barleys' or the similar-sounding 'barrels' was named 42 times, 'thumbs' or 'thumbs up'—which is the truce sign—20 times, and no other term was mentioned more than five times.

At Portsmouth it was soon clear that the common term is 'creams'—two of the other terms being puns on creams; while 'olly-olly-ee' is properly a call to end a game, and other terms were the recollections of children who had been to primary schools in other areas.

When a sample class of 30 children were questioned at Welwyn, 29 of the 30 gave either 'fains' or 'fainites':

24 gave 'fains' (sometimes spelt 'veins') as first or only truce term

5 gave 'fainites' (sometimes spelt 'vainites')

1 only gave 'pax'.

Investigations at other schools confirm that one term is usually predominant.

Bus Tickets

Although some ancient auguries are now no longer heeded, it is probable that as many ways of foretelling the future are employed today as at any time in the past, for when old divinations become impracticable, new wonders, more in keeping with the times, arise to take their place. Thus a plurality of traditions concerning friendship and fortune are now centred on bus and tram tickets. All over Britain the half-price community hold that the serial number of a ticket possesses intimate significance for the person to whom it is issued, and, since children probably predict the future more often with tickets than with anything else, it seems proper to describe this phenomenon in detail.

The serial numbers most prized are those in which the sum of the digits is twenty-one, and tickets bearing such numbers are even thought to influence the future:

'If on getting on a bus and purchasing a bus ticket I find that the number of the issue of the ticket adds up to 21 then I always keep that ticket as a kind of charm that will bring me luck.'

Girl, 13, Pontypool.

'If the numbers on your ticket add up to 21 you are lucky.'

Girl, 11, Lydney.

'If the number on your bus ticket adds up to 21 you will be lucky all the month.'

Boy, 12, Wandsworth.

A Brixton boy adds that it is especially lucky if the letters in front of the serial number are the person's initials. A Brighton girl says that if the total comes to 21 it means 'one will get another boy friend'. A Watford girl says it means one will be married.

If the serial numbers add up to other totals they may also have significance, particularly multiples of seven:

'If the figures on your bus tickets add up to 7 or a denomination of 7 it is lucky.'

Boy, 13, Upminster.

'If the numbers add up to 7 it means a wish, 14 a kiss, 21 a letter, 28 a parcel.'

Girl, 15, Ipswich.

Inevitably:

'If the numbers on the bus ticket add up to 13 bad luck is forecast for the future.'

Boy, 12, Lambeth.

The actual figures in the serial number are also noted, the most auspicious again being the number seven.

'If the last number of ticket is a 7 you are going to have a lucky day.'

Boy, 12, Southwark.

Many south-east London boys confirm this, also children in the Home Counties and at Oxford. A number of boys at Croydon state that they collect such tickets. One boy says that he collects them for a blind person; and several say that a person should keep on collecting them until he has a million such tickets.

An Upminster boy, aged 13, says: 'If the 7 is the second figure the owner will marry soon or has a secret lover.'

A girl, 14, from Cumberland, says that if a ticket has the figures 1, 2, 4, or 5 on it 'it means you are in love'. Twelve-year-olds in Sheffield say that if two figures are the same and next to each other 'you have a wish'. A North Weald boy says that it is lucky if all the figures are the same.

The general opinion, however, is that twenty-one is the important number, and in some cities the receipt of such a ticket gives, or is supposed to give, peculiar privileges. In Aberdeen for instance:

'If any girl receives a ticket on which the numbers add up to twenty-one she keeps it until she meets the boy she admires the most and gives it to him. This means she loves him.'

Girl, aged 15.

'If a person has a car ticket where the figures add up to twenty-one and she gives it to a person of the opposite sex, it means that she loves whomever she gave it to and she will be married at twenty-one.'

Girl, aged 14.

The significance of this token is sometimes taken a stage further, the response of the person to whom it is offered being of consequence.

'A well-known superstition is counting on tramcar tickets. If they amount to twenty-one we keep it and give it to a boy. If he throws it away he throws away one's love, but if he keeps it he keeps one's love.'

Girl, aged 14.

Other girls in Aberdeen say that if he tears it in half and 'returns half of it to her, that means he loves her'. But all emphasize that *'Twenty-one is the only number used for this'*. It is a practice which has also been reported from Bath, Brighton, Fife, Glasgow, Liverpool, London, Newcastle, Peterborough, Pontypool, and Swansea. Sometimes, particularly amongst boys, it is expected that the sign of reciprocated affection should be more explicit. A boy, aged 12, from Southwark declares:

'If you get a ticket with the numbers adding up to 21, you can get a kiss off your girl friend.'

This statement is confirmed by other London lads, thus: 'If get 21 G.F. will give kiss in exchange'—'Every bus ticket adding up to 21 is worth one kiss'—'Drop behind a girl and demand a kiss'. One lad says: 'If you have a bus ticket adding up to 21, then you should be allowed to kiss your girl, but it doesn't always work.'

In Swansea, the girls elaborate:

'If the number adds up to twenty-one and you give the ticket to your boy friend he must kiss you. If he likes you he gives it back to you and you then kiss him, and so on.'

They also say:

'If you have a ticket whose numbers add up to twenty-nine your boy friend should take you to the pictures.'

'If you have twenty-one tickets adding up to twenty-one you ask him to come to your twenty-first birthday party.'

An Ealing girl states:

'If the total is 21 it means "I love you", but if it is 19 it means "I hate you". You give them to people you love or hate. Other totals also have meanings but these are the only two I know.'

In Aberdeen, Manchester, Oxford, and Swansea, it is also the custom to work out the initials of the well-beloved:

'If the number on the ticket does not add up to twenty-one it is usual to see which letter of the alphabet corresponds with the number on one's ticket and whichever letter it is will be the first in one's future husband's name.'

Girl, 14, Aberdeen.

In Swansea, where some buses use ribbon tickets, the girls examine the smaller code number to give them the initial of the boy friend's Christian name; and they use the route number on the ticket to give the initial of his surname.

In many cities (perhaps in most cities) bus tickets are further used for an even more comprehensive divination, two methods being predominant. In the first, the serial numbers are translated literally as they stand:

'The first two figures on the top is the age you will get married the third how much money you earn a week and the forth how many children you will have.'

Boy, 12, Peckham.

Not all children agree with this. The usual formula is that the first two numbers on the ticket give the age when a person will be married, the third gives the number of children, and the fourth the weekly wage earned by self or husband. Thus the number 2158 means that a person will be married at 21, have five children, and earn £8 per week.

Other such formulas, adopted by individualists, are liable to give more newsworthy predictions:

'5964=5 wives, 9 boys, 6 girls and £4 a week'—*Boy, 12, Brixton.*

'6609=marry when you are 6, have 6 wives, no children, and live 9 more years'—*Boy 13, Croydon.*

'26406=get married twice, have six children, live in forty different houses, earn £6 a week'—*Girl 12, Ipswich.*

In the other method the future is worked out with the aid of an old folk rhyme, and the method affords an interesting example of the urbanization of a rural superstition, for the rhyme is one which country people have long recited when a company of magpies is observed. A 10-year-old Birmingham girl writes:

'The way we tell our furtune is to keep our bus tickets and add up the numbers at the top, see how many times seven gos into the number, see how many you have over. Say this little ryhmn, and that is your furture. The rhymn is—

> One for sorrow,
> Two for joy,
> Three for a letter,
> Four for a boy,
> Five for silver,
> Six for gold,
> Seven for a secret, that's never been told.'

This is the usual verse and procedure. Also reported from Bath, Bedford, Doncaster, Leicester, London, Oxford, Sheffield, Warwick, and from Hull, where children are said to have used this rhyme with tram tickets since about 1920.

Only a few variations have been found. In Coleraine, Ireland, they add up the numbers, and then add again (e.g. 6154, added together=16, added together again=7) and then recite:

> One for sorrow, two for joy,
> Three for a kiss and four for a boy,
> Five for silver, six for gold,
> Seven for a secret never to be told.

> Eight for a letter from over the sea,
> Nine for a lover as true as can be.

On the outskirts of Birmingham some children see how many times *five* goes into the number, and then recite the rhyme quoted by the 10-year-old above, with the addition:

> Eight for a bracelet, nine for a ring,
> Ten for a person that can sing.

And at a youth club in Ipswich teenagers have the sophisticated version:

> One for sorrow, two for joy,
> Three for a letter, four for a boy,
> Five for a sweetheart, six for a kiss,
> Seven for an evening full of bliss.

Thus do children in the twentieth century, many of whom have never seen a magpie in their lives, unwittingly sustain a rustic rhythm which was known in the days of Dr. Johnson. And almost certainly the lines have greater currency today, in their new application, than they had in the pastoral days before the Industrial Revolution.

Language and the Development of Thinking

One of the aspects of language development which this collection of readings aims to emphasize is that children use language to fill out their understanding of the world. By using language, children are not limited to what they can hear and see immediately around them. They can refer to objects, people, events that are not present i.e. not physically present or in the past or future as far as time is concerned. In the following extract from Lewis's *Language, Thought and Personality in Infancy and Childhood*, the author looks at the function of language as the child physically and cognitively explores the world around him.

11

M. M. LEWIS
Language and Exploration

(Let us consider) the child beginning to use semi-conventional forms such as *tee, pushie, goggie*, as means of directing his own and other people's attention to particular 'things', 'situations'. A sound-pattern used in this way is a kind of demonstrative act— a sort of pointing. It is of course a step beyond actual pointing and certainly it is a great deal more effective in communication; for not only does it draw the attention of another person but the manner in which it is spoken, its intonational character, expresses and symbolizes the nature of the child's concern with the thing, the situation.

What the child must needs move on to now is the ability to draw attention to something which is not present; present neither for him nor for his listener; something beyond the actual here or now, or both. As he achieves this the child makes a further notable advance in the transformation of his speech from expression to a means of symbolization.[1]

We turn to the earlier stages of this development as they can be observed in infancy.

The Growth of Reference to what is Absent

When for the first time we notice a child saying a word which clearly relates to something absent, this may seem to us, the on-lookers, a suddenly and completely new step. But here again, what has entered his life is not a new form of behaviour, but a more effective instrument for communication—he is now using an

M. M. Lewis: Extract from *Language, Thought and Personality in Infancy and Childhood*, London: Harrap and New York: Basic Books Inc., 1963, Chapter 5. © M. M. Lewis.
[1] Brain 1961, 3 takes reference to the absent to be the essential attribute of a symbol as distinct from a sign. Speaking of the cries of non-human animals, he says, 'They are never symbols; that is, they have no power to represent things in their absence.'

adopted word as he has already been using one of his own sound-groups. What is new is the word, and with it the additional power and effectiveness it gives to his ability to communicate, in drawing attention to what is absent.

Observation shows that, as in other aspects of linguistic development, there are a number of interrelated contributory factors. Of these the most important are the child's own rudimentary reference to what is absent, beginning far back in his history; the reinforcement of this by the constant attempts of others to direct his attention to what is absent; and the emergence of linguistic intercourse—speech in response to speech.

(a) Rudimentary reference to the absent

This is already implicit in a child's early utterance, in his manipulative use of discomfort-cries. When, for instance, a child cries *mama* as a means of bringing his absent mother to his side, he is, we may reasonably suppose, already in a rudimentary way also directing his own attention to her before she comes within reach of his sight or hearing. This direction towards something absent certainly gains in power, in precision and effectiveness as the child, in communication with others, comes to substitute conventional, or semi-conventional, words for his own speech-forms.

Thus the first clear case of K's spontaneous reference to an absent thing by means of a semi-conventional word was at 1;4,17. At breakfast-time he was accustomed to have honey, for which his word for some time had been *ha*. This morning, no honey was on the table. Turning towards the cupboard in which the honey was kept, he said *ha!*—certainly a manipulative demand.

It is evident that it is a great gain for the child if he uses a semi-conventional word such as *ha* instead of a widely-ranging speech-form such as *mama* or *eh! eh!*—which might, on this occasion, be taken to refer to any one of a number of things in the cupboard. When he says *ha* he is more 'likely to be understood'—that is, a response from others is both more likely to occur and to be more appropriate to his need. Further, because its reference is narrower and more specific—that is, linked with this particular object, the honey—it becomes for the child, in his own inner speech, a more adequate means of referring to the absent honey. When now someone says *ha* or *honey* to him, there is a stronger tendency for him to direct his behaviour towards the honey, even though it is absent. This brings us to the second contributory factor—the manner in which the child is incited to refer to absent things by the remarks and behaviour of others.

(b) Incitement by others

In the course of ordinary family life, we are constantly speaking to the child about things that are absent, with the intention of directing his behaviour towards them. When at last we succeed, it is because we have managed, once again, to modify an already well-established pattern of behaviour—the child's response to a word or phrase referring wholly to the present situation.

We have already seen how K was being taught, in play, to respond to the phrase *Baby, give mummy crustie!* There came a time when he responded appropriately to such a phrase when it involved an object not actually present to his senses.

> 1;1,5. The child was playing on the floor. His ball was in a corner of the room, where it had lain unheeded by him all day. His mother said, *Baby, where's ballie?* The child turned and crawled towards the ball. On the way there he halted at the coal-box, a favourite plaything. His mother repeated the question, whereupon he resumed his journey, seized the ball and looked up at her. (Lewis 1951, p. 234.)

This is truly a remarkable event, the importance of which in a child's development can hardly be exaggerated. It is, however, mysterious only if we ignore what has led up to it. The question *Where's ballie?* has caused the child to perform an act, to engage in a series of movements culminating in grasping the ball. The detailed record of observations shows that this child, during at least four months before this episode, has regularly responded appropriately to the phrase when the ball was present. There can be little doubt that in the course of these occasions the word *ballie* has become linked with his experience of the ball when he has heard the word spoken and said it to himself. We can well believe that a connection has been established between his recall of the experience of the ball and his 'internalization' of the word. Now, even when the ball is out of sight, the word uttered by his mother incites him to direct his behaviour towards it.

This development is fostered by another contributory factor, the growth of linguistic intercourse—the interchange of speech as a form of behaviour in itself, less tied to the actual present situation and ultimately independent of it. The child engages in communication freed from the dominance of what is present to his senses.

(c) The emergence of linguistic intercourse

Here again, observation shows that what may seem to be a new pattern of behaviour is in fact the development of earlier patterns. The child has now come to respond to speech by speech. Leading up to this there are, we find, two successive phases. First, the child learns to respond to speech by acts; then by acts and speech and, from this, by speech alone.

Response to speech by acts we have seen in such cases as *Baby, where's ballie?*—the child responding to speech by an action concerned with something not actually present to his senses. Sooner or later we find the child responding to speech by a pattern of behaviour which includes speech. K, for instance, had learnt to respond to *Peep-bo*, said by his mother, by covering his face with his hands and then withdrawing them. At 1;1,8 (three days after the episode of *Baby, where's ballie?*) he not only made the appropriate movements, but also said *eh-bo!*

Now, in ordinary circumstances, those about the child are constantly inciting him to respond in this way to speech by speech. At first, this will only happen when what is said is concerned with the present situation. For instance, at 1;5,10, K, pointing to the fire, said in a delighted tone, *Aha! fa!* When his mother, also pointing to the fire, asked, *What's that?* he replied, *fa!*

The child then learns to respond to speech by speech which refers to something absent, but with clues in the present situation. At 1;6.9. K's mother, standing by a drawer in which chocolate was kept, said, *I've got something nice for you!* to which he replied *gogga.* Finally, the child learns to respond to speech by speech when there is nothing in the present situation to support his reply. Five days after the last episode, K's mother said to him *What would baby like?* to which he replied, *gogga*. He has begun to respond to speech by speech, when the whole pattern of intercourse is relatively free from the present physical situation. The remark of the other person is itself sufficient to evoke his spoken response.

It is evident that in intercourse of this kind the child is being incited to direct his utterance towards what is absent. Having earlier learnt—as by *Baby, where's ballie?*—to direct his behaviour towards what is absent, he now learns to make a spoken reference towards what is absent. The step that he has taken is obviously of the greatest importance for his further development. It opens up for him the vast possibilities of conversation with others, in which there is reference to a universe beyond the immediate spatial and temporal present. The significance of this for the growth of his thought—and, indeed, of all his behaviour—can hardly be overestimated. But, as we have seen, it is not a sudden new creation in the child's life. Like his every other achievement, it arises from the conjunction of modes of behaviour already present in his earlier experience.

The beginning of reference to past and to future
From the growth of ability to symbolize the spatially absent there emerges the ability to symbolize what is temporally remote. As a child learns to converse with others about the 'there', he also learns to speak about the 'then' and the 'to-be'.

The rudiments of reference to the past are already to be found on occasions when a child's speech is directed towards what is spatially absent. For instance, when he says *ha!*, turning towards the cupboard in which honey is usually kept, this is likely to include some recall of a previous perception of the honey in the cupboard. To say *gogga*, while standing by the drawer where chocolate is kept, is likely to include some recall of a previous perception of chocolate in the drawer.

But in these cases the object which is recalled as having existed in the past also persists in the present. Mother has only to open the cupboard and there is the honey. What we have now to see is how a child comes to refer to what is past and gone; what can be brought into the present only through the power of thought.

There can be no doubt that, without any intervention by others, a child will, in some measure, recall the past—that he will 'turn round upon his own schemata', symbolizing the past for himself, perhaps by non-verbal symbols. But there is also no doubt that the development of a child's verbal reference to the past is greatly aided by the fact that others so frequently speak to him about the past. It would seem likely that a child would be very much slower in communication concerning the past if we did not lead him in that direction.

It is interesting to notice that much of our reference to the past in talking to a child occurs in play with him—in a sort of game of question-and-answer. Take a typical instance, from the record of K at 1;8,22.

Adult	Child
Where's Da gone?	*goh!* (gone!)
Where?	*Da*
Yes, but where?	*cool!* (school!)

We enjoy this game of trying to get the child to give the right answer and feel that he is very clever when he succeeds. What a wonderful memory, he has, bless him! To remember that Da goes to school!

A more detached and critical person might point out that this interchange may be merely verbal, that the child is merely imitating words he has heard—*Da has gone to school*—without understanding them. There is surely some truth in this; but we must also recognize that purely verbal interchange, as a sort of game, is a factor in bringing about real linguistic intercourse. What it does is to accustom the child to utter patterns of speech whose only reference is to the past. Here, as everywhere, the child in learning language in intercourse with others, is provided with symbols which promote his thinking.

Thus in the growth of a child's reference to the past there is, once more, the convergence of factors springing from the child himself and his social environment. The child himself recalls and symbolizes to himself past experiences. Others incite him to respond to and speak words which also recall the past. There comes a time when spontaneously he will speak about the past. With K, this first seems to have occurred at 2;0,20. On returning from a walk he said *mo-u-ka*. His father asked *motor-car?*, to which he replied *No!* When his father then asked *moo-cow?* he replied with satisfaction, *moo-ka!*

When the child says *mo-u-ka* he is repeating the word that he has uttered, either openly or to himself, on seeing the cow during his walk. The first reply of his father, *motor-car?* is not corroborative—it does not match his word or what it means for him. But when he obtains the reply *moo-cow?* he not only has the satisfaction of being understood, but his reference to the absent cow is also reinforced. It is in conversation of this kind, as we try to understand a child and work with him to achieve mutual comprehension, that we help him to refer more and more effectively to the past. Through linguistic intercourse, there is social reinforcement of his memory.

In somewhat similar fashion we promote his reference to the future. The main contributory factors are parallel to those that operate in the growth of reference to the past. First there is the child's own rudimentary reference to the future. Secondly there is incitement to make this reference, through linguistic intercourse with others. Finally there comes a time when he spontaneously refers to the future.

Here again we have space to cite only typical instances. A child is already making a rudimentary reference to the future when he is using a word manipulatively in order to secure something not actually present. When, for example, K at breakfast-time turned towards the cupboard containing honey and said *ha!*, he was looking forward to receiving the honey. More clearly still, some months later (at 1;8,24), as his mother was preparing to take him out, he said *gogga!*, asking for and anticipating the buying of chocolate.

Meanwhile, in intercourse with the child, others are constantly reinforcing his forward-looking reference. For instance, at 1;6,3, K began climbing upstairs at his usual bath-time. His mother asked, *Where are you going?* to which he replied *ba!* (bath). Anyone who has lived with children could give innumerable examples of this kind of question-and-answer, which, we notice, is exactly parallel to conversations referring to the past, such as *Where's Da gone?—Cool!*

There is one point worth mentioning here that perhaps has not received the attention it deserves. In our questions referring to the past, as compared with those referring to the future, there are differences in our intonation, probably also in our gestures and bodily attitudes. It may well be, that a child learns to respond to these differences—that he is led to make a backward or forward reference by these characteristics of utterances, as well as by the actual words used.

Finally there comes a time when a child makes a spontaneous reference to the future. Thus K at 2;1,23 was told a story by his mother and had it repeated a second and third time. Then he said, *K tell it now!*

In tracing the development of reference to the future we must notice that this is helped by the fact that, for a child, the future so often resembles the past. The child who anticipates chocolate when he says *gogga*, or his bath when he says *ba*, or says *K tell it now!* when he wishes to tell the story, is anticipating that the present situation will have the same sequel as a similar situation has had in the past. His imagination of the future is based upon his memory of the past—as is, indeed, all prediction throughout life.

What, most of all, fosters his forward-looking reference is the sort of response his attempts at this receive from us. It helps him if we reply by words or deeds or both. It helps him if our words show that we understand him; still more, if what we do satisfies him. If after he has said *gogga*, chocolate appears; or after *K tell it now!* he is allowed to tell the story, clearly his tendency to refer to the future is likely to be promoted. There is here, just as in the growth of reference to the past, social reinforcement of forward-looking reference.

The functions of questions

Perhaps the most powerful means of social reinforcement, in promoting his reference to what is present, to what is absent, to the past and to the future, is the question-and-answer which forms so large a part of our communication with him, from the time when we first begin to interchange speech with him.

Questioning is a form of behaviour, not always symbolized by an interrogative form of words. As Nathan Isaacs has said, 'For the psychologist, questions should before everything else be psychic *events*. His problems should be: What are their causes and functions? In what situations do they arise? What is their relation to these situations?' This is particularly in point in describing the beginnings of questioning. The stages of development are certainly not simply marked by the appearance of interrogative words, Where? What? Why? and the rest. For at first a child often questions without using any interrogative form. Sometimes, on the other hand, he uses an interrogative word without asking a question. We cannot judge the development of questioning by the order of the acquisition of interrogative words—it is the activity of questioning, however expressed, which is our concern.

What is a question—what sort of behaviour is it, as we find it in everyday life? It is, of course, a form of instrumental language, an utterance by which we attempt to secure action from others. But the responsive action sought is of a special kind. The questioner needs to fill a gap in his knowledge or, at least, to test what he already supposes. This knowledge that the questioner seeks is either his goal in itself or a preliminary to action. Instead of thinking on his own—perceiving, remembering, imagining, reasoning—the questioner brings others into co-operation with him. He calls upon them to help him in exploring a situation, either to get to know more about the situation itself or as a means to further action.

Now it need hardly be said that the functions of questions, as we find them in adult life, are likely to be different, or present only, in rudimentary forms, in infancy. Our present topic is precisely this, to trace the process by which the various functions of questions emerge in a child's linguistic behaviour.

Observations make it clear that questioning is a specialization of tendencies already present in this linguistic behaviour. At an early stage, a child begins rudimentary questioning; he responds to the questions of others and to their incitement and encouragement of his own questioning. He asks questions about the immediate present situation; then the scope of his questioning is enlarged beyond the immediate situation to what is absent in time and space. Throughout all this, imitation and play are important factors.

The rudiments of questioning

As in so many other aspects of language development, a child begins his rudimentary questioning before he adopts conventional speech. Unfortunately, here again, because it is pre-conventional, this rudimentary questioning has received little attention. I have to cite my own observations.

> 1;6,3.   K was looking at a picture-book with his mother. She asked, *Where's eggie?* whereupon he pointed to a picture of an egg. Coming to a picture of a horse he looked up enquiringly at his mother, who said, *Horse.* Coming then to a picture of a jug, he pointed to it and looked up at her. She remained silent. Then he said, *eh . . . eh . . . eh!* urgently, pointing all the time until she answered, *Jug.*

This observation, which we may reasonably take as typical of many children, is illuminating in a number of ways. We see the child's mother asking him questions to which he replies by simple pointing, without language. He then imitates her to the extent of looking at her interrogatively and this evokes her reply. When he tries again, however, his mother deliberately refuses to respond until he makes a *spoken* interrogation. By her manner and attitude, and in the urgency of his need to secure a response, she brings him to the point of utterance. His *eh . . . eh . . . eh!* is as yet hardly a question; it is, perhaps, no more than a demand that she shall reply, but it has the rudiments of questioning in it. It is manipulative, in that the child is using speech as a means of securing action from another person. The important development is this— that the action he hopes to secure is a *reply*, an act of speech. Only a linguistic response will satisfy him. The interchange with his mother is rudimentary question-and-answer, though still no more than a sort of game.

A further development is the child's use of speech as a means of securing a reply that he already expects. For instance:

> 1;9,2.   There are two low cupboards side by side, one of which is forbidden to him. He points to this cupboard saying *eh, eh* (a customary way with him of indicating a wish or request). When his mother replies *No!* he points to the permitted cupboard, again saying *eh, eh.* His mother replies *Yes!* All this episode is repeated about a dozen times. Later there is a similar episode in connection with a forbidden bottle and a permitted box.

Let us notice here the beginning of questioning as a substitute for physical, non-linguistic behaviour. Instead of opening the cupboard door, the child speaks. He calls upon his mother to help him in exploring the situation by symbolizing it with him. The replies he obtains are satisfying in themselves because they fit into the pattern of the game; but they are also something more than this—potentially, a guide to further action. They are likely to influence his play with these cupboards in the future.

Throughout this development we see the three factors mentioned above—play, imitation and the co-operation of others. The rudimentary questioning is a form of play, enjoyed for its own sake. It is imitative play—the child asks questions in the manner in which he himself has been questioned. Most important of all is his mother's willingness to play this game with him; we see that she deliberately causes him to express his interrogation through speech. And when he utters his rudimentary question, she takes the trouble to make a verbal reply, even though a non-verbal reply might have sufficed—a nod or shake of the head. As always, the speed and efficacy of a child's linguistic development is immeasurably influenced by the adult co-operation that he receives.

The transition to conventional speech

Again, as throughout linguistic development, the growth of questioning from a child's primitive utterance is reinforced and facilitated by his adoption of conventional speech. In particular, as he comes to use questioning as an instrument for the symbolical exploration of his environment, he realizes that one form of interrogation is specially valuable—questions directed to securing the names of things.

So we come to one of the most striking characteristics of children in their second and third years—their indefatigable concern with naming-questions. M. E. Smith, for instance, recording some three thousand questions of children of this age, found that one-fifth were directed to obtain the name of an object or person.[1] William Stern, the pioneer of the modern study of children's language, saw this onset of naming-questions as one of the great

[1] The details are: 94 per cent of the questions concerned the immediate situation; 46 per cent referred to human action or relationships; 20 per cent were naming-questions (Smith 1933, 201). Davis 1932, analysing 3650 questions of seventy-three children between 3;0 and 12;0 found that 88 per cent concerned the immediate situation.

moments in a child's life. The child discovers 'that every thing has a name'; that to every object there belongs a lasting symbol, by means of which we can indicate the object and communicate about it.[1]

Stern appears to believe that children as early as the second year arrive at this formulated generalization. This would seem to be too adult, too intellectualized, a view of cognitive development at this stage; but perhaps Stern means no more than that children behave 'as though' they had made this discovery—and this we can well accept.

There is no need to give examples of naming-questions. Anyone who has had anything to do with a young child will be only too familiar with them. Certainly at first, and often for a long time to come, a child will ask for the name of one thing after another, as a sort of game. Not infrequently he will know the name before he asks for it and will seem merely to be seeking the satisfaction of this affirmatory interchange. But what is learnt in play can subsequently be used as an instrument to satisfy other needs.

Questioning as exploration

Among these needs, none is more imperative than the child's desire to explore his environment; at first, what is immediately present; later, what is remote in place and time. Already, while he is playing the game of question-and-answer, he is learning that questioning is a means of exploration. Asking for names is a simple kind of exploration—the child builds up, with the help of others, a verbal universe which symbolizes his environment. Even before he asks questions he will have begun to learn names by everyday trial-and-error—as we saw, for instance, K learning the names of animals. Then he begins to do it more directly by asking questions.

Some of these questions help him to extend the exploration of his environment beyond the immediate present situation. We have seen that before this, his reference to what is absent will have begun in the course of everyday interchange, in his attempts to satisfy his manipulative and declarative needs. Now he finds that

[1] Stern 1924, 162 and (a fuller account) 1922, 176. Among others, Vygotsky 1962 has criticized Stern's view that a child in his second year arrives at a generalization as to the naming-function of words. Wallon's paper is an excellent account of the basic affective, functional, imitative and social factors in the development of questioning.

an instrument that more directly helps him to symbolize what is absent, is the question that asks *Where?*—although at first he may not use this interrogative word.

> 1;10,3. K asked his mother, *Daddy?* She replied, *Gone ta-ta.* He then asked, *Kah?* (Carrie?). His mother replied, *Kitchen.* She then said, *Where's mummy?* He replied, pointing to her, *eh, eh, eh!*

We see here several different forms of behaviour, already habitual to the child, combining to produce questioning that refers to what is absent. First, there is the interplay of imitation. For a long time past, the child has himself been asked Where-questions—beginning as early as 1;1,5 with *Where's ballie?* Now at 1;10,3 he imitates by asking Where-questions of his mother. His first two she answers; at his third, she imitates him, asking him in turn, *Where's mummy?* Secondly there is an interesting development of manipulative function. When the child asks *Where's daddy?* he has something of the same manipulative intention as when he said *ha!* for the unseen honey. But there is now this difference, that his request results, not in the production of his father, but in a verbal reply from his mother. As soon as a child receives such a verbal reply, his manipulative utterance begins to have the function of interrogation—a verbal demand which secures a verbal response. Finally, we see that there is still an element of play in this interchange. The child is obviously no less interested in the game of question-and-answer than in the whereabouts of his father or Carrie.

Clearly, the chief result of obtaining replies to his Where-questions is this, that the child finds that through these questions he can take the initiative in causing another person to refer to something within their common environment and yet beyond the immediate situation. By securing social co-operation of this kind he extends his area of reference, building up a structure of symbolization of what is absent.

From beginnings such as these, there are two lines of development in the use of questions as a means of referring to what is absent. The child aids his own reference by addressing questions to himself, and he also asks questions to bring others into co-operation with him in referring to the absent.

Instances of K's communication with himself:

2;2,23.   Looking through a picture-book, he finds the picture of a teddy bear. Shuts the book and says: *Ever can teddy bear be?* He repeats this many times.

2;3,5.   Playing the game of hiding a pencil in a book: *Ever can you be, little pencil?*

2;4,18.   Looking for his toy, 'Billy-boy': *Billy-boy, where Garkie put it? Where is it?*

2;4,19.   Playing with his train, looking for the string: *Where's the string?*[1]

This kind of chatter, so characteristic of children throughout infancy, is not merely an accompaniment to action: the question the child asks himself is one element within the total action—the verbal part of the game.[2] The words help to direct the child's perception and motor activity. The words also help to bring what the child cannot see into relation with what he can see—the absent in relation to the present. If we say that the child is 'thinking aloud', we must recognize that there is likely to be a two-way relation here between words and thought. On the one hand, the child utters words which he recalls internally from similar past experiences. On the other hand, the utterance of the words may be followed by 'internalization' of them, so that the child is helped to think more effectively about what is absent—so that what is out of sight need not be out of mind.

If now we look at the questions asked of others we see an important line of development. The information received becomes, rather than an aid to an immediate physical activity, an incentive to further speech by the child.

Instances are:

2;5,0.   Looking for a strip of felt, K asks his father, *Where is it?* When it is shown to him he says, *There it is.*

[1] For the full record see Lewis 1951, 365. Here no attempt has been made to render the child's pronunciation.

[2] This function of self-addressed questions became clear to me from my own observations, first published in 1937 (Lewis 1951, 254), where I suggest that this is an important aspect of Piaget's 'egocentric' language. Vigotsky 1939, 39 emphasizes the same point in his criticism of Piaget; Luria, following him, calls language of this kind 'synpractic'; Luria and Yudovich 1959, 19; Luria 1961.

2;2,3. His mother has returned from a visit to a friend. He asks, *Auntie ya?* (Auntie there?). His mother replies, *Yes!* whereupon he says, *Want it auntie. Go ask her!*

2;7,9. He has been out to tea the previous day with his mother. Today she has been out alone. On her return he asks, *Has mummy been out to tea?* She replies, *Yes.*

The child's goal here may well be said to be knowledge as an end in itself. The question he asks has the intention of obtaining confirmation or denial of what he already supposes. The affirmatory answer he receives is sufficient in itself, giving him the knowledge he seeks. But if his mother's answer had been in the negative, he might have gone on with further questioning until a satisfying answer was reached.

With information-seeking interrogation of this kind we are at the beginning of that vast proliferation of questions so characteristic of this period in a child's life. In some children, as with K, it may begin as early as the middle of the third year; with others, later. Differences in the speed and the volume of this development are likely to be due to differences in temperament, intelligence, verbal ability and imitativeness and—running through all these—the extent of incitement and co-operation the child receives from those about him. There must be retardation in the development of a child's exploration of his world, present and absent, if he is not questioned and if his own questions remain unanswered. For a deaf child, or a child in an institution, this may mean a severe restriction of enterprise in reaching out beyond his immediate experience.

The differentiation of questions

In normally favourable conditions, a child's questions become more diverse in function and he acquires specific interrogative words. But since interrogative forms and functions do not at first always coincide, the course of development may not be simple and direct. As the child's interrogative needs become more specific, he may or may not express these by means of the conventional words. At the same time, in imitating conventional interrogative words he may or may not use these with the conventional functions. The process by which he comes to use the interrogative forms of the mother tongue with their conventional functions may be long and arduous, in some cases extending over several years.

In general, the main features of this course of development are these. The child has interrogative needs which he has been expressing, though crudely and ineffectively, by the rudimentary means at his disposal. Meanwhile, others are constantly questioning him and each other; the child imitates the interrogative forms that he hears, sometimes as a kind of game sometimes as real questioning. Gradually he finds that specific kinds of interrogation bring specific kinds of response. For instance, What-questions supply names; Where-questions bring indications of location; and Who-did-this-questions and Why-questions bring information about the source or the goal of actions. He becomes more clearly aware of these various sequences of question and answer, and so learns to use specific forms of questioning to secure specific types of response.

Three kinds of interrogative behaviour may be distinguished. First, the child continues to play the game of question-and-answer; he asks what we may call 'pseudo-questions'—questions the answers to which he already knows and which he asks simply for the pleasure of the verbal interchange with someone. Secondly, he continues to ask questions to test the correctness of what he believes—a rudimentary form of testing a hypothesis. Finally, he asks questions by which he seeks real information—what he as yet does not know.

In actually observing a child, it is not always possible to draw clear lines of separation between these kinds of interrogative activity. Instances from the record of K will illustrate this.

(a) *Naming-questions*

2;6,17. With his mother he is playing the game of 'Counting', i.e., naming things. He says, *Could mummy count this and this?* She replies, *You count first?* He points and asks, *What is it?* She replies, *What?* whereupon he says, *Milk.* All this is repeated with one object after another.

If his mother had not been so persistent, one might well have thought that he really did not know the names of the various objects. On the other hand, there is little doubt that in the following instance we have a real question:

2;7,15. He points to word after word in a book of nursery-rhymes, asking each time, *What does this say?*

(b) *Where-questions*

Two observations on the same day—the first probably playful, the second probably really seeking information:

2;9,3. He says to his mother, *Do you know where R's bicycle is?* When she answers *No!* he continues, *R's bicycle is at Auntie M's.*

When his father awakens him in the morning he says, *Where's mummy?* His father replies, *In bed*, whereupon he says, *I want to say, Good morning.*

(c) *Questions concerning sources of actions*

A very important development in a child's life is the emergence of questions and answers concerned with the sources of actions. The child begins to ask Why-questions, and to answer questions of this kind with 'Because . . .' These exchanges might appear to imply that the child has begun to have clear ideas of causality. But here, no more than in other aspects of linguistic development are children's words to be taken at their face value. Close observation of the circumstances in which these questions and answers occur, and of a child's linguistic and general development at the time, lead to the conclusion that what the child says is not so much an expression of an existing notion of cause-and-effect, as a means by which the growth of ideas of causality may be fostered.

A child approaches ideas of cause-and-effect by various kinds of questions that demand information, and it is the answers that he gets to his questions that do much to connect cause and effect for him.

Sometimes the question simply asks for an explanation of an action observed by the child:

2;9,8. His father goes to a drawer and opens it. K asks, *What do you want daddy?*

But quite often the child has a glimmering of the answer and is asking for reinforcement and expansion of his knowledge:

2;9,9. Seeing his father putting on his spectacles, K asks, *What you putting those glasses on for?*

Taken by itself this might seem to be a genuine request for information. But in this case we happen to have a record of an earlier observation:

> 2;5,12. His father has his spectacles off. K says, *Daddy put glasses on.*

Since the child has seen his father putting on his spectacles he most probably has seen this followed by the reading of a book or newspaper. So that when he now asks why his father is putting on his glasses he has, we may suppose, at least some notion of the answer, 'To read . . .'. If this is so, the question has been directed to secure confirmation of what, to some extent, the child already supposes.

In many cases this function of a child's question is beyond doubt. For instance:

> 2;8,12. K, to his mother, *Who bought that frock?* She replies, *Mummy,* whereupon he says, *No, Lily!* (He has accompanied Lily, the maid, when she called for the dress.)

The child, in asking the question, already has his own answer to it. He has experienced a schema of events which, in recall, he can formulate in words. In putting a part of this as a question, he is seeking to have the rest of his inner formulation confirmed by someone else—it is a kind of game. But when his mother's reply does not, in fact, match his own inner statement, he supplies his own answer.

Often we deliberately make him do this. Instead of answering his request for information, we turn the question upon him, causing him to supply the answer, which he is perfectly able to do. For instance:

> 2;10,18. While eating soup: *Mummy, why do we use a spoon?* Mother: *Why?* K: *'Cause we can't drink it with our hands.*
>
> 2;9,0. His mother, referring to a projected excursion on Sunday: *Perhaps Lily will come too.* K: *Lily can't come.* Mother: *Why?* K: *'Cause of George.* (George is the young man who calls on Lily on Sundays!)

In these two instances the child has answered our Why-question with a Because-answer. But are we warranted in supposing that he has a clear awareness of cause-and-effect in these situations? It seems much more likely that in each case he is aware of a juxtaposition of events and can formulate this. It seems likely that he is not yet aware that we use a spoon *because* we don't drink soup with our hands: he is saying that these two things occur together—we don't drink soup with our hands, we use a spoon. Likewise when he says that Lily can't come because of George he is, surely, saying not that George is the cause of Lily's inability to come out, but rather that when George calls on Sundays, Lily stays at home.

This is in keeping with Piaget's contention that at first children are aware only of juxtaposition where later they recognize causality. More than anyone else, Piaget has made clear to us how much a child's progress in the development of ideas of causality depends upon his intercourse with other people. 'It is precisely to the extent that verbal-conceptual thought is transformed by its collective nature that it becomes capable of proof and search for truth, in contradistinction to the practical character of the acts of sensorimotor intelligence and their search for success or satisfaction.'[1] But what Piaget does not, perhaps, sufficiently stress is that in a child's early questions his nebulous and inchoate ideas of causality are made more explicit by his imitation of the language which adults use to express causality.

The process of development here is similar to the growth of awareness of spatial relationships. By asking and answering Where-questions imitatively, in play, a child is led to enquire more and more specifically about the location of absent things and so to form for himself a patterned structure of objects in space. In the same way, his imitation of Why-questions and Because-answers, often in play, fosters his growing awareness of causal relationships.

In the course of the present chapter, what we have been witnessing is the progressive influence of language upon the child's schemata. While he is as yet poor in language, he already has some rudimentary symbolization of the world about him; some dawning reference to what is absent, past or yet to come; some formulation of the linkage of certain events together. In our intercourse with him, the mother tongue helps him to become more

[1] Piaget 1955, 360.

clearly aware of spatial, temporal and even causal relationships by giving him the symbols for them—the linguistic forms by means of which we are accustomed to symbolize these relationships. Often it is his adoption, in imitation, of a verbal form that brings a structure of relationships into a relatively amorphous schema. If it is not true to say that words give birth to his ideas, at least this is true, that through words his ideas grow and ramify and become more clearly related to each other.

In his early questions a child may certainly be seeking information, but just as often—if not more frequently—practising the formulation of events that he can already tentatively make for himself. He is rapidly building up for himself a structure of knowledge, a system of symbolization. He is incited to do this by others in their questions to him; he practises question-and-answer in play with them and by himself; and he often asks questions, the answers to which he already knows, seeking as it were social approval or rejection of his own answers. It may be said that he is experimenting all the time to discover what may or may not be admitted to his system of knowledge. At first this experimenting may be a half-blind groping by trial-and-error; gradually, through social co-operation, it becomes more clear-sighted and more immediately and effectively directed towards its goals.

References

Brain, R. (1961) *Speech Disorders*, London: Butterworth.
Davis, E. A. (1932) *Child Development*, **3**.
Lewis, M. M. (1951) *Infant Speech* (2nd ed.), London: Routledge.
Luria, A. R. (1961) 'The role of speech in the regulation of normal and abnormal behaviour'. In B. Simon and J. Simon, *Educational Psychology in the USSR*, London: Routledge.
Luria, A. R. and Yudovich, F. Ia. (1959) *Speech and the Development of Mental Processes in the Child*, London: Staples Press.
Piaget, J. (1955) *The Child's Construction of Reality*, New York: Basic Books.
Smith, M. E. (1933) *Child Development*, **4**.
Stern, W. (1924) *Psychology of Early Childhood*, London: Allen & Unwin.
Vygotsky, L. S. (1939) *Psychiatry*, **2**.
— (1962) *Thought and Language*, New York: Wiley.

12 A. R. LURIA
The Directive Function of Speech in Development and Dissolution

A controversy has been active for many years concerning the relationship between language and thought, or between thought and language. Specifically the argument is about which comes first—the thought or the word. Vygotsky and Piaget take opposing sides in the debate. Vygotsky considers that it is well-nigh impossible for a child to abstract all the concepts that are coded by language without the word. He suggests that the word acts as a coat hanger on which the child hangs a concept. With further instances of the concept the child is able to organize his thoughts in terms of the word. In Vygotsky's writing there are two main types of concepts—'spontaneous concepts' in which the word is immediately linked to the child's own experience from very early on; and 'scientific concepts' which are generally learned with formal education through words. With 'scientific concepts' the child is told the word first and then, by reading about it, makes it part of his experience. In a way the opposite is true for 'spontaneous concepts' in that the child first has the experience and then is given a word to code that experience or concept.

Piaget, on the other hand, sees thought as being the result of internalized actions which are in turn dependent upon the level of development of the child's *non-verbal cognitive and perceptual abilities*. For Piaget, language can 'increase the powers of thought in range and rapidity' because language can refer to objects and concepts not present in time or (sapce,) but that is all. In the end, Piaget says, language use depends upon certain non-verbal psychological developments. In effect he is saying that the concept must precede the word, for the language, of which the word is but part, is preceded by the development of intelligence, i.e.

> through the actions of the child on the environment and the interiorization of these actions to form the operational structures (Inhelder *et al.* 1966, p. 163).

In Reading 12, Luria, a member of the Russian school of psycho-

A. R. Luria: Extract from 'The directive function of speech in development and dissolution' *Word*, 15, 1959, pp. 341–52.

linguistics, employs a series of experiments to explore the relationships between words and their functions in the cognitive development of the child.

Inhelder, B. *et al.* 'On cognitive development' *American Psychologist*, 1966, **21**, 160–4.

Along with the semantic and syntactic functions of speech, it is necessary to distinguish also its pragmatic or directive function. In the development of behaviour this function manifests itself in the fact that a word gives rise to new temporary connections in the brain and directs the system of activity of the child that has mastered it.

It was a full quarter of a century ago that the eminent Soviet psychologist Vygotsky pointed out the role played by the words of adults in the development of the child's mental processes and formulated his well-known thesis that what the child at first does with the help, and on the instructions, of the adult, he later begins to do by himself, supporting himself with his own speech; that speech as a form of communication with adults later becomes a means of organizing the child's own behaviour; and that the function which was previously divided between two people later becomes an internal function of human behaviour. In the years that have elapsed since Vygotsky's death the problem of the role of the word in the organization of mental life has been the subject of numerous Soviet investigations.

There arises, however, the question of how this pragmatic, directive function of the word is formed, and how its formation relates to the formation of the significative or generalizing functions of the word. A brief review of the pertinent experiments forms the topic of the present communication.

1. A child at the beginning of its second year of life is already in command of a considerable number of words. He understands such expressions as *cup, cat, fish, horse,* and can without difficulty hand someone the object if it is mentioned. But is the pragmatic, directive function of speech at this stage as effective as its significative, nominative function? Can the cited word always direct the child's activity with full effectiveness?

An answer to this question is suggested by the experiments which we have carried out in collaboration with A. G. Polijakova.

Before a child aged 1; 2 to 1; 4, we placed some object, e.g. a toy *fish*, and asked him to hand it to us; the child did this without particular difficulty. We then asked him, in the same situation, to hand us the *cat*. The child at first looked at us in disbelief, then began to look around until he found the object which had been named. It would seem that the adult word fully determined the child's action.

Let us, however, repeat this experiment in a somewhat more complicated situation. Let us place before the child two objects: a toy *fish* at some distance from it, and half way towards the fish a brightly coloured toy *cat*. If in this situation we ask a child of 1; 0 to 1; 2 to hand us the *fish*, his behaviour will be different. The uttered word will evoke in him an orientational reaction, and his glance will be fixed on the fish; but his hand, stretched out towards the fish, will stop half way, turn towards the cat, and instead of giving us the fish that was requested, the child will grasp the *cat* and offer it to the experimenter. The directive function of the word will be maintained only up to the moment when it comes into conflict with the conditions of the external situation. While the word easily directs behaviour in a situation that lacks conflict, it loses its directive role if the immediate orientational reaction is evoked by a more closely located, or brighter, or more interesting object.

It is only at the age of 1; 4 to 1; 6 that this phenomenon disappears and the selective effect of words is maintained even in conditions in which the components of the situation conflict with it.

We can easily disturb the directive function of the word in still another way. It is known that the word physiologically excites a certain system of connections in the cortex. In the normal, mature nervous system these connections possess considerable mobility and easily replace each other. As has been shown in many investigations, the mobility of the connections evoked by the word (or, as I. P. Pavlov called it, by the second signal system of reality), is even greater than the mobility of connections evoked by immediate signals.

However, the mobility of nervous processes in a very small child is still quite inadequate, and connections evoked by the word possess a considerable inertia at the early stages of development.

Taking this inadequacy of the mobility of connections in the early stages of development as a premise, we can measure the effectiveness of the directive function of the word.

We place before a child of 1; 0 to 1; 2 two toys: a fish and a horse, this time placing them at the same distance and giving them dimensions and colours that are equally attractive. We ask the child to give us the *fish*: he does this easily. We repeat this experiment three or four times, and the effect remains the same. In exactly the same tone of voice, we now utter a different instruction and ask the child to hand us the *horse*. Despite the fact that the meaning of this word is well known to the child, the inertia of the connections evoked by the first word is so great that in many cases the child again offers the experimenter the fish. The directive function of the changed verbal instructions is here vitiated by the inertia of the connection that has been established.[1]

The loss of the directive function of a word whose meaning is well known can also be observed in an experiment involving actions designated by verbs. If we give a child of 1; 2 to 1; 4 a stick on which rings are placed and we instruct him, 'Put on the ring', he does this easily. With equal ease he will, in another situation, execute the instruction, 'Take off the ring'. However, if the child has several times *put on* a ring and is holding the next ring in his hands, the instruction '*Take off* the ring' loses its directive meaning and begins to function non-specifically, merely accelerating the activity of *putting on* the ring onto the stick (Poljakova's and Ljamina's experiment).

The directive role of the word at an early age is maintained only if the word does not conflict with the inert connections which arose at an earlier instruction or which began with the child's own activity.

2. Experimental research can do more than ascertain the bare fact that the directive role of words is not fully effective at an early age. Such research can also measure the relative effectiveness of verbal signals as compared to the directive role of immediate, visual sig-

---

[1] In a number of cases such an experiment may not give the desired results. This happens when the dominant role in the child's behaviour continues to be played by the *immediate orientational response to objects*. In such cases the child will alternately hand the experimenter now this object, now the other, and the directive function of speech will fail to be exercised from the start.

nals. In order to make this comparison as vivid as possible, we pass on to some experiments with somewhat older children—aged from 1; 4 to 1; 6 on the one hand, and from 1; 8 to 2; 0, on the other hand.

Let us first establish how effective the orienting (attention directing) and directive role of a visual signal and its trace can be at this stage. We place before a child two inverted objects, a cup and a tumbler of non-transparent plastic. As the child watches, we hide a coin under the cup, which is placed to the left, and we ask the child to 'find' it. For a child of 1; 4 to 1; 6, this constitutes an interesting and meaningful task, which he solves without difficulty. We repeat this experiment three or four times, each time holding the coin under the cup within sight of the child. The solution will invariably be successful. Now, without interrupting the experiment, we change its conditions and hide the coin not under the cup on the left, but under the tumbler on the right. A certain proportion of children of the younger group will follow not the changed visual signal (more precisely, its trace), but the *influence of the inert motor stereotype*, and will put out their hands towards the cup on the left, carrying out the habitual movement reinforced in the previous experiment; only then will they turn to the tumbler under which the coin is hidden.

Let us now weaken the influence of the visual signal. We repeat the first experiment, but impose a short, 10-second delay between the hiding of the coin under the cup and the execution of the movement. This forces the child to act according to the *traces* of the visual signal whose effectiveness we are considering. The majority of children in the younger group successfully execute this task; only a few, the very youngest, cease to subordinate their actions to the visual instruction and begin to grasp both objects, losing track of the task of finding the coin that is hidden under one of them.

However, we again modify the conditions and after repeating the experiment three or four times with the cup and the 10-second delay we hide the coin under the tumbler located on the right, all within sight of the child. The picture now changes substantially. The ten-second delay turns out to be sufficient for the visual signal to yield its place to the decisive influence of the reinforced motor habit. The overwhelming majority of children now repeat the movement directed towards the cup on the left, ceasing to be directed by the image of the coin hidden under the tumbler on the right.

This orienting, directive influence of the visual signal is maintained better among children of the older group (1; 8 to 2; 0). Even when the execution of the movement is delayed, they solve the task well, directing their search to the object under which they saw the coin being hidden. This means that the orienting, directive role of the visual image becomes so effective at the end of the second year of life that the child submits to it completely, and successfully overcomes the inertia of the motor connections which have arisen.

A completely different picture appears in those cases where we replace the immediate, visual signals by verbal ones. For this purpose we again place before the child the two abovementioned objects, a cup and a tumbler, but this time unseen by the child, we slip the coin under the left-hand cup. In order to orient, i.e. to direct the actions of the child, we now draw upon a word rather than a visual image. We tell the child: 'The coin is under the cup. . . . Find the coin!' This instruction attunes the child completely and the game continues, but its results turn out to be profoundly different. While the trace of an immediate visual impression caused all children of the younger group to reach with assurance for the cup under which they saw the coin being hidden, the verbal instruction turns out to be wholly insufficient for this directive role: a considerable proportion of the children of this age lose track of the task and begin to grasp *both* objects before them. When we repeated the experiment with a ten-second delay in the execution of the action, this loss of directed activity among the children of the younger group was almost universal.

We then returned to the experiments with the immediate (non-delayed) execution of the action. When we reinforced the required reaction by repeating the instructions several times, 'The coin is under the cup. . . . Find the coin!', the children of the younger group turned out to be capable of executing it in an organized way: the word achieved the required directive function, and the children reached for the object named. However, if we altered the verbal instruction and, without changing the intonation, said 'Now the coin is under the tumbler. . . . Find it!', only an insignificant proportion of the children changed their movements, while the great majority repeated their previous movement. When a ten-second delay was imposed on the execution of the task, all the children of the younger group failed to let their action follow the changed verbal instruction; they continued to execute the stereotyped movement that had been reinforced in the previous experiment and, as before, turned to the cup on the left.

The children of the older group (1; 8 to 2 years), who solved these tasks with uniform success when the directive role was played by a visual signal (in experiments with delayed as well as with immediate execution), turned out to lag behind when they had to execute the task according to verbal instructions. They did carry out both tasks well if they were allowed to make the necessary movement immediately; then they would turn to the cup after the instruction 'The coin is under the cup. . . . Find the coin!' and to the tumbler if the instruction was 'The coin is under the tumbler. . . . Find the coin!' However, it was enough to delay the execution of the instructions by ten seconds for this orienting, directive role of the verbal instruction to be insufficiently effective. After three repetitions of the experiment with the instruction 'The coin is under the cup. . . . Find the coin!' the transition to another command—'The coin is under the tumbler. . . . Find the coin!'—deprived the verbal instruction of its directive role, and the child continued inertly to execute the former habitual movement. In these cases the kinaesthetic stereotype which had been worked out earlier overcame the insufficiently established effect of the word.

A comparative analysis of the orienting or directive functions of visual and verbal signals allows us to see how late the directive role of the word is formed in early childhood.

3: While the directive function of straightforward, 'deictic' speech is already formed around the age of 2, the kind of speech that involves more complicated preliminary connections—connections which precede the action and organize it in advance—acquires a regulative function considerably later, and its development occupies the entire third and partly the fourth year of life.

This time let us turn to a child with a more complicated, involved instruction. 'When the light flashes, you will press the ball (rubber bulb)' or ' . . . you will raise your hand.' Such a verbal instruction, formulated this time in a syntactically complex, 'conditional' sentence, does not require any immediate realization of an action. It must close a preliminary verbal connection, giving to the appearance of a stimulus ('light') a conditional meaning of the signal for action ('you will press the ball'). The directive role is played here not by a separate word, but by a relation, a synthesis of words entering into a sentence; instead of an immediate, 'triggering' role it acquires a preliminary, conditional, 'pretriggering' function.

It has been shown experimentally that the possibility of establishing such a pretriggering system of connections on the basis of speech—not to speak of the possibility of subordinating further conditional reactions to it—is something unattainable for a child of 2 to 2½ years, and sometimes even for a 3-year-old child.

The younger children of this group (1; 10 to 2 years) appear unable to realize that synthesis of separate elements which is required by the instruction formulated in the sentence. Each individual word contained in the sentence evokes in the child an immediate orienting reaction, and as soon as he hears the beginning of the sentence, 'When the light flashes . . .,' the child begins to look for the light with its eyes; when he hears the end of the sentence—'. . . you will press the ball'—he immediately presses the device in his hand. At this stage the separate words have already acquired an effective triggering function, but the creation, by means of words, of a preliminary pretriggering system of connections, which requires the inhibition of immediate reactions and their separation into individual fragments, turns out to be unattainable. This is why the actual presentation of a light signal—the flash of light—does not at this stage lead to a conditioned movement, and evokes only an immediate orienting reaction: the child begins simply to inspect the light, which has not yet become for him a conditional signal for the pressing of the ball.

It would, however, be incorrect to believe that the formation of this more complex form of directive speech—the closing of conditional, pretriggering connections—depends entirely on the ability to relate words which comprise a sentence, i.e. to do the work of synthesizing the elements of a sentence into a single system. Even when a child, some time later, is able to do this synthesizing work and begins to 'understand' the meaning of the whole sentence well, the effective directive role of the sentence can still remain absent for a long time.

Let us adduce the experiments which demonstrate this interesting fact.

We present a child at the end of the third year of his life (2; 8 to 2; 10) with an instruction of this kind, and we see a picture which differs basically from the one that we have just described. A child at this age will as a rule make the required connection without particular difficulty, and when the light flashes he will press the ball; however, he will be unable to stop the movements which have been triggered by speech and he will very soon begin to press the ball regardless of the signal, continuing involuntarily to repeat the previous movements. Even the repetition of the instruction or the reinforcement of the inhibitory link which is hidden in it—even the request to 'Press *only* when the light flashes' and '*Not to press* when there is no light'—all this turns out to be powerless to stop the motor excitation that has begun; on the contrary, this excitation is sometimes even reinforced by the inhibitory instruction, which in the given case turns out still to lack its inhibitory meaning and continues to act non-specifically, only strengthening the dominant motor response.

While speech at this time has already acquired an effective connection closing triggering function, it has thus not yet acquired an effective inhibitory role.

This weakness of the inhibitory function of speech, as was shown by the observations of Tikhomirov in 1958, can be seen most vividly by means of special experiments. Let us complicate the instruction described above and present it to a child of 3 to 3½ years. We will ask it to press the ball every time a red light goes on, and not to press it when a blue light goes on; in other words, we will place the child in circumstances in which speech requires a complex *selective* reaction—positive with respect to one signal (red) and inhibitory with respect to another (blue). We let the child repeat the instruction and we are persuaded that all the information included in the sentence has reached him and is retained. Does this mean that it also possesses an effective directive role?

The experiment shows that this practical correspondence between the semantic meaning of the sentence and its directive role does not appear for a long time. Having understood the meaning of the instruction and repeating it correctly, the child is practically unable to execute it: the excitation provoked by the signal turns out to be so considerable and diffuse that after only a few attempts the blue signal, too, begins to evoke in the child impulsive motor responses. At first he attempts to control them but later, as his excitement grows while the directive function of the inhibitory verbal instruction weakens, he begins to perform the movements without any restraint.

In clashing with the inert excitation evoked by a positive signal, the inhibitory link in the verbal instruction is crushed. At first the child retains the entire instruction, but though he repeats it correctly, he is nevertheless unable to subordinate his actions to it. It is not uncommon for the inert excitation evoked by the positive part of the instruction to become so overwhelming that, under the influence of his own impulsive reaction, the child loses the inhibitory link contained in the verbal signal and begins to assure the experimenter that the instruction required him to press the ball in response to both signals presented to him.

Thus the insufficient mobility of the child's neurodynamics at first destroys the directive role of the verbal instruction, and later distorts the entire system of links contained in it.

4. The question now arises: Can we reinforce the regulating function of verbal connections, and if so, how can this be done most effectively? The solution of this question may bring us closer to the description of certain mechanisms of the directive function of speech.

The experiments carried out by Paramonova in 1956 showed that there are very simple means for heightening the directive influence of speech when the effect of the traces of a verbal instruction turn out to be insufficient.

Let us carry out an experiment of the kind already described with a 3-year-old child. We ask him to press a ball in response to every red signal and to refrain from pressing it in response to every blue one. We introduce only one change into this experiment: we accompany each flash of the red light with the direct command 'Press!' and every flash of the blue lamp with a similar command, 'Don't press!' If such plainly directed speech is introduced, it allows the child quickly to work out a fairly effective system of selective reactions. What could not be attained through preliminary connections evoked by a verbal instruction turns out to be easily attainable if we draw upon the immediate influence of verbal commands. In direct speech, the directive function has been fairly effectively established; its influence is therefore capable of concentrating the course of nervous processes and of producing a differentiated habit.

In the experiments just described we drew upon the directive function of verbal commands in order to make more precise the influence of verbal instructions and to secure the organized course of the child's motor responses. Could we not, however, for this purpose draw upon the *child's own speech* and have it support the traces of the verbal instruction, which weaken relatively fast? After all, as Vygotsky has already shown, the function which at first is distributed between two people can easily turn into an internal psychological system, and what a child today does with help, he will tomorrow be able to do on his own. The investigation of the *directive possibilities of the child's own speech* can uncover a new and essential side of his linguistic development.

We repeat the experiment described, but introduce some substantial changes. In order to make it easier for the child to carry out his task correctly, we ask him *to give himself supplementary verbal commands*, accompanying each appearance of a red signal with the word 'Press!', and the appearance of each blue signal with the words 'Don't press!' Will this utilization of the child's own commands reinforce the action of the verbal instruction and strengthen its directive role?

The experiment shows that it is not so simple to obtain a directive influence from the child's own speech, and that over the first years of life the directive role of the child's own speech undergoes a complex course of development.

Let us begin with children of 2 to $2\frac{1}{2}$ years and simplify our experiment for this purpose. We ask the child to respond to each flash of the red light by pressing the ball; but in order to remove those excessive movements which, as we have indicated above, are not subject to the control of an inhibitory instruction, we ask the child to accompany each motor reaction with the word 'Press!' (or even with something easier to pronounce, such as 'Now!', to which we assign the meaning of a self-command). The experiments of S. V. Jakovleva in 1958 have shown that the active speech of a child at this age is so insufficiently developed, and the underlying neurodynamics so inert, that the child of 2 to 2½ years of age still finds difficulty in coordinating his verbal commands with the signal and frequently begins to utter excessive, stereotyped commands. It is significant that even if the child succeeds and begins to say 'Press!' (or 'Now!') only when the signal appears, his entire energy is diverted to the utterance of this word, and the motor reaction which is supposed to be associated with it becomes extinct. The child at this age cannot yet create a *system* of neural processes that includes both verbal and motor links, and the word does not play any directive role.

As O. K. Tikhomirov's experiments in 1958 showed, it is only at 3 years of age that the neurodynamics which underlie the speech processes are sufficiently mobile for the child to time his own verbal command with the signal and for the command to exert a directive influence on the motor response as it becomes a mobile link in a unified system with it. While the child is unable to control his excessive, diffuse pressings of the ball according to the preliminary instruction, he easily achieves this control when he begins to give himself the commands 'Press!' and 'Don't press!'. In concentrating the diffuse excitation, the child's own verbal responses, functioning on a feedback principle, here acquire their directive function.

However, is this directive function of the child's own speech fully-fledged? Control experiments have answered this question in the negative and have permitted us to see more deeply into the mechanisms of the early forms of the directive function of speech.

Let us return again to the more complicated experiment described above. We present a child of 3 to 3½ years with the instruction to press a ball every time a red light flashes and to refrain from pressing it when there is a blue flash, but we give him the possibility of accompanying each red signal with his affirmative command 'Press!' and every blue signal with his own inhibitory command, 'Don't press!' Does the directive role of the child's *inhibitory* verbal response have the same, full value as his *positive* verbal response?

The experiments which have been conducted for this purpose have disclosed some very substantial peculiarities of the regulating effect of the child's own speech. The verbal responses 'Press' and 'Don't press' turn out to have a complex structure. Physiologically they are, first of all, motor responses of the speech apparatus and are thus always connected with the positive phase of an innervation. But in virtue of their *meanings* they are systems of connections which, in the former case, have a positive, and in the latter case, an inhibitory signal value. Which side of the child's own speech—the motor ('impulsive') or semantic ('selective') side—here influences the motor processes and acquires the directive role?

The experiments of O. K. Tikhomirov yield an answer to this question. A child of 3 to 3½ years easily responds to each light signal with the required word, but in uttering the command 'Don't press' in response to the blue signal, he not only fails to restrain his motor responses, but *presses the ball even harder.* Consequently, the child's own verbal reaction 'Don't press' exerts its influence not in its semantic aspect, i.e. not by the selective connections which are behind it, but by its immediate 'impulsive' impact. This is why the directive influence of a child's own speech at this stage still has a non-selective, non-specific character.

At least one more year must pass before the directive role goes over to the selective system of semantic connections which are behind the word, and—as Tikhomirov has observed—it is only at the age of 4 to 4½ years that the verbal response 'Don't press' actually acquires the inhibitory effect specific to speech.

However, for this stage of development one circumstance is typical: as soon as the directive role passes to the semantic aspect of speech and that aspect becomes dominant, external speech becomes superfluous. The directive role is taken over by those inner connections which lie behind the word, and they now begin to display their selective effect in directing the further motor responses of the child.

The development of the pragmatic, directive aspect of speech constitutes a new chapter in psychology and psycholinguistics. It still has almost no facts to operate with that are derived from systematic investigation. However, by establishing the fact that by no means all the information carried by speech *ipso facto* acquires a directive value in determining human behaviour, and by investigating the formation patterns of this directive role of speech, this chapter has already opened important new vistas for the scientific investigation of the organization of human behaviour.

13 JOHN B. CARROLL and JOSEPH B. CASAGRANDE
Language Structuring
Experience

This is one of the few experiments on the Whorf hypothesis with young children. The authors investigated how children of different cultures performed a categorization of objects test. They started with the hypothesis that because a person's 'world-view' is to some extent moulded by the particular language he speaks, certain categorization tests with children from different cultures will reveal differences in categorization procedures. In Navaho the forms of verbs of handling must be selected in accordance with the shape of the object of the verb. In view of the requirement it seemed reasonable to the authors that Navaho children would be able to discriminate between forms and shapes of objects before English speaking children of the same age who do not have to make this obligatory distinction.

The results are not entirely conclusive and Carroll (1958) suggests that although language can have an effect in influencing the strengths of various stimuli it cannot radically alter actual perceptual discrimination. Carroll describes the effect of language on experience as a lattice rather than a mould; he says:

> This lattice, as it were, may obscure little bits of our experience, but it lets through the rest in larger or smaller hunks, perhaps, clarifying some parts, clouding other parts, and suggesting a larger pattern for still another. All the while, however, we see the pattern of the whole and are as little bothered by the lattice as if it were a screen installed on our front porch (Carroll 1958, p. 33).

Carroll, J. B. 'Some psychological effects of language structure'. In P. Jock & J. Zubin (eds.) *Psychopathology of Communication*, New York: Grune & Stratton, 1958.

More than fifty years ago George Santayana wrote in his essay *The Sense of Beauty*: 'Grammar, philosophically studied, is akin

John B. Carroll and Joseph B. Casagrande: Extract from 'The function of language classifications in behavior'. In E. E. Maccoby, T. M. Newcomb, E. L. Hartley (eds.) *Readings in Social Psychology*, 3rd edition, Holt, Rinehart, Winston, 1958, pp. 18–31.

to the deepest metaphysics, because in revealing the constitution of speech, it reveals the constitution of thought and the hierarchy of those categories by which we conceive the world' (p. 169). The world of experience is characterized by a logic that deals with continua; our experiences present themselves to us in almost limitless variations and shadings; and there are no boundaries between the parts of experience except those which are created by our perceptions.

If a language is to be used for efficient person-to-person communication about the world of experience, it must operate with a logic that deals with discrete entities—a logic of criteriality which distinguishes experiences on certain arbitrary and agreed-upon terms. When we give proper names to individual persons, pet animals, and geographical locations, we are responding to an extreme need for discreteness and specific differentiation, but most of the time we are well satisfied to convey our experiences by means of a relatively small number (a few thousand, say) of general categories into which we learn to fit them. As a first approximation we may regard each word of a language like English as the name of a category of experience: *horse, petunia, he, ecstasy, reprimand, green, very,* and *nevertheless* are all categories of experience. Not all categories of experience are symbolized by discrete words; some are represented by grammatical phenomena such as are indicated in the following contrasts: *horse* v. *horse's; petunia* v. *petunias; he* v. *him; ecstasy* v. *ecstatic; reprimand* v. *reprimanded; green* v. *greener; the very old man* v. *the very idea;* and the classic *dog bites man* v. *man bites dog.*

If we agree that the categories of a language are 'arbitrary' in the sense that they could be replaced by other, equally acceptable ways of categorizing experience, we could begin to inquire to what extent the several thousand languages of the world have similar categories. How many languages have a distinct, generic term for *horse?* How many languages have only a term for what we would call *quadruped,* applying it alike to horses, dogs, wolves, giraffes and adding appropriate qualifying terms? Are there languages which have no generic term for *horse* but only terms for particular breeds and conditions of horses? (We are told that Arabic is such a language.) Or let us take a grammatical problem: do all languages distinguish singular and plural? (No, Chinese does not.) Are there languages which have more levels of grammatical number than our two? (Yes; some languages have four 'numbers', singular, dual, trial, and plural.) Investigations along these lines are not to be undertaken lightly, for they require an immense sophistication in the techniques of linguistic science. We can nevertheless predict the major outlines of the results. There would be many semantic areas of remarkable (though rarely complete) uniformity among languages, while other areas would tend to show considerable diversity. The linguist Morris Swadesh has surveyed a wide variety of languages in an effort to arrive at a list of concepts for which one would be fairly sure to find a distinct word or word-like form in every language. His final list of 100 such concepts includes things like: personal pronouns: *I, thou, we, he, ye, they;* position and movement: *come, sit, give, fly, stand, hold, fall, swim;* natural objects and phenomena: *ice, salt, star, sun, wind;* descriptives: *old, dry, good, new, warm, rotten, cold;* miscellaneous: *name, other, not, burn, blow, freeze, swell, road, kill.* But even in observing this apparent uniformity, we must not be misled into thinking that there are exact semantic correspondences between languages. English *horse,* French *cheval,* and German *Pferd* may have different ranges of application and different semantic overtones; the measurement of such differences is a problem beyond the scope of this paper.[1] Further, we can find rather obvious lacks of correspondence when we look at the different ranges of meaning covered by the English *proceed* v. French *procéder* ('to proceed' but also 'to behave or conduct oneself'), or English *experience* v. French *expérience* ('experience' but also 'experiment'). It would appear that the categories of one language are sometimes 'untranslatable' into another language; even if we ignore such problems as finding the difference between the English and the Russian concepts of democracy, there remain such cases as German *Gemütlichkeit* and French *acharnement* which are presumably incapable of exact rendering in English. Even such a simple concept as that represented by the word *too* is extremely clumsy to express in Amharic, the official language of Ethiopia. In the realm of grammar, Edward Sapir's classic work *Language* will suggest the extent to which

---

[1] The 'semantic differential' technique devised by Osgood may be particularly useful here. See C. E. Osgood, G. J. Suci, and P. H. Tannenbaum, *The Measurement of Meaning* (Urbana: University of Illinois Press, 1957).

languages differ among themselves in grammatical concepts. Although Sapir felt that 'no language wholly fails to distinguish noun and verb', his writings suggest that there are few basic concepts which universally find expression in the grammatical structures of languages. This is not to say that there are grammatical concepts which cannot be expressed in all languages; in general, any grammatical concept found in one language can be expressed somehow in every language, even if the expression is a little awkward or periphrastic. Languages do differ remarkably, however, in the grammatical concepts which are mandatory: for example, the use of the singular-plural distinction is said to be mandatory in English but completely optional in Chinese. If someone says 'I'm going out to hunt bear', he is dispensing with the singular-plural distinction and talking in the pattern of Chinese—which happens to be convenient because he does not know whether he will bag one bear or more than one.

The real question for the social psychologist is this: Is the behaviour of a person (aside from his language behaviour) a function of the language he happens to speak? Granted that languages differ in the ways we have described, what effects will these differences have on the way a person thinks, the way he deals with other people, or the way he deals with his environment?

The notion that language makes an important difference in behaviour has a long history, beginning with the writings of the German philologist W. von Humboldt more than a century ago. In more recent times, the linguist Benjamin Lee Whorf has been the chief exponent of what he termed 'linguistic relativity':

> . . . the background linguistic system (in other words, the grammar) of each language is not merely a reproducing instrument for voicing ideas but rather is itself the shaper of ideas, the programme and guide for the individual's mental activity, for his analysis of impressions, for his synthesis of his mental stock in trade. Formulation of ideas is not an independent process, strictly rational in the old sense, but is part of a particular grammar and differs, from slightly to greatly, between different grammars.[1]

[1] J. B. Carroll (ed.) *Language, Thought and Reality*, New York: Wiley, 1956·
212f.

The linguistic relativity hypothesis is a special case of the culture-personality theory. Substituting terms in Smith, Bruner, and White's précis of culture-personality theory, we may express it this way: Each language creates a special plight to which the individual must adjust. The human plight is in no sense universal save in this fact: that however different the language may be, it has certain common problems with which to deal—time, space, quantity, action, state, etc. But each language handles these problems differently and develops special ways of communicating. These ways of communicating create special needs, special responses, and lead to the development of special modes of thinking.

The alternative to the linguistic relativity hypothesis would be a statement that the behaviour of a person is not a function of the language he happens to speak or be speaking, that his modes of categorizing experience and dealing with his world operate independently of language, that language is simply a way of communicating something which is in every way prior to its codification in language.

This paper reports two experiments designed to explore, in a preliminary way, to what extent and under what conditions the linguistic relativity hypothesis can be accepted.

In order to find evidence to support the linguistic relativity hypothesis it is not sufficient merely to point to differences between languages and assume that users of those languages have correspondingly different mental experiences; if we are not to be guilty of circular inference, it is necessary to show some correspondence between the presence or absence of a certain linguistic phenomenon and the presence or absence of a certain kind of 'non-linguistic' response. This being the case, we must be clear as to what we mean by a non-linguistic response. Unfortunately, it is extremely difficult to define this rigorously. We might be tempted to do so by saying that a non-linguistic response is one which can be elicited without the intervention of any symbolic system, but as soon as we realize that the bells, buzzers, lights, levers, and food pellets through which we elicit the behaviour of dogs and rats may be regarded as symbolic systems, this definition would serve to exclude large classes of responses which we would still like to call 'non-linguistic'. When we come to examine the actual behaviours used in our experiments, we will find that their 'non-linguistic' character resides in the fact that they are neutral, as it were, with respect to the special symbolic systems against which they are being tested. For example, in the second experiment to be presented, a child is asked to tell whether a blue rope 'goes best with' a blue stick or a yellow rope. Now, by appropriate reinforcement techniques, we could teach the child always to choose on the basis of form or always to choose on the basis of colour, and we could do this without using English or Navaho or any other special symbolic systems. Suppose, again, we were studying differences in the arithmetical abilities of children who had learned the decimal system and of children who had learned only the system of Roman numerals. The arithmetical behaviour being studied is analogous to our 'non-linguistic' behaviour because it is neutral to any one special system of arithmetical symbolism in the sense that it is possible to operate in either system, though not necessarily with the same efficiency.

As Brown and Lenneberg have suggested,[1] two approaches present themselves for the testing of the linguistic relativity hypothesis. Brown and Lenneberg used the first of these—an 'intralinguistic' approach which, capitalizing on the fact that the speakers of a given language manifest differences in their knowledge and use of that language, attempts to show that these differences are correlated with certain other behaviours. In both experiments reported here, we have used the second approach—an 'interlinguistic' design in which nonlinguistic behaviours of speakers of two different languages are compared. Use of this second approach entails an advantage and a danger: it may become possible to select linguistic features in two languages which are strikingly and fundamentally different, but it becomes difficult to assure oneself that any observed behavioural correlates are *not* due to irrelevant factors such as dissimilar cultural backgrounds and experiences.

Experiment I

In the Hopi language, still spoken in the pueblos of northeastern Arizona, the semantic domains of verbs for various kinds of

[1] R. W. Brown and E. H Lenneberg, 'A Study in Language and Cognition' *J. Abnorm. & Soc. Psychol.*, 1954, XLIX, 454–62.

physical activities have structures quite different from the corresponding domains in English. In speaking of *breaking*, the Hopi must use verbs depending upon whether there is one fission or many fissions (a distinction not unlike that between 'break' and 'shatter'). He uses the same verb for *spilling* and for *pouring*, but must use a different verb depending upon whether the material being spilled or poured is liquid or non-liquid. He can use the same verb in speaking of denting an object like a fender and in speaking of pressing a doorbell. The question posed in this experiment was whether these linguistic features would show corresponding features of nonlinguistic behaviour in speakers of Hopi when contrasted with speakers of English. The 'non-linguistic' behaviour chosen for study was that of sorting or classifying pictures of the actions represented by verbs of breaking, spilling, pressing, and similar physical activities.

Method

Line drawings were prepared, representing various physical actions such as falling, breaking, dropping, etc. These drawings were then assembled in sets of three, or triads, in such a way that, on the basis of comparative linguistic analysis, it could be hypothesized that in each triad native speakers of Hopi would tend to put a different pair of pictures together as contrasted with native speakers of English.

The test was administered individually to 14 Hopi adults (age range 24 to over 66) who were known to be fluent speakers of Hopi. All could speak English with varying degrees of competence, but regarded themselves as more fluent in Hopi. The test was also administered to 28 'Anglos' (as they are called in the Southwest) consisting of 12 adults of comparable degree of education in a rural New England community and 16 graduate students at Harvard University.

The test was introduced as an experiment in 'how we think' and started with six pre-test items, of which the first is shown as Figure 1. The three pictures were presented as physically separated photographs which could be shuffled and arranged at the will of the subject, who was asked simply to decide which two of the three pictures went together. The subjects had no difficulty in

FIGURE 1   FIGURE 2

FIGURE 3   FIGURE 4

Sample Items from Experiment I

seeing that the two pictures of falling objects went together. The remaining five pre-test items were designed to reveal whether the subjects understood the task and to make it clear that they were to respond on the basis of the action or type of action represented rather than incidental features of any objects depicted. The test proper consisted of 17 'critical' items and five 'control' items about which no linguistic hypothesis was formulated. (We shall omit further discussion of the control items because they showed no interesting differences between Hopis and Anglos.)

The subjects were also asked to tell why their choices went together. No suggestion was given that the experiment had anything to do with language, and most of the Hopis responded in English. Occasionally, however, subjects volunteered that it seemed to 'work better' to 'think in Hopi', and gave their verbalizations in Hopi. The results, therefore, consist not only of the choices made by the subjects but also (except for three or four cases) the stated reasons for the choices.

Results

The nature of the results and some of the problems in their interpretation may be first illustrated by presenting data for one of the 'critical' items in detail. The pictures for Item 20 are presented in Figure 2.

The linguistic basis for this item resides in the fact that in Hopi there is a verb *'u'ta* which means 'to close an opening', and this is the verb normally used for placing covers on open boxes, closing lids, closing holes in tubes or walls, etc.; in contrast, placing a cover on something for protection against dust or damage is represented by the verbs *na:kwapna* or *nönöma*. In English, however, we tend to use *cover* regardless of whether we are covering an opening or not, and we tend to reserve *close* for the situation where an opening can be more or less exactly fitted with a lid or other special stoppage (also for special cases like *closing a book*). On this basis it was hypothesized that Hopis would tend to put together pictures *A* and *C*, while Anglos would tend to put together pictures *B* and *C*.

In presenting this item to Anglo subjects, it was necessary to explain (without mentioning or suggesting the verbs 'cover' or 'close') that in picture *C* a woman was placing a wicker plaque over a box of food (the traditional Hopi *piki* corn bread).

Table 1 shows the number of subjects in various classifications making each of three possible groupings, together with a classification of the reasons for these choices.

The small numbers of cases make statistical significance testing difficult if not impossible, but even if we are to make a statistical test, it must be recognized that a given response may mean different

TABLE 1
Choices and reasons for choices for the item of Figure 2

Group	'Hopi' response A & C combined		'English' response: B & C combined		Neutral: A & B combined	
14 Hopi adults	3	Both *'u'ta*	2	Both	1	Both will
	1	Neither is		covering		be tightly
		na:kwapna	2	(Not given)		covered
	1	Both are	–		1	Both being
		boxes	(N=4)			covered
	1	Both hold-			–	
		ing the lid			(N=2)	
	2	(Not given)				
	–					
	(N=8)					
12 Rural Anglos	4	Both are	4	Both	1	Both cover-
		boxes		covering,		ing
	2	Both		*v.* closing	1	Both more
		covering		or shut-		familiar
		with lids		ting	–	
	–		–		(N=2)	
	(N=6)		(N=4)			
16 Grad. students	1	Putting on	8	Both	1	Both (cus-
		a *flat*		covering,		tomarily)
		cover		*v.* closing		'used and
	3	(Not		or shut-		covered'
		given)		ting		*v.* one-
	–		1	Both put-		time
	(N=4)			ting on		covering
				top	–	
			1	Both 'deal-	(N=1)	
				ing with		
				entire		
				structure'		
			1	(Not		
				given)		
			–			
			(N=11)			

things. Thus, at least three Hopis put pictures *A* and *C* together on the ground that both show *'u'ta* 'closing an opening', but to at least four Anglos pictures *A* and *C* go together because they show boxes. The most striking result here is the fact that Hopis tend *not* to put pictures *B* and *C* together, while Anglos, particularly educated ones, show a strong tendency to do so. Only four out of 14 Hopis put pictures *B* and *C* together, while 11 out of 16 college-educated Anglos did so. We can look at the reasons for the choices more closely. Only four out of the 14 Hopis mentioned any kind of 'covering' in giving their reasons (whatever their choice), while 17 out of 28 Anglos did—a result significant below the 10-per cent level.

Although limited, these results suggest that speakers of Hopi tend to organize their perceptions of situations such as those pictured in Figure 1 in terms of 'closing openings' instead of 'putting covers on things'.

There were several other critical items showing results tending to favour our hypothesis. For the pictures of Figure 3, it was expected that Hopis would tend to pair *A* and *C* because both represent the action called *leluwi*, 'to apply or spread over a surface', while Anglos would pair *B* and *C* because they both show 'painting'. (Hopi has a word for painting, but its use is restricted to cases where one paints a picture or a design, as distinct from covering a surface with paint.) Six of the 14 Hopis paired *A* and *C*, while only four of all 28 Anglos did so; of these four, two paired on the basis of the fact that both showed the use of a tool versus the use of one's hands; the significance of this result is at just below the 5-per-cent level by Fisher's test. Actually, a more striking result was unanticipated: Anglos had a strong tendency to pair either *B* and *C* or *A* and *B* because they felt both members of these pairs represented 'decorating' versus mere painting or covering. 'Artistic creation' was also mentioned as a basis for these choices.

Another item showing interesting results is shown in Figure 4. As has been mentioned 'spilling' (accidentally) and 'pouring' (intentionally) are not distinguished in Hopi; there is a way of translating the idea of 'accidentally' but this is handled as a separate expression instead of being built into the verb, as in English. Hopi uses slightly different forms for pouring: *wehekna*, 'to pour liquid', and *wa:hokna*, 'to pour sand, gravel, or other non-liquid loose things', but the form for dropping something is entirely different: *po:sna*. We found that eight out of 14 Hopis (57 per cent) paired pictures *A* and *C*, consonant with the linguistic forms; these figures contrast with the finding that only seven out of 28 Anglos, or 25 per cent, made this pairing. The probability of chance occurrence of a result as extreme as this, determined by the χ^2 test with continuity-correction, is less than 10 per cent. At least 16 of the 20 Anglos who paired pictures *B* and *C* explained that there was unintentional, accidental action in both of them, while only two Hopis drew attention to this accidental character of the action. Instead, Hopis rarely seemed concerned about whether the man in picture *A meant* to pour out the peaches, while Anglos frequently queried the experimenter about this.

Admitting the results from all 17 'critical' items as evidence, we present in Table 2 a summary to show the extent to which our hypotheses were favoured by the data. There is probably not a truly significant difference between the 29 per cent representing the tendency of the Hopi subjects to make the expected 'Hopi' response of pairing pictures *A* and *C* and the 22·6 per cent and 24·0 per cent, values for the two Anglo groups, but the trend is at least one of those tantalizingly modest ones which can be characterized only as being 'in the predicted direction'.

Upon re-examination of the purely linguistic data and consideration of certain unanticipated difficulties which had arisen in the subjects' interpretations of the drawings, it was possible to weed out five items which had gone sour, so to speak, leaving 12 critical items for which the results are presented in the lower part of Table 2. Here we see a sturdier trend in favour of our general hypothesis, although the results are still far from striking. It is not really legitimate to treat Table 2 as a contingency table and apply a χ^2 test, because the events represented there are not necessarily independent; were we to assume that all the choices are independent, however, and were we then to apply a χ^2 test to the lower part of Table 2, we would find that the probability of this χ^2 being exceeded by chance would be less than 0·01.

The results encourage us to think that not only do we have a promising technique for studying the linguistic relativity hypothesis, but we also have an indication that in further and more extensive trials of this method we may obtain greater assurances that language categories influence at least one variety of nonlinguistic behaviour. Several suggestions towards improvement

TABLE 2
Total frequency of pairing

		'Hopi' response: A & C	'Anglo' response: B & C	Neutral: A & B	Total
17 'critical items'	14 Hopi	69 (29·0%)	126 (52·9%)	43 (18·1%)	238
	12 Rural Anglos	46 (22·6)	119 (58·3)	39 (19·1)	204
	16 Educated Anglos	65 (24·0)	156 (57·5)	50 (18·5)	271
12 'critical items' with 'good hypotheses'	14 Hopi	57 (34·0)	80 (47·6)	31 (18·4)	168
	12 Rural Anglos	31 (21·5)	85 (59·0)	28 (19·5)	144
	16 Educated Anglos	36 (18·8)	122 (63·9)	33 (17·3)	191

of the experimental methodology may be offered: (1) drawings should be given extensive pre-tests to insure that they are interpreted similarly by all subjects; (2) the experiment should utilize contrasting groups of monolinguals (rather than bilinguals as we had to use here); and (3) subjects should be asked to choose which of two pictures, *A* or *B*, go best with a fixed third picture, *C*. (This procedure is used in Experiment II.)

Experiment II

This second experiment was an attempt to show that behaviour can be influenced by a grammatical phenomenon as well as a purely lexical or semantic phenomenon.

It is obligatory in the Navaho language, when using verbs of *handling*, to employ a particular one of a set of verbal forms according to the shape or some other essential attribute of the object about which one is speaking. Thus, if I ask you in Navaho to hand me an object, I must use the appropriate verb stem depending on the nature of the object. If it is a long flexible object such as a piece of string, I must say *šańléh*: if it is a long rigid object such as a stick, I must say *šańtįįh*: if it is a flat flexible material such as a paper or cloth, I must say *šańitcóós*, and so on.

The groups of words in Navaho which together regularly take one or another of these verb stems, say the family of words for all long, rigid objects, carry no linguistic marker of their class membership. They comprise what Whorf[1] has called a 'covert class', as distinguished from an 'overt class' such as gender in Latin with the familiar *–us, –i, –a, –ae* case and number suffixes. Nor, in the absence of native grammarians, are there any terms in Navaho for these categories themselves. This like many another grammatical rule operates well below the level of conscious awareness. Although most Navaho-speaking children, even at the age of three or four, used these forms unerringly, they were unable to tell why they used a particular form with any particular object. Even though a child could not name an object, or may not have seen one like it before, in most cases he used the correct verb form according to the nature of the object.

Because of this obligatory categorization of objects in Navaho, it seemed reasonable that Navaho-speaking children would learn to discriminate the 'form' attributes of objects at an earlier age than their English-speaking compeers. The finding of American[2] and European[3] psychologists that children tend first to distinguish objects on the basis of size and colour might—at least at the level of verbal facility in dealing with these variables—be partly an artifact of the particular language they use. The hypothesis was, then, that this feature of the Navaho language would affect the relative potency, or order of emergence of such concepts as colour, size, shape or form, and number in the Navaho-speaking child, as compared with English-speaking Navaho children of the same age, and that Navaho-speaking children would be more

[1] Carroll, op. cit., pp. 87–101.

[2] C. R. Brian and F. L. Goodenough, 'The relative potency of color and form perception at various ages' *J. Exper. Psychol.*, 1929, XII, 197–213.

[3] A. Descœudres, 'Couleur, forme, ou nombre' *Arch. de Psychol.*, 1914, XIV, 305–41.

inclined than the latter to perceive formal similarities between objects.

This hypothesis was tested using a variety of experimental materials and several different procedures, of which only one will be reported here. Although the test was expressly adapted to Navaho, the design as well as the basic hypothesis could be extended to other languages since nearly all languages have obligatory categories.

The procedure whose results we will report here was called 'Ambiguous Sets' and was actually interposed between several other procedures well after the child had become accustomed to the experimental situation.

Method

Ten pairs of objects (coloured wooden blocks, sticks, and pieces of rope) were used, each of which differed significantly in two respects, e.g., colour and size, colour and shape, size and shape, or shape and Navaho verb-form classification. These pairs of objects were arranged before the child, one pair at a time. After being presented with a pair of objects, the child was shown a third object similar to each member of the pair in only one of the two relevant characteristics, but of course matching neither, and was asked to tell the experimenter which of the pair went best with the object shown to him. For example, one of the pairs consisted of a yellow stick and a piece of blue rope of comparable size. The child was then shown a yellow rope, and the basis of his choice could be either colour or the Navaho verb-form classification— since different verbal forms are used for a length of rope and a stick. The ten sets of objects were presented in the alphabetical order of the letters shown in Table 3, with the exception that the first set presented was set *O*, and the last was set *P*.

The subjects were 135 Navaho children ranging from three to about ten years of age, drawn from the vicinity of Fort Defiance and Window Rock, Arizona, on the Navaho reservation. On the basis of a bilingualism test and other criteria of language dominance, the 135 subjects were divided into five groups; monolingual in Navaho, Navaho-predominant, balanced bilingual, English-predominant, and English monolingual. For purposes of statistical analysis Navaho monolinguals and Navaho-predominant were grouped together (59 subjects), as were the English monolinguals and English-predominants (43). The remaining 33 subjects were classed as 'balanced bilinguals' and this group included a number of individuals whose language status was dubious.

The experiment was conducted in Navaho or, with appropriate modifications in the instructions, in English, as indicated. An interpreter was used with Navaho-speaking children, although the experimenter was able to give instructions in Navaho for some of the procedures used. Most of the testing was done in the children's homes—usually Navaho hogans of the traditional sort—and in the presence of parents, grandparents, siblings, and other interested and very curious onlookers.

Although the establishment of contrasting groups of Navaho children on the basis of language dominance was regarded as providing adequate control, a supplementary control group was obtained by testing 47 white American middle-class children in the Boston metropolitan area, with an age range roughly comparable to that of the Navaho children.

Results

The children were not at all baffled by the ambiguity inherent in the task; their choices were invariably made with little or no hesitation.

The data were analysed both item by item and by age. In considering the results, shown in Table 3, it must be remembered that it was our hypothesis that Navaho-dominant children would be more likely to make their choices on the basis of similarity in shape and verb-stem classification than on the basis of size or colour. Thus, for the first seven sets listed in Table 3, we would expect the Navaho-dominant children to choose the object listed under (a), the 'Navaho choice'. This prediction is borne out by the data, for the differences between the two groups of Navaho children are all in the expected direction, and five are significant (by a two-tailed χ^2 test) at better than the 5-per-cent level. The most striking differences come for those sets of objects that involve a contrast embodied in the Navaho system of verbal categories: sets O and P where the contrast is between colour and material and verb stem, and sets *H* and *N* where the contrast is between colour and verb stem, material being the same, comparing objects of the long-rigid class, and of the so-called 'round object' class. The less striking differences involve contrasts which are not formally recognized in Navaho grammar since the same verb stem is used in talking about the cubes and pyramids of set *K*.

In sets *G*, *J*, and *M* our hypothesis would not lead us to predict any difference between the groups; they may be regarded as control items. Both groups of children show a marked preference for colour rather than size in sets *G* and *J*. Set *M* shows a significant difference between the two Navaho groups, possibly explicable on the basis of the greater potency of colour for the English-dominant children, the contrast of the blue and yellow of set *G* and the blue and white of set *J* being more marked than that between the black and dark blue of set *M*.

Table 4 shows that there are important and consistent developmental trends for the seven critical sets involving the contrast between shape or verb form and colour—a trend which gives added significance to the differences between the Navaho-dominant and English-dominant groups noted above, since the Navaho-dominant children averaged almost a year younger. In both the Navaho groups (the data for white Americans will be discussed below) the trend is towards the increasing perceptual saliency of shape or form, as compared with colour, with increasing age. The curve starts lower and remains lower for English-dominant Navaho children, although it rises rather rapidly after the age of seven. Navaho children stay ahead of their English-speaking age mates, although the two curves tend to converge as age increases.

Thus far discussion has been restricted to the results for two contrasting groups of Navaho children. These groups had been established in the hope that maximum possible control would be gained over the variables of race, culture, and environment which might affect the results. All the children tested were from the same rather small area on the Navaho reservation; the parents of nearly every child were both Navaho, except for the few cases in which one of the parents was a member of some other American Indian tribe. To be sure, the cultural variable could be only imperfectly controlled—the English-dominant children were almost

TABLE 3
Results of the 'Ambiguous Sets' experiment

Set	Attributes contrasted	Objects in set			Percent of 'a' choices			
		Comparison model	Alternative choices (a)	(b)	Navaho-dominant Navahos (N=59)	English-dominant Navahos (N=43)	P*	White American children (N=47)
O	Verb-stem, colour	blue rope	yellow rope	blue stick	70·7	39·5	<0·01	83·0
P	,,	yellow rope	blue rope	yellow stick	70·7	39·5	<0·01	80·7
H	,,	blue stick	yellow stick	blue cylinder	71·2	44·2	<0·01	76·6
N	,,	blue stick	yellow stick	blue oblong block	72·4	44·2	<0·01	82·9

I	shape, size	small blue cube	medium blue cube	small blue sphere	79·7	60·5	<0·05	72·4
L		small blue cylinder	large blue cylinder	small blue oblong	59·4	44·2	>0·10	82·9
K	shape, colour	medium blue cube	medium white cube	medium blue pyramid	45·7	39·5	>0·10	70·2
G	size, colour	medium blue cube	medium yellow cube	small blue cube	21·0	23·2	>0·10	74·4
J	,, ,,	medium blue cube	medium white cube	large blue cube	15·2	14·0	>0·10	55·3
M	,, ,,	medium blue cube	medium black cube	small blue cube	59·3	30·2	<0·01	74·4

*This is the probability that χ^2 as obtained in a 2 × 2 table comparing the two groups of Navahos would be equalled or exceeded under the hypothesis of no difference.

inevitably more acculturated to the local variant of white American culture than were the Navaho-dominant children, but certainly the culture contrast is not as great as between Navaho-speaking children and English-speaking white children, say, from the Eastern United States. However, we may well ask how the performance of these Navaho children compares with that of children speaking

TABLE 4

Percentage of 'a' choices in the first seven sets, by age level

Age	Navaho-dominant Navahos		English-dominant Navahos		White American children	
	N*	per cent	N*	per cent	N*	per cent
3 } 4 }	14	64	7	33	{ 8 { 10	45 69
5	13	57	9	38	10	91
6	12	64	5	34	8	93
7	9	71	9	36	4	100
8	6	74	5	49	5	83
9–10	5	81	8	75	2	93

* Note that this N is the number of cases yielding data; each case contributes seven responses, and the percentages are computed on the basis of the total number of responses.

English or another language on the same or a comparable test. In an experiment closely similar in materials and procedures to the one reported here, Clara Brian and Florence Goodenough,[1] found a marked preference for colour over form for American children aged three to six. At age three years six months, 33·6 per cent of choices were for form over colour; at age four, 24·7 per cent for form over colour; and at age four years six months, 36 per cent (as compared with 64 per cent for Navaho-dominant children in this age group and 33 per cent for English-dominant children of the same age group). The Brian and Goodenough results are also in substantial agreement with those of Alice Descœudres working with French-speaking children more than 40 years ago.

When we compare our Navaho results with those obtained for

[1] Brian and Goodenough, op. cit.

47 white American children in the Boston area, we find that the responses of the white American children are more similar to those for the Navaho-dominant children than for the English-dominant children; as we may see from the last column of Table 3, they consistently tend to choose object 'a' on the basis of form or shape in preference to colour and size. The white children today, however, can hardly be considered a fair control group for the Indian children, for their cultural background of experiences with forms and colours is enormously different. Early and continued practice with toys of the form-board variety is likely to impress the white American child with the importance of form and size as contrasted with a 'secondary' quality like colour. Further, social class is known to be correlated with tendency to choose form over colour,[1] and our white American children tended to be from the upper middle class. Nevertheless, it is interesting to observe in Table 4 that the white American children show the same developmental trend as either group of Navaho children. As a matter of fact, at the earliest age level, the three- and four-year-old Navaho-dominant children outstrip their white American age mates in preferring form to colour.

If we consider only the two groups over which we have exercised the maximum control over the variables we presume to be relevant, the Navaho-dominant and English-dominant Navaho children, we have shown that language patterning seems to be correlated with a tendency to match objects on the basis of form rather than colour or size. When we also consider the data from white American children, as well as the age trends, we may amend our hypothesis in possibly the following form: The tendency of a child to match objects on the basis of form or material rather than size or colour increases with age and may be enhanced by either of two kinds of experiences; (a) learning to speak a language, like Navaho, which because of the central role played by form and material in its grammatical structure, requires the learner to make certain discriminations of form and material in the earlier stages of language learning in order to make himself understood at all; or (b) practice with toys and other objects involving the fitting of forms and shapes, and the resultant greater reinforcement received

[1] S. Honkavaara, 'A Critical Re-evaluation of the Color or Form Reaction and Disproving of the Hypotheses Connected with It' *J. Psychol.*, 1958, XLV, 25–36

from form-matching. If our results are accepted as supporting this revised hypothesis, they indicate, we believe, that the potential influence of linguistic patterning on cognitive functioning and on the conceptual development of the child, as he is inducted by his language into the world of experience, is a fruitful area for further study.

H. G. FURTH
Thinking without Language

We have already looked at the plight of 'wolf-children' brought up
without language in a severely deprived environment, we now turn to
look at deaf children and their problems in a normal environment.
Furth's book *Thinking without Language* examines the implications of
deafness on the ability to think and progress in an educational situation.
An important conclusion that Furth comes to in his book is that deaf
children, and others without language, are able to think and to communicate certain of their mental operations. What remains unclear is
just what areas of cognition are most dependent on language for their
creation, development and outward and inward communication.

Deaf persons have in the past been likened to dumb animals and
relegated to the category of the demented. They were considered
legally and humanly incompetent. This attitude was based on the
assumption that speech is the distinguishing mark of the rational
as compared to the irrational animal. What has been primarily
responsible for our changed attitude towards the deaf? It was
chiefly the discovery that speech could be taught to at least some
of the deaf. This empirical fact demonstrated conclusively that
deafness is not necessarily connected with lack of intelligence.

Yet today speech or language is still the passport required to
admit the deaf into the society of fully developed human beings.
At least this is the philosophy underlying our present educational
and rehabilitative process. This also is the attitude we inculcate
implicitly in parents of deaf children, in society at large and last
but not least in the deaf person himself. From this angle, we perceive a certain basic similarity between our present viewpoint and
that of past centuries *vis-à-vis* the deaf. In effect we are still saying
to them: 'On condition that you learn our language, we are willing
to accept you.' The principal difference is that while this feat was

H. G. Furth: Extract from 'Practical implications' in his *Thinking without
Language*. Collier-Macmillan, 1966, pp. 202–15. © Hans G. Furth, 1966.

not considered possible in the past, today it is thought to be the normal and predominant situation among the deaf.

This attitude is constantly nourished by theories of scholars who extol language as the source and medium of civilization and intelligence. One can hardly blame educators and speech therapists if they take their lead from such exponents of learning.

Actually the general failure of the deaf to acquire linguistic competence poses a remarkable challenge, not only to educators, but to scientists. The latter have not seriously investigated this problem and the former are left to attribute the failure in a rather superficial manner to low intelligence, poor teaching methods, minimal brain damage, or to some mysterious law of least effort, according to which children would not learn to walk if we permitted them to crawl!

Here is an instance of what Festinger called cognitive dissonance. On one hand we honestly desire to accept the deaf child and help him attain maturity by the only means at our disposal, namely language. On the other hand, facts demonstrate that the vast majority of the deaf never acquire linguistic competence. Quite obviously the educator is at an impasse. Even apart from the oral-manual controversy which forces all specialists in this field to take sides and puts them on the defensive—certainly not an atmosphere conducive to realistic objective appraisal—what else can the teacher do but insist on more and more language? For language is the only means, he is told, of making the deaf acceptable to our society. As for the facts of the deaf pupil's very limited progress, there is a subtle tendency to suppress them. They are known, of course, but not discussed too openly or too definitely. They are treated like sex in Freud's Vienna. Thus reading norms are published for the deaf but they are not directly compared to the achievement of hearing children. One hears statements to the effect that the deaf are two or three years behind, or one consoles parents with the small number of words a hearing child in second grade is able to *read*, as though this were comparable to the number of words a deaf child *knows*.

These defence mechanisms are but minor factors in comparison with the potentially harmful effect of our unrealistic attitude on the deaf themselves and their immediate families. If experts are divided, how can the already distraught parent decide among them? If scholars teach that language is the most important factor contributing to intellectual development, how can the ordinary person disagree? If the speech teacher stresses the need for constant unrelenting effort towards oral speech, what parent would still search for non-verbal methods of education for his deaf child?

We cannot forget about the child himself who is given to understand that he will be accepted by his parents and society at large only if he learns language. The primary need for healthy development of any child, particularly one with a disability, is acceptance of himself as a person. This acceptance should not be made conditional on an aspect of behaviour directly connected with the child's disability and therefore beyond his control. Such acceptance is rarely accorded deaf children unless they are born to unusual parents. Our educational and scientific atmosphere does not permit us really to accept deafness.

The oral educational philosophy is bound to be detrimental to the relationship of the deaf child to his parents. It is hard for any parent to accept the fact that his child is deaf or otherwise permanently disabled. This particular disability, moreover, unlike some others, usually is diagnosed only after many months or years of anxious doubt, unrealistic hopes, not to mention financial burdens and untold inconveniences. This cannot help but have its effect on the young child to whose already great handicap must be added the burden of doubts about his own worth, as he witnesses his parents' distress and feels his isolation from other family members.

Those guiding the education of the deaf child impress very early on the parents' mind the all-importance of the speech and language factor. To my knowledge hearing parents of deaf children are never encouraged to learn the sign language of the deaf. Thus the deaf child and his parents, directed to stress speech and lip reading and discouraged from using manual signs, are left to their own devices in communicating with one another. Many parents try faithfully, in what they believe is their child's best interest, to follow the teacher's advice. Meantime, the child is growing and reaches the age of five or six years. The level of communication of which he is capable by means of speech is of the most primitive types hardly above the signals by which we communicate with our pets. The child implicitly understands that his parents and the hearing society they represent will not love him as he is, but will accept him only if he learns speech. Thus he is deprived of the unconditional acceptance that is the foundation of normal healthy development for any child.

By the time the child enters school the battle for mastery of language is already largely lost. The child's intelligence has been developing without benefit of language. He now spends years and years in school, constantly exposed to formal linguistic training, and progressing at a snail's pace to that almost inevitable ceiling of Grade 3 reading level. He is still below the level that would enable him readily to form and comprehend connected language.

However, at the same time, in school he meets for the first time other children like himself, playmates and friends who accept him without requiring verbal language. Outside of class hours he learns to socialize with other children and to communicate in his own way. The large residential schools, willingly or unwillingly, become for most deaf children a substitute for society and family. Many parents recognize this when after years of vain attempts to reach their child through language, they are relieved to see him in congenial surroundings.

Helped by the presence of companions and by the extra-classroom activity provided by the school, most deaf adolescents make a remarkable adjustment in the face of what must surely be considered heavy odds. They have not learned the language society has so insistently foisted upon them, but they consider that the failure lies with society, not with them. The deaf adult exhibits a certain hostility towards the hearing world which may offend our sensibility and good will. Yet is this not an almost unavoidable reaction by which the deaf individual upholds his dignity and counteracts the devaluatory attitude of society? If the deaf person unhesitatingly accepted society's norms, he would have to consider himself less of a person for not having language. The American who is deaf is rightly proud of his independence and his status as a responsible citizen and is unwilling to accept an inferior status of dependency. This is in contrast to the situation of the deaf in other countries and of persons with other disabilities such as blindness, who for reasons not pertinent to this discussion are unfortunately more ready to accept the false standard of society and consequently their own dependency.

Perhaps the linguistic failure of the deaf becomes more understandable when one realizes the irony of our position in wanting to accept deafness but not accepting deficiency in language. To say that the deaf associate experiences of frustration and failure with formal language learning is to understate the case. Yet no failing experience interferes with a hearing child's acquisition of language. The following statement is admittedly speculation but it is in accord with all we know about the psychology of language acquisition: The deaf child fails to acquire language because it is taught too late, in an unreasonable medium, in an unnatural way, and by the wrong person.

The biologically appropriate time for learning a first language is before the age of 3 or $3\frac{1}{2}$, during the period when the infant's intelligence blossoms in symbol formation. While scholars may be impressed by the fact that some deaf children can acquire linguistic competence at a considerably later age, I am willing to note these as exceptions and accept the biological norm. Then too, it is unreasonable to expect deaf children to learn by means of visible lip movements alone. Lip movements are inadequate even for the best of lip readers who must fill in large gaps in the visible information by educated guesses and intellectual effort. A more easily discriminable method seems absolutely necessary. Thirdly, the very idea of giving formal teaching before one can communicate informally with a child is contrary to the child's psychological status. Children learn admirably when the learning serves a psychological function and becomes incorporated into their thinking structure, but formal learning—divorced from an informal communication—is quite foreign much before the age of eight and rarely leads to lasting success.

Finally, children should acquire their first language in the environment in which they make the first giant steps in the intellective and symbolic grasp of reality. A late beginning in learning language necessarily divorces the learning of the first means of communication from the learning of specific social and emotional reactions to significant persons in their immediate society.

It is a rather sad commentary on the present educational situation that the example of Soviet Russia was required before any attempt to introduce manual spelling at an early age became acceptable in American schools for the deaf. This is a measure of the appeal of an ideal deaf person, one whose oral behaviour would not betray his deafness any more than his outward appearance gives a clue as to his inability to hear. This ideal not only insisted on linguistic competence but on speech expression and speech reception as well. Manual spelling *is* English language. Yet any school introducing this method with small children ten years ago would have been forced to abandon this method as not sufficiently 'oral'.

One important reason for the dominance of the oral method may be mentioned. Some eighty years ago when the oral method began to assert itself and quickly became predominant in all schools for the deaf, the picture of the deaf population in these schools was quite different from what it is today. Oralism could never have gained such impetus if the majority of deaf children had come to school then as they do now without any linguistic competence. Thanks to modern medicine acquired deafness after the age of early language acquisition is now rare. But quite the opposite situation prevailed eighty years ago, or even thirty years ago. Then most of the pupils at schools for the deaf had lost their hearing after the age of natural language acquisition. Hence, most of the deaf knew their mother tongue before they became deaf and with these deafened persons it made sense to insist so strongly on preserving speech and learning lip reading.

Today there are only a handful of deafened children. The greatest need of the deaf child now is not speech but language, and it is only by a distortion of its original purpose that the oral method holds sway as the ordinary and preferred way of acquiring linguistic competence.

Yet as the oral method has now, for better or worse, reached its dominant position in the education of the deaf, the presence of even one profoundly deaf student who succeeds well by the oral method is sufficient to insure its continued prevalence. This permits educators to point to their outstanding pupils as living arguments in support of the pure oral approach. To others this is very much like singling out Paderewski and Horowitz to a parent and saying: 'Look how well they play the piano! If they can do it, why not your child?'

The so-called oral-manual controversy in the education of the deaf is not really a controversy that can be settled on its practical merit since there is no such thing as a truly manual education.

One can read compromise statements which reflect the thinking of many educators, such as: 'All deaf children must first be given the opportunity of an oral education. If by age twelve they show little sign of success, one may use manual methods of education.' One wonders whether any thought at all is being given to the developing mind of the twelve-year-old child. The fixation on the one secondary aspect of language, namely speech, in preference to everything else, including linguistic competence, is indeed baffling. This oral preoccupation must strike a neutral observer as irrational. It is like some strange custom or institution which is encouraged within a community although perceived as harmful by an outsider.

Even learning one's mother tongue through manual spelling in a formal school setting at five years of age as is now practised in a few schools, is too late and too unnatural a procedure to result in general success. At that age, the effort is already remedial learning rather than first language learning. A wise educator of the deaf once remarked that the more intelligent deaf child may be hindered by his very intelligence from acquiring verbal language. By this he implied that linguistic competence is rooted in the beginnings of intellectual life as an acquired symbolic medium and frame of social expression. If society does not provide the child with conventional symbols, he can still develop intellectually, but the symbol system which embodies his thinking will be different from the verbal system, so much so that the two systems may be actively opposed.

Perhaps we could learn much about that private symbol system of the deaf if we were content to study their manual signing in an objective fashion without comparing it to the 'mature' verbal language of our society and calling it by contrast 'primitive' and 'concrete'. Apart from this it would seem to be a most significant fact, worthy of scientific attention, that signing is learned by practically all the deaf while the verbal language is mastered by only a few.

The additional general observation can be made that all infants learn any language to which they are exposed in a natural way during the first three years, provided the important sensory cues are transmitted and internally processed. It would seem to follow quite logically that a deaf child too could learn society's language

in an almost infallible way. If parents were taught to make a discriminable sign for each word while they speak it, this procedure
would almost necessarily teach the deaf child the natural language.
In this manner the deaf child would come to use signs in the same
way in which we use morphemes and the transition from these
signs to written English would be a matter of transliteration
rather than translation. That is, the child would sign according to
the English syntax, not according to the popular sign language in
common use. Thus the greatest obstacle to learning English
would be removed because deaf children would already have
learned to comprehend and express themselves in English syntax.
Comprehension of syntactical rules, it will be recalled, rather than
memory of single words, is currently the great obstacle which so
few deaf children learn to overcome.

Objections to this proposal may invoke the idea of least effort:
'Children permitted to use a manual, easily discriminable form of
communication will not be motivated to work at the arduous task
of receptive and expressive speech.' Even though this argument is
patently fallacious, it is hard to see how one could prefer a situation
in which 90 per cent of the deaf do not know language and perhaps
4 per cent are excellent in both aspects of speech, to a situation in
which 90 per cent of the deaf conceivably would have linguistic
competence and possibly only 3 per cent would be proficient
speech artists.

A second objection is somewhat more serious. Does signing
according to English syntax exist, and would parents be willing
to use it? As to the last point, I am convinced that parents, once
they are made to understand the real situation, will be co-operative,
just as in the past they listened to other advice. Besides, there does
not seem to be any other way in which parents can demonstrate
to their deaf child that they accept him and are willing to communicate with him on his own terms. Such parents would not
anxiously base their hopes on the slender chance of an unlikely
event. They would enjoy living contact with the child who needs
only to be exposed to discriminable cues to pick up language like
any other normal child. The signing which is proposed would not
be as difficult to learn as a foreign language. It would be English in
which frequently used words or morphemes would have simple,
gesture-like signs. Some spelling would obviously be necessary

and some manual signs for syntactical features now completely neglected in the conventional sign language would have to be devised.

Use of such manual signs, in addition to encouraging the
learning of English linguistic structure, would also actually enhance the use of speech or hearing aids. The need for symbolic
imitation and comprehension is so strong that a two-year-old
child will not voluntarily neglect any cues which would facilitate
meaningful symbolic communication. An additional benefit of this
suggested programme would be a possible insight into the per-
plexing problem of so-called 'aphasic' children, i.e., children
whose hearing sensitivity is presumed to be adequate but who
cannot make use of the sounds they apparently 'hear'. If there is a
cerebral centre which mediates linguistic behaviour, would truly
aphasic children be separated from deaf children by the fact that
they cannot learn to *sign* the English language?

These considerations concerning a realistic programme of teaching language to the deaf were prompted by a survey of the present
situation prevailing throughout the modern world and a more
adequate scientific description of the natural development of
thinking and language as outlined in previous chapters. A more
direct application of conclusions derived from experimental work
on the thinking of the deaf is the need to question seriously our
educational method which stresses and relies almost exclusively
upon verbal skill. Tradition has been rather heavily loaded with
educational disciplines deriving their existence from linguistic
habits. We need only look back over endless controversies which
today strike us as semantic follies. Perhaps such emphasis could be
condoned as long as education was limited to the few presumed
to be sophisticated in their use of language. But with the development of free and compulsory education for all, some of the verbal
rigour was relaxed and an increase in the use of audio-visual and
other concrete aids have become common. Yet in spite of these
liberalizing trends, the basic tendency to equate scholastic learning
with verbal learning is still very much in evidence.

Underlying this general emphasis on verbal learning was the
ready association of thinking and language which prevailed in one
form or another throughout the history of Western thought and
education. The history of the deaf stands out as one exceptionally
glaring instance of man's inability to see beyond the confines of his

own theoretical assumptions. The evidence brought together in these pages is not intended to devaluate language or displace it from its legitimate place in the education of verbal persons, but to clear the way for a scientific appreciation of the thinking process upon which verbal learning should take place.

The amount of unthinking verbal learning in our schools at every grade level from kindergarten to university is still vast. For every student who thinks clearly and has difficulty communicating his thought verbally, there are easily a hundred others who say things they have not thought through. Such use of linguistic behaviour is expected in ordinary conversation or routine everyday life, but it plays havoc with an education which purports to train thinking.

Leaving the general educational situation aside, society is still faced with great numbers of children who for one reason or another are deficient, not in linguistic competence as the deaf are, but in various linguistic skills. There are the millions of mentally retarded, the millions of culturally deprived, the emotionally disturbed, and the children with articulation disorders, or reading difficulties. All these and other children with linguistic deficiencies pose special educational problems. We admit such children are particularly deficient in linguistic behaviour and then, as if to punish them for this, we focus our educational curriculum on their weakest point.

How many hours are wasted because instructions are framed in a verbal medium whose linguistic meaning baffles the child so that he does not even come to the point of considering the subject matter under discussion? How can thinking ensue from the recognition of a problem if the message does not get through and the real problem is the linguistic obstacle of comprehending the message? In a similar vein, many wrong verbal answers reveal a lack of verbal skill more than a lack of thinking.

These points are particularly pertinent at the younger age levels, before the child's intelligence in operational thinking frees him from too exclusive a dependence on specific symbolic representations and on perceptually present situations. If at this level linguistic skill is not firmly established, the child will be particularly handicapped by the fact that language symbols are not readily transformed into representational images. A deaf child's failure to solve the verbal problem which asks for the way in which 'thermometer' and 'scales' are alike is simply due to his ignorance of the key words, as well as of their syntactical connection. A child somewhat lacking in linguistic skill for various reasons may be so preoccupied with the effort to comprehend the verbal message that the relevant thinking to produce the common concept and its corresponding verbal term does not even take place.

Just as linguistic competence cannot be drilled into the growing deaf child, ineptness in linguistic usage cannot be remedied by constant exposure to formal verbal teaching. On the contrary, the net effect of such a procedure is to make formal teaching even more distasteful to the child, widening the gulf between language and the development of thinking. For children in any way deficient in linguistic usage, educational procedures should concentrate on the stronger part of their intellectual structure, not exclusively on verbal means.

This plea for non-verbal teaching methods is no longer completely novel, as is demonstrated by the recent upsurge of interest in the Montessori method, and by new teaching methods for mathematics which practically eliminate verbal language. The need for letting children discover principles of thinking through activity is now frequently mentioned.

If educators firmly accepted the notion that thinking is first and foremost doing, acting, behaving, or internally operating rather than just knowing the right word, and if they agreed that education should primarily teach and develop thinking according to a child's optimal potential, they would more readily seek non-verbal teaching methods, particularly in cases where linguistic skill is retarded or absent.

At the Center for Research in Thinking and Language, we are currently planning a course in thinking, a non-verbal training curriculum for discovery, inference, conceptual control, transfer, symbolic transformation and combination, to be given to deaf or otherwise linguistically handicapped children. Its purpose will be to develop thinking skills in pupils otherwise exposed to practically no formal educational training except rote memory of linguistic symbols. The advantages of such a procedure are obvious and manifold, and many educators have expressed their interest in co-operating with it.

Not least among the fruits of such an endeavour would be a clearer insight into the actual intellectual potential of linguistically handicapped persons. In general we have been satisfied to point out what they could not do. The experimental studies reported here, however, are but an indication that thinking is going on in the linguistically handicapped deaf. To study the limits of this thinking and to observe more closely its processes and strategies necessitate that the psychologist venture into training and education.

Language and Meaning

The debate conducted by Halliday in Reading 15 is central to this collection of readings. It is only necessary to read the comment of Braine's introduction to his survey of language acquisition quoted by Halliday on page 223. As Halliday points out, the implication of Braine's remarks is that language is a 'commodity of some kind that the child has to gain possession of in the course of maturation'. Halliday does not see language as a mere commodity. He sees it occupying 'the central role in the process of social learning'.

15 M. A. K. HALLIDAY
Learning to Mean

Introductory

Considered in the perspective of language development as a whole, the latest period of intensive study in this field—the last decade and more—has been characterized by what may, in time, come to seem a rather one-sided concentration on grammatical structure. The question that has most frequently been asked is, 'How does the child acquire structure?'[1] The implication has been that this is really the heart of the language learning process; and also perhaps, in the use of the term 'acquisition', that structure, and therefore language itself, is a commodity of some kind that the child has to gain possession of in the course of maturation.

The dominant standpoint has been a psycholinguistic one; and the dominant issue, at least in the United States where much of the most important work has been carried out, that between 'nativist' and 'environmentalist' interpretations (Osser 1970), although there seems to be no necessary connection between these as general philosophical positions and the particular models of the processes involved in the learning of linguistic structure that have been most typically associated with them (cf. Braine 1971, esp. § 3). The nativist view lays more stress on a specific innate language-learning capacity; it does not follow from this that the child necessarily learns by setting up hypothetical rules of grammar and matching them against what he hears, but there has been a widely-held interpretation along these lines. Environmentalist views, by contrast, emphasize the aspect of language learning which relates it to other learning tasks, and stress its dependence on environmental conditions; again, this is often assumed to imply

M. A. K. Halliday: Extract from 'Learning how to mean' in Eric H. and Elizabeth Lenneberg (eds.) *Foundations of Language Development*, Paris: UNESCO, 1975.

[1] For example, Braine (1971: 8) introduces his comprehensive survey of work on 'the acquisition of language' with the words '. . . this review is concerned only with the acquisition of linguistic structure. Thus, work on child language where the concern is with social or intellectual development will not be reviewed. Even within the area defined, the subject of lexical development will be reviewed only very sketchily.' No mention is made of the development of the semantic system.

an associationist, stimulus-response model of the learning process, although there is no essential connection between the two.

In the investigation of how the child learns grammatical structure, attention has naturally been focused on the nature of the earliest structures which the child produces for himself, where he combines certain elements—typically but not necessarily words—which he also uses in isolation, or in other combinations. There are in principle two ways of looking at these, the one adult-oriented and the other child-oriented. The child's structures may be represented either as approximations to the forms of the adult language, or as independent structures *sui generis*. The first approach, which is in a sense presupposed by a nativist view, involves treating many of the child's utterances, perhaps all of them at a certain stage, as ill-formed; they are analysed as the product of distortions of various kinds, particularly the deletion of elements. This brings out their relationship to the adult forms, but it blocks the way to the recognition and interpretation of the child's own system. In the second approach, the child's earliest structures are analysed as combinations of elements forming a system in their own right, typically based on the contrast between closed and open-ended classes; the best-known example is Braine's (1963) 'pivotal' model, with its categories of 'pivot' and 'open'. Such an analysis has been criticized on the grounds that it fails to account for ambiguous forms (e.g. Bloom 1970: *mummy sock* = (i) 'mummy's sock', (ii) 'mummy is putting my socks on'); but this is an aspect of a more general limitation, namely that it does not account for the meaning of what the child says. Nor does it easily suggest how, or why, the child moves from his own into the adult system; if language development is primarily the acquisition of structure, why does the child learn one set of structures in order to discard them in favour of another? For an excellent discussion of these and related issues, see Brown 1974.

None of the above objections is very serious, provided it is recognized, first, that structural analysis is a highly abstract exercise, in which both types of representation are valid and each affords its own insight; and secondly—a related point—that language development is much more than the acquisition of structure. But, by the same token, the form of representation of the grammatical structures of the child's language is then no longer the central issue. The fundamental question is, 'How does the child learn language?' In other words, how does he master the adult linguistic system—in which grammar is just one part, and structure is just one part of grammar? How does he build up a multiple coding system consisting of content, form, and expression of meaning relations, the representation of these as lexico-structural configurations, and the realization of these, in turn, as phonological patterns?

A consideration of this question in its broader context is embodied in what Roger Brown calls a 'rich interpretation' of children's language: the approach to language development through the investigation of meaning. This is not, of course, a new idea. But when the psychologists' traditional two-level model of language (as sound and meaning) came to be overtaken by that of structuralist linguistics—which was still in terms of two levels, but this time of sound and form—it rather receded into the background.[1] With the now general recognition of the basically tri-stratal nature of the linguistic system (and Prague theory, glossematics, system-structure theory, tagmemics, stratification theory and the later versions of transformation theory are all variants on this theme), the semantic perspective has been restored. The 'rich interpretation' may still rest on a structural analysis of the utterances of children's speech; but if so, this is an analysis at the semological level in which the elements of structure are functional in character. Most typically, perhaps, they are the transitivity functions of the clause, such as Agent and Process (Schlesinger 1971); but it is worth commenting here that all functional categories, whether those of transitivity, like Fillmore's (1968) 'cases', or those of thematic structure (Gruber 1967), and including traditional notions like subject and modifier, are semantic in origin (Halliday 1970) and could therefore figure appropriately in such a description.

[1] Just how far the latter view prevailed can be seen in the following quotation from Ervin and Miller (1963: 108): 'The most important contribution that modern linguistics has brought to child language studies is the coception of what a language is. A language is a system that can be described nternally in terms of two primary parts or levels—the phonological (sound sys in) and the grammatical. A complete description of a language would include tem count of all possible phonological sequences and also a set of rules by whan accanh predict all the possible sentences in that language.'

The approach to structure through meaning may also be either child-oriented or adult-oriented. For example, the utterance *now room* (see below), which could be glossed as 'now let's go to (play in) (daddy's) room', could be analysed on the adult model as something like Imperative + Process + Agent + Locative + Temporal, with Imperative, Process and Agent deleted; or, in its own terms, as something like Request for joint action + Arena, with nothing omitted or 'understood'.

Once again, these are abstract representations and neither can be said to be wrong. But a child-oriented semantic analysis of the latter kind, which is very suggestive, carries certain further implications. Since the elements of the structure are not being explained as (approximations to) those of the adult language, there is presumably some other source from which they are derived and in terms of which they have any meaning. Why, for example, would we postulate an element such as 'Request for joint action'? This is explicable only if one of the functions of language is to call for action on the part of others, to regulate their behaviour in some way. No doubt this is true; but to make it explicit implies some specification of the total set of functions of language, some kind of a functional hypothesis which is not just a list of uses of language but a system of developmental functions from each of which a range of meanings, or 'meaning potential', is derived.

At this point the attempt to understand the structure of the child's utterances leads directly into questions about the linguistic system as a whole, and specifically about the functions for which that system first develops. There is an important link between the two senses of 'function', first as in 'functions in structure' and second as in 'functions of language'; the former, when interpreted semantically, imply the latter. But whether or not the line of approach is through considerations of structure, once the interest is focused on how the child learns a system of meanings this points to some investigation in functional terms. It becomes necessary to look beyond the language itself, but to do so without presupposing a particular conceptual framework, because this is precisely what the child is using language to construct; and herein lies the value of a functional approach. Early language development may be interpreted as the child's progressive mastery of a functional potential.

There is yet a further implication here, one which takes us into the social foundations of language. If, for example, language is used, from an early stage, to regulate the behaviour of others, and it is suggested that the mastery of this function is one of the essential steps in the developmental process, this assumes some general framework of social structure and social processes in terms of which a function such as 'regulatory' would make sense. More particularly—since we are concerned with the language of the child—it presupposes a concept of cultural transmission within which the role of language in the transmission process may be highlighted and defined. Here the concept of meaning, and of learning to mean, is in the last analysis interpreted in sociological terms, in the context of some chain of dependence such as: social order—transmission of the social order to the child—role of language in the transmission process—functions of language in relation to this role—meanings derived from these functions.

In this way the functional interpretation of the child's meanings implies what might be termed a sociolinguistic approach (cf. Osser 1970), in which the learning of language is seen as a process of interaction between the child and other human beings. From this perspective, which is complementary to the psycholinguistic one (in no sense contradictory), the focus of attention is on the linguistic system as a whole, considered as having a (functionally organized) meaning potential, or semantic system, at one end, and a vocal potential, or phonological system, at the other. In this context, structure no longer occupies the centre of the stage; it enters in because it is one form of the realization of meanings. This has certain important consequences for the investigation of language development. The analysis does not depend on utterances of more than one element, that is, on combinations of words as structural units. This is significant because, although the word in the sense of a lexical item or lexeme (i.e. vocabulary) soon comes to play an essential part in the development of the linguistic system, the word as a structural unit, which is a different concept, does not, or nothing like so prominently: it is merely one type of constituent among others, and the young child has no special awareness of words as constituents (this point is brought out by Braine (1971:87), who for some reason finds it surprising). From the functional point of view, as soon as there are meaningful expressions there is language, and the investigation can begin at a time before words and structures have evolved to take over the burden of realization.

It then emerges that the child already has a linguistic system before he has any words or structures at all.[1] He is capable of expressing a range of meanings which at first seem difficult to pin down, because they do not translate easily into adult language, but which become quite transparent when interpreted functionally, in the light of the question 'What has the child learnt to do by means of language?'. The transition from this first phase into the adult system can also be explained in functional terms, although it is necessary to modify the concept of function very considerably in passing from the developmental origins of the system, where 'function' equals 'use', to the highly abstract sense in which we can talk of the functional organization of the adult language. However, this modification in the concept 'function of language' is itself one of the major sources of insight into the process whereby the adult system evolves from that of the child.

In what follows we shall suggest a tentative framework for a functional, or sociolinguistic, account of early language development. This will recognize three phases: Phase I, the child's initial functional-linguistic system; Phase II, the transition from this system to that of the adult language; Phase III, the learning of the adult language. The account does not presuppose any one particular psychological model of language acquisition or theory of learning. Linguistically, it assumes some form of a realizational model of language; the descriptive techniques used were those of system-structure theory, with the 'system' (a set of options with a condition of entry) as the basic concept (Firth 1957), but such a representation can be readily interpreted in stratificational terms (Lamb 1970; Reich 1970). The sociological standpoint is derived from the findings and the theoretical work of Bernstein (1969–70; 1971a; 1971b). But the particular impetus for the detailed study of a developing language system, which provides the observational basis for this sketch, came from working over a number of years

---

[1] Cf. Leopold (1939–49, I: 22), '. . . meanings were always developed before sound-forms'. As it stands this is difficult to interpret; but I take it to mean 'before the appearance of sound-forms recognizably derived from the adult language'.

with teachers of English as a mother tongue, who were attempting to grapple with the fundamental problem of language in education (for the results of their work see Mackay, Thompson and Schaub 1970; Doughty, Pearce and Thornton 1971). Their experience showed that we are still far from understanding the essential patterns of language development in the pre-school child, in the deeper sense of being able to answer the question, 'How does the child learn how to mean?'

Phase I: Functional Origins

Developmental Functions: A Hypothesis

Seen from a sociolinguistic viewpoint, the learning of the mother tongue appears to comprise three phases of development. The first of these consists in mastering certain basic functions of language, each one having a small range of alternatives, or 'meaning potential', associated with it.

A tentative system of developmental (Phase I) functions was suggested, as follows (Halliday 1969):

Instrumental	'I want'
Regulatory	'do as I tell you'
Interactional	'me and you'
Personal	'here I come'
Heuristic	'tell me why'
Imaginative	'let's pretend'
Informative	'I've got something to tell you'

The hypothesis was that these functions would appear, approximately in the order listed, and in any case with the 'informative' (originally called 'representational') significantly last; that, in Phase I, they would appear as discrete, with each expression (and therefore each utterance) having just one function; and that the mastery of all of them—with the possible exception of the last— would be both a necessary and a sufficient condition for the transition to the adult system. The implication of this is that these functions of language represent universals of human culture, which may in turn have further implications for an understanding of the evolution of language.

The hypothesis was tested, and the pattern of development from Phase I to Phase III followed through in detail, in an intensive study of the language development of one subject, Nigel, from 9 to 24 months. This will be the main source of information for the present account.

The Functional Interpretation of Child Language

The criteria adopted for regarding a vocalization by the child as an utterance (i.e. as language) were: an observable and constant relation between content and expression, such that, for each content/expression pair, the expression was observed in at least three unambiguous instances and the content was interpretable in functional terms. (In practice the distinction between random vocalizations and systematic forms proved to be obvious, and the latter were observed with far more than minimal frequency.) This means that the content was, in each case, derivable as a possible option in meaning from some point of origin that could reasonably be interpreted as a context for effective verbal action (Firth 1950), whether or not in the above list. We may compare here Leopold's observation (1939–49 I: 21) that his daughter at eight months showed 'the intention of communication, which must be considered the chief criterion of language'. On the above criteria, Nigel's vocalizations at 9 months were still pre-linguistic, or just on the threshold of language. At 10½ months, however, he had a language, consisting of a meaning potential in each of four functions. We shall refer to this as NL 1, meaning 'Nigel's Language 1' (Figure 1).

At this stage, there is no grammar. That is to say, there is no level of linguistic 'form' (syntax, morphology, vocabulary) intermediate between the content and the expression. In stratificational terms, the child has a semology and a phonology but not yet a lexology. Furthermore, the system owes nothing to the English language (a possible exception being [bø] 'I want my toy bird'); the sounds are spontaneous and, in general, unexplained, although two or three are attested as imitations of natural sounds which the child has heard himself make and then put to systematic use. (Parenthetically, it should be noted that a phonetic alphabet such as the IPA notation is quite inappropriate as a means of

NL 1 (9–10½ months)

CONTENT		EXPRESSION		GLOSS
Function	*Content systems*	*Articulation*	*Tone (falling)*	
Instrumental	demand (general)	['nãnãnã]	mid	give me that
	demand for bird	[bø]	mid	give me my bird
Regulatory	normal	[ə̃]	mid	do that (again)
	intensified	[m͡nŋ]	high wide	do that right now
Interactional	initiating — friendliness	[ø], ['dø], ['do]	mid narrow	nice to see you (shall we look at this together?)
	initiating — impatience	[ənnn]	mid	nice to see you—at last
	response	[ɛ], [ə]	low	yes it's me
Personal	withdrawal	[g̊ʷɣyg̊ʷɣyg̊ʷɣy]	low narrow	I'm sleepy
	participation — pleasure — general	[a]	low	that's nice
	participation — pleasure — taste	[n͡ŋ]	low	that tastes nice
	participation — interest — general	[ø]	low	that's interesting
	participation — interest — specific	[d̊o], [bø], [ø]	low	look it's moving (? dog, bird)

Figure 1

representing the child's speech sounds at this stage; it is far too specific. What is wanted is a system of notation showing generalized postures and prosodic values.)

Rather, it might be said that the expression owes nothing to the English language. As far as the content is concerned, the English language probably has played a part, by virtue of the fact that it embodies meanings such as 'I want that' somewhere in its semantic system, and the adult hearer therefore recognizes and responds to such meanings. It is of course immaterial, in this regard, whether such meanings are or are not cultural and linguistic universals.

Nigel's language was studied continuously and the description recast every $1\frac{1}{2}$ months, this being the interval that appeared to be optimal: with a longer interval one might fail to note significant steps in the progression, while with a shorter one, one would be too much at the mercy of random non-occurrences in the data. Table I shows the number of options within each function at each stage from NL 1 (9–$10\frac{1}{2}$ months) to NL 5, the end of Phase I (15–$16\frac{1}{2}$ months). Those for NL 6, which is considered to be the beginning of Phase II, are added for comparison, although it should be stressed that they are not only less reliable but also, as will emerge from what follows, less significant as an index of the system.

Characteristics of Phase I Systems

The set of options comprising NL 1 represents what a very small child can do with language—which is quite a lot, in relation to his total behaviour potential. He can use language to satisfy his own material needs, in terms of goods or services (instrumental); to exert control over the behaviour of others (regulatory); to establish and maintain contact with those that matter to him (interactional); and to express his own individuality and self-awareness (personal). Moreover, any one option may have a very considerable range; not only in the sense that it can be used very frequently (i.e. on numerous occasions, not counting repetitions within one occasion: it is necessary to distinguish 'instances' from 'tokens' at this stage), but also, and more significantly, in the sense that many of the options are very general in their applicability. There

TABLE 1

	Instru-mental	Regu-latory	Inter-actional	Per-sonal	Heur-istic	Imagin-ative	Infor-mative	Total
Phase I								
NL 1 (9–10½ months)	2	2	3	5	—	—	—	12
NL 2 (10½–12 months)	3	2	6	9	—	—	—	20
NL 3 (12–13½ months)	5	6	7	9	(?)	—	—	27
NL 4 (13½–15 months)	5	6	7	10	(?)	2	—	30
NL 5 (15–16½ months)	10	6	14	17	—	3	—	50
Phase II								
NL 6 (16½–18 months)	29	28	17	65*	1	4	—	144

* Note: this figure includes all expressions used in observation and recall, reinterpreted in Phase II as 'mathetic' (deriving from personal-heuristic).

is a tendency, in fact, for each function to include an unmarked option whose meaning is equivalent to the general meaning of the function in question: for example, in the instrumental function there is one option meaning simply 'I want that', where the object of desire is clear from the context—contrasting with one or more specific options such as 'I want my bird'. There are various modifications of this pattern; for instance there may be one unmarked term for an initiating context and another for a response ('yes I do want that'). But the principle is clearly operative, and perhaps anticipates the 'good reason' principle, that of 'select this option unless there is a good reason for selecting some other one', that is such a fundamental feature of adult language.

The functions observed in Nigel's Phase I turn out to be those of the initial hypothesis. This will cease to be true in Phase II, but in one important respect the hypothesis fails already—there is no sign of a developmental progression within the first four functions. As a matter of fact the only two expressions recorded before nine months that fulfil the criteria for language were in the interactional and personal areas. Furthermore, the imaginative function seems to appear before the heuristic, although a re-interpretation of certain elements (the 'problem area' referred to in the next paragraph) in the light of Phase II observations suggests that this may be wrong, and that the heuristic function begins to appear at NL 4 ($13\frac{1}{2}$–15 months), at the same time as the imaginative. The two are closely related: the heuristic function is language in the exploration of the objective environment—of the 'non-self' that has been separated off from the self through the personal function—while the imaginative is language used to create an environment of one's own, which may be one of sound or of meaning and which leads eventually into story, song and poetry. Finally, the informative function has not appeared at all. What does emerge as some sort of developmental sequence, in Nigel's case, is (i) that the first four functions listed clearly precede the rest, and (ii) that all others precede the informative. The informative function does not appear until nearly the end of Phase II, round about NL 9 (21–$22\frac{1}{2}$ months); but this was not entirely unexpected, since the use of language to convey information is clearly a derivative function, one which presupposes various special conditions including, for one thing, the concept of dialogue.

The functions themselves, however, emerge with remarkable clarity. Not only did it prove surprisingly easy to apply the general criteria for identifying a vocal act as language (since the learning of a system cannot be regarded as a function of that system, anything interpreted as linguistic practising was automatically excluded—Nigel in fact did very little of this); it was possible, throughout NL 1–5, to assign utterances to expressions, expressions to meanings and meanings to functions with relatively little doubt or ambiguity. There was one significant exception to this, a problem area lying at the border of the interactional and the personal functions, which proved extremely difficult to systematize; subsequent interpretation suggests that it was, in fact, the origin of heuristic language, or rather of a more general learning function that is discussed more fully below. Otherwise, although the functions clearly overlap in principle, or at least shade into one another, the value of an element at all levels in the system was usually not difficult to establish.

More important, the fact that the meanings could be derived from functions that were set up on extra-linguistic grounds justified our regarding these early utterances as expressions of language—a step that is necessary if we are to understand the genesis of language as a whole. Phase II, which corresponds to what has usually, in recent years, been taken as the (unexplained) point of origin of the system, is here regarded as being already transitional, and explained as a reinterpretation of the elementary functions in a more generalized form. Ultimately, these evolve into the abstract functional components of the adult grammatical system; and these components then serve as the medium for the encoding, in grammar, of the original functions in their concrete extensions as what we would call simply 'uses of language'.

Phase II: The Transition

The transition to the adult system begins, with Nigel, at NL 6 (16½–18 months). This phase is characterized by two main features: (i) a shift in the functional orientation, which is described below, and (ii) major and very rapid advances in vocabulary, in structure, and in dialogue.

Vocabulary and structure are in principle the same thing. What emerges at this point is a grammar, in the traditional sense of this term as a level of linguistic 'form' (the lexological stratum). This is a system intermediate between the content and the expression, and it is the distinguishing characteristic of human, adult language. The options in the grammatical system are realized as structure and vocabulary, with vocabulary, as a rule, expressing the more specific choices.

Vocabulary

NL 6 has some 80–100 new meanings, and, for the first time, the majority of the meanings are expressed by means of lexical items—the expressions are English words. In the first instance these are used holophrastically which in the present context is defined in functional terms: the lexical item forms by itself an utterance that is functionally independent and complete. With Nigel, this did not continue very long; he happened to be one of those children who hardly go through a 'holophrastic stage', for whom the holophrase is merely the limiting case of a linguistic structure. In any case the holophrase is, in itself, of little importance; but it serves to reveal the very crucial step whereby the child introduces words—that is, a vocabulary—into his linguistic system.

Why does the child learn words? Do they fit into and enrich the existing functional pattern, or are they demanded by the opening up of new functional possibilities? The answer seems to be, not unexpectedly, both. Many of the words that are learnt first are called for by existing functions. Of these the majority, in Nigel's case, are at first restricted to one function only, e.g. *cat* means only 'hullo, cat!' (interactional), *syrup* means only 'I want my syrup' (instrumental); a few begin to appear in more than one function, at different times, e.g. *hole* means now 'make a hole' (instrumental), now 'I want to (go out for a walk and) put things in holes' (regulatory) and now 'look, there's a hole' (personal-heuristic; see below); and just once or twice we find a combination of functions in a single instance, e.g. *cake* meaning 'look, there's a cake—and I want some!' This last is very striking when it first occurs. With the adult, all utterances are plurifunctional; but for a child the ability to mean two things at once marks a great advance. Thus, as far as the existing functions arec oncerned, the learning of vocabulary (i) engenders new meanings within these functions and (ii) allows for functions to be combined. The latter will then impose definite requirements on the nature of linguistic structure, since the principal role of structure, in the grammar, is that of mapping one functional meaning on to another.

However, many of the new words—the majority, in Nigel's case—do not fit into the earlier functional pattern. In the first place, they have clearly not been learnt for pragmatic contexts. Indeed many of them are not particularly appropriate to the instrumental or regulatory functions, e.g. *bubble, toe, star, hot, weathercock*; and even those that are do not appear in these functions until later on—the words *dog* and *bus*, for example, although perfectly well understood as also referring to certain toys, are not used to ask for those toys, or in any other pragmatic sense.

It might be surmised, then, that the impetus to the learning of new words would come from the emergence of the informative function, from the child's desire to use language for conveying information. But this is not so. At 18 months Nigel has no conception of language as a means of communicating an experience to someone who has not shared that experience with him; it is only much later that he internalizes the fact that language can be used in this way. A further possibility might be that the child is simply practising, using new words just in order to learn them. This also must be rejected, if it implies that the child is learning language in order to learn language; he cannot seriously be thought to be storing up verbal wealth for future uses he as yet knows nothing about. But the notion of learning is the relevant one, provided it is interpreted as learning in general, not simply the learning of language. For Nigel, the main functional impetus behind the move into the lexical mode is, very distinctly, that of learning about his environment. Most of the new vocabulary is used, at first, solely in the context of observation and recall: 'I see/hear . . .', including 'I saw/heard . . .'.

In terms of the developmental functions, this appears to be a blend of the personal and the heuristic, resulting from some such process as the following. First, the self is separated from the 'non-self' (the environment). Second, a meaning potential arises in respect of each: personal reactions, e.g. 'pleasure', and attention to external phenomena, e.g. 'look'. Third, new meanings arise through the combination of the two: involvement with, and reaction to, features of the environment, e.g. 'look, that's interesting!' Fourth, the child develops a linguistic semiotic for the interpretation and structuring of the environment in terms of his own experience.

Hence the new words function mainly as a means of categorizing observed phenomena. Many of them represent items having properties that are difficult to assimilate to experience, typically movement (e.g. *dog, bee, train, bubble*) and visual or auditory prominence (e.g. *tower, light, bus, drill*); while others are simply phenomena that are central to the child's personal explorations—in Nigel's case, particularly things in pictures. The child is constructing a heuristic hypothesis about the environment, in the form of an experiential semantic system whose meanings are realized through words and structures, and which is used in contexts of observation and recall—and before long also of prediction.[1]

This 'learning' function of language—perhaps we might refer to it as the 'mathetic' function—appears to arise as a synthesis of the two principal non-pragmatic Phase I functions: the personal, which is the self-oriented one, and the heuristic, which is other-oriented. Nigel's earliest instances, at the beginning of Phase II, are markedly other-oriented; but this function soon becomes a means of exploring the self as well, and so takes up, on a higher level, the meaning of the original Phase I 'personal' function. We can trace the history of this mathetic function of language in Nigel's case from the very beginning; it is of interest because it

---

[1] In a recent article, Ingram (1971) proposes adapting Fillmore's 'case' theory of structural function to one-element utterances, with a category of 'semantic transitivity', corresponding in general to the concept of 'Process' as a structural role (Halliday, 1970); he then suggests that the child identifies objects in terms of their potential 'semantic function' (that is, their role in transitivity), e.g. their ability to move, or to operate on other objects, and that this defines for the child concepts such as 'Agent' and 'animate'. This agrees in principle with what is being suggested here, although Ingram's account of transitivity seems to be too simple; but Ingram fails to relate his notions to the language-function perspective of the child—on the one hand his assumption seems to be that 'semantic' can be equated with 'ideational', while on the other hand many of his own examples are of utterances having a predominantly pragmatic function.

reveals what was, for one child, the primary mode of entry into grammar.

Prominent in NL 1 is an interactional option in which some pleasurable experience, usually a picture, is used as the channel for contact with another person: [dɔ̀] etc.; glossed as 'nice to see you, and shall we look at this together?' In NL 2, this apparently splits into two meanings, though still with considerable overlap: one having an interactional emphasis, [dɔ̀], [ɛ̀ya] etc., 'nice to see you (and look at this!)', the other personal [dɔ̀], [dɛ̀o] etc., 'that's nice', reacting to a picture or bright object and not requiring the presence of a second participant. By NL 3, the former has become simply a greeting, and the expression for it is replaced, in NL 4, by *hullo* [ālouwā], alongside which appear individualized expressions of greeting *mummy, daddy, Anna*. The latter remains as an expression of personal interest; but meanwhile a third form arises at the intersection of the two, [ādà], [adādādà] etc., which represents the earliest type of *linguistic* interaction, glossed as 'look at this—now you say its name'—used only where the object is familiar and the name already (receptively) known. In NL 5, this naming request specializes out and becomes the form of demand for a new name, [ædȳdà] 'what's that?'; and this is used constantly as a heuristic device. Meanwhile, alongside the general expression of personal interest there have appeared a few specific variants, 'look that's a . . .' which are expressed by English words. At first these occur only in familiar contexts, again typically pictures; but in NL 6 they come to be used in the categorization of new experience, in the form of observation and recall: 'I see a . . .', 'I saw a . . .'. Then, within a very short time (less than one month), and still largely in this same mathetic function, the vocabulary begins to be backed up by structures. We can thus follow through, with Nigel, the process whereby the use of names to record and comment on what is observed, which is a universal feature of child language at a certain stage, arises out of meanings and functions that already existed for the child before any vocabulary had been learnt at all.

Structure

With Nigel, the structural explosion followed very closely on the lexical one. That it is part of the same general process, the envelopment of a stratum of 'grammar' intermediate between the content and the expression, is shown, however, not so much by the short-ness of this interval—which with some children is much longer— but by the fact that both vocabulary and structure first appear in the same functional contexts. All that was said, in functional terms, about the learning of vocabulary could apply to structure also.[1]

The origin and early development of structure will be touched upon here only in so far as it relates to the functional perspective. At the outset of Phase II, Nigel displayed two types of proto-structure, or rather two variants of the same type: a specific expression, within a certain function, combined either (i) with a gesture or (ii) with a general expression from the same function. Examples: [dà:bī] *Dvořak* + beating time (music gesture), 'I want the Dvořak record on' (instrumental function); [ndà] *star* + shaking head (negation gesture), 'I can't see the star' (personal); [ὲ lɔu] (command + *hole*), 'make a hole' (regulatory); [ù æyi:] (excitement + *egg*), '[ʌ æyi] an egg,' (personal). Shortly after this came word strings; these were of two words only, e.g. [bʌbu nɔumɔ] (*bubble, no-more*) 'the bubbles have gone away' except when in lists, when there might be as many as six, e.g. *stick, hole, stone, train, ball, bus* 'I saw sticks, etc.'; and each word still has its own independent (falling) tone contour. The first 'true' struc-ture, in the sense of a string of words on a single tone contour, appeared at 19 months, just four weeks after the first major excursion into vocabulary; and within two more weeks various types of structure were being produced, as in the following sets of examples:

(1)   mummy come, more meat, butter on, squeeze orange, mend train, help juice ('help me with the juice'), come over-there,

---

[1] Despite a commonly held belief to the contrary, the speech which the child hears around him is, in the typical instance, coherent, well-informed and con-textually relevant. In interaction with adults he is not, in general, surrounded by intellectual discourse, with its backtracking, anacolutha, high lexical density and hesitant planning; but by the fluent, smoothly grammatical and richly structured utterances of informal everyday conversation. (Of the first hundred clauses spoken in Nigel's presence on one particular day, only three were in some way 'deviant'.) He has abundant evidence with which to construct the grammatical system of his language. What he hears from other children, natur-ally, is different—but in ways which serve as a guide for his own efforts. This is not, of course, an argument against the nativist hypothesis; it merely removes one of the arguments that has been used to claim the necessity of a nativist interpretation.

now room ('now let's go to the room'), star for-you ('make a star for me'), more meat please

(2) green car, two book ('two books'), mummy book ('mummy's book'), bee flower ('there's a bee on the flower'), bubble round-round ('the bubbles are going round and round'), tiny red light, two fast train.

These structures fall into two distinct groups, on functional criteria. Those under (1) are 'pragmatic', and correspond to the instrumental and regulatory functions of Phase I; while those of (2) are what we have called 'mathetic', deriving from the personal-heuristic functions.

Quite unexpectedly, this binary grouping was made fully explicit by Nigel himself, when within the same two-week period (the end of NL 7, 19 to 19½ months) he introduced an entirely new distinction into his speech, that between falling and rising tone. From this point on, all pragmatic utterances were spoken on a rising tone and all non-pragmatic (mathetic) ones on a falling tone. The distinction was fully systematic, and was maintained intact for some months; it provided a striking corroboration of the significance of pragmatic/mathetic as a major functional opposition. If Nigel is at all typical, this opposition (though not, of course, Nigel's particular form of realization of it) seems to be fundamental to the transition to Phase III, the adult system; we shall return to it below. Here it is relevant because it enables us to see the development of structure in Phase II as an integral part of the total language-learning process.

What is the relation of linguistic structure to the functions of language? Let us take the examples, from Nigel at the beginning of Phase II (NL 7, 18–19½ months), of *more meat, two book* and *green car*. All three seem at first sight to display an identical structure, whether this is stated in child-oriented terms, e.g. Pivot + Open, or in adult-oriented terms, e.g. Modifier + Head. But *more meat* occurs only in a pragmatic function, while the other two occur only in a mathetic function. Moreover this is a general pattern; we find *more omelet, more bread* etc. all likewise pragmatic only, and *two train, mummy book* ('mummy's book'), *green peg, red car* etc. all mathetic only. It is this functional specialization which relates these structures to the earlier stage of language learning. By a subsequent step, they become functionally derestricted, so that the structure represented by *more meat* becomes compatible with the mathetic sense 'Look here's some . . .', and that of *green car* with the pragmatic sense of 'I want the . . .'. At first, however, each structure is tied exclusively to just one function or the other.

The structural analysis of *more meat* might be 'Request + Object of desire', relating it to the instrumental function from which it derives. The elements of the structure are pragmatic not experiential ones. By contrast, *green car* may be analysed in experiential terms, as perhaps 'Visual property + Object observed'. In terms of the introductory discussion, this interpretation of structure is child-oriented semantic: semantic in order to relate it to function, child-oriented to show the part it plays developmentally, which is obscured if we assume from the start a final outcome in the shape of a structure of the adult language. Exactly how a structure such as that represented by *more meat*, initially pragmatic, comes later to take on a non-pragmatic function, first in alternation and then in combination with the pragmatic, is an interesting and difficult question; presumably in this instance the request element *more* comes to be reinterpreted experientially as a comparative quantifier (in Nigel's case, via the aspectual sense 'I want (you) to go on . . . ing', e.g. *more play rao* 'I want us to go on playing lions'); while the request function is generalized and taken over by the modal system in the grammar (in Nigel's case, via the systematic use of the rising tone). We have chosen here what is probably a rather simple example; but the point is a general one. In the beginning, all Nigel's structures, like his vocabulary, are functionally specific; they are either pragmatic (set (1) above), or mathetic (set (2)). Only after an interval are they transferred to the other function; and this takes place, not by a shift out of one box into another, but rather by a recasting of the concept of 'function' on to a more abstract plane so that all expressions become, in effect, plurifunctional.

Herein lies the essential unity of structure and vocabulary. Words and structures, or rather 'words-and-structures', i.e. lexico-grammatical units, are the expression of options at a new level appearing in the child's linguistic system intermediate between meaning and sound. This is the stratum of linguistic form, or grammar; and it appears that grammar develops, with the child, as the means of incorporating the functional potential into the heart of the linguistic system. It allows for meanings which derive from different functions to be encoded together, as integrated structures, so that every expression becomes, in principle, functionally complex. Grammar makes it possible to mean more than one thing at a time.

Dialogue

The early development of the grammatical system has been fairly thoroughly explored, as the succeeding chapters describe. What has been much less explored, though of fundamental importance, is how the child learns dialogue.

Nigel learnt to engage in dialogue at the same time as he started to learn vocabulary, towards the end of NL 6 (just before 18 months); and dialogue could serve as well as vocabulary to mark the beginning of his Phase II. There was some 'proto-dialogue' in Phase I: at NL 2, Nigel had three specific responses, to calls, greetings and gifts, and by NL 5 he could answer questions of the type 'do you want . . .?', 'shall I . . .?', i.e. those where the answers required were instrumental, regulatory or interactional in function. But he could not initiate dialogue; nor could he give responses of a purely linguistic kind.[1]

Dialogue can be viewed as, essentially, the adoption and assignment of roles. The roles in question are social roles, but of a special kind: they exist only in and through language, as communication roles—speaker, addressee, respondent, questioner, persuader and the like. But they are of general significance developmentally, since they serve both as a channel and as a model for social interaction. Whenever someone speaks, he normally takes on the role of addresser ('I'm talking to you'), and assigns the role of listener ('attend'); but in dialogue these roles have to be made more specific, not merely 'I'm talking to you' but, for example, 'I am demanding information, and you are to respond by supplying it'. Dialogue involves purely linguistic forms of

---

[1] He could not, in other words, respond to utterances where the response would have lain outside his functional potential. He could express the meanings 'yes' and 'no' in the senses of 'yes I want that', 'no I don't want that' (instrumental), or 'yes do that', 'no don't do that' (regulatory). But he had no general polarity (positive/negative) system; nor could he respond to any question seeking information, such as 'did you see a car?' or 'what did you see?'.

personal interaction; at the same time, it exemplifies the general principle whereby people adopt roles, assign them, and accept or reject those that are assigned to them.

The mysteries of dialogue were unravelled by Nigel in the two-week period at the opening of NL 7 (18–18½ months). At the end of this time he could:

1. respond to a WH- question (provided the answer was already known to the questioner), e.g. 'What are you eating?' Nigel: *banana.*

2. respond to a command, e.g. 'Take the toothpaste to Daddy and go and get your bib.' Nigel does so, saying: *daddy . . . noddy . . . train,* i.e. 'Daddy, (give) noddy (toothpaste to him, and go and get your bib with the) train (on it)'.

3. respond to a statement, e.g. 'You went on a train yesterday'. Nigel signals attention, by repeating, and continues the conversation: *train . . . byebye,* i.e. 'yes, I went on a train, and then (when I got off) the train went away'.

4. respond to a response, e.g. Nigel: *gravel.* Response: 'Yes, you had some gravel in your hand'. Nigel: *ooh,* i.e. 'it hurt me'.

5. initiate dialogue, e.g. Nigel: *what's that?* Response: 'That's butter.' Nigel repeats: *butter.*

The question 'what's that?' is, however, his only option for initiating dialogue at this stage. Apart from this, it is outside his functional potential to demand a linguistic response: he cannot yet assign specific communication roles. But he has gone some way in being able to accept those that are assigned to him.[1] As long as the child's responses are limited to exchanges such as:

('Nigel!') Nigel: [ə̀] 'yes I'm here'

('Do you want some cheese?') Nigel: [nò] 'no I don't want it'

('Shall I put the lorry in the box for you?') Nigel: [à] 'yes do' he is simply using language in its original extralinguistic functions; this is not yet true dialogue. The ability to respond to a WH-question, however, is a significant innovation; the child has mastered the principle of the purely communicative functions of language, and is beginning to take on roles that are defined by

---

[1] Nigel cannot at this stage respond explicitly to a yes/no question. But he sometimes does so by implication, e.g. 'Are you going shopping?' Nigel: *bread . . . egg* i.e. 'I'm going to buy bread and eggs'.

language itself. This is the first step towards the 'informative' use of language, which is late in appearing precisely because it is language in a function that is solely defined by language—a complex and difficult notion.

Once the child can engage in dialogue, new possibilities arise in relation to the functions he has already mastered: the elaboration of existing options, persistence and change in functional 'tactics' and so on. Dialogue also plays an essential part in the development of the generalized mathetic function, not only making it possible for the child to ask for new names but also allowing for systematic exploration of the environment and extended patterns of verbal recall. But no less important than this is the role of dialogue in anticipating and leading into Phase III, the mastery of the adult system. Through its embodiment of linguistic role-playing, dialogue opens the way to the options of mood (declarative, interrogative etc.), and thus to the entire interpersonal component in the language system. This is the component whereby the speaker intrudes or, as it were, builds himself into the linguistic structure, expressing his relations with other participants, his attitudes and judgements, his commitments, desires and the like (Halliday 1972). Thus in the course of Phase II, with the help of an increasing amount of imitative, role-playing speech—and also of sheer argument, which plays an essential part—the child learns to participate linguistically, and to intrude his own angle, his individuality and his personal involvement into the linguistic structure. In this way language becomes for him an effective channel of social learning, a means of participating in and receiving the culture. Meanings are expressed as verbal interaction in social contexts; this is the essential condition for the transmission of culture, and makes it possible for certain types of context to play a critical part in the socialization process (Bernstein 1971a).

Phase II is thus characterized by two major advances towards the adult linguistic system. On the one hand, the child adds a grammar, a level of linguistic form (syntax and vocabulary) intermediate between content and expression, so developing the basic tri-stratal organization of the adult language. The grammar is a system of potential, a network of options that is capable of 'receiving' from the content level and 'transmitting' to the expression;[1]

[1] Or the other way round, in the reception of speech. Our concern here is with

in so doing it forms structure, accepting options from various functionally distinct content systems and interpreting these into integrated structure patterns. It is a nexus of systems and structures, as defined by Firth (1957). On the other hand, the child learns dialogue: he learns to adopt, accept and assign linguistic roles, and thus to measure linguistic success in linguistic terms. From now on, success consists no longer simply in obtaining the desired material object or piece of behaviour, but rather in playing one's part: in freely accepting the roles that one is assigned, and getting others to accept those that one has assigned to them.

Phase II can be said to end when the child has mastered the principles of grammar and of dialogue, and thus effectively completed the transition to the adult language system. (He is still, of course, only just beginning his mastery of the adult language.) But Phase II is transitional also in the functional sense, in that the child is moving from the original set of discrete developmental functions, where 'function' equals 'use', through an intermediate stage leading to the more abstract concept of 'function' that lies at the heart of the adult language. Naturally the two aspects of the transition, the functional and the systemic, are closely interconnected; they are the two sides of the developmental process. The development of the functions, however, is significant for interpreting the development of the system—in the sense that language evolves in the way it does because of what is has to do. In the final section, we will sketch out in tentative fashion the nature of the child's functional progression into the adult language.

Phase III: Into Language

Functions of the Adult System

Can we relate the 'function' of Phase I, where it refers to a set of simple, unintegrated *uses* of language, instrumental, regulatory and so on, to 'function' in the sense of the highly abstract,

productive language, and relatively little is yet known about the processes whereby the child develops his understanding of what is said to and around him. But it is likely that the crucial step here too is the development of this third, intermediate level in his own linguistic coding system.

integrated networks of relations that make up the adult language system?

The answer will depend on our interpretation of 'function' in the adult language. Functional theories of language have attempted as a rule, not so much to explain the nature of language in functional terms, as to explain types of language use; their points of departure have been, for example, ethnographic (Malinowski 1923), psychological (Bühler 1934), ethological (Morris 1967) or educational (Lewis 1947; Britton 1970). But although the categories and terminologies differ, all of these incorporate in some form or other a basic distinction between an ideational (representational, referential, cognitive, denotative) and an interpersonal (expressive-conative, orectic, evocative, connotative) function of language.

If we now adapt this functional perspective to a consideration of the nature of language itself, we find that the adult linguistic system is in fact founded on a functional plurality. In particular, it is structured around the two-way distinction of ideational and interpersonal. The grammar of an adult language is a tripartite network of options, deriving from these two basic functions together with a third, that of creating text—the textual or, we could equally well say, 'textural' function of language. This last is not treated in most functional theories because it is intrinsic to language; it is an enabling function, providing the conditions whereby the other functions can effectively be served. The textual function arises out of the very nature of language, and we need not therefore look for its independent origin in the developmental process. The question then becomes: how does the child progress from the functional pattern of his Phase I linguistic system to the ideational—interpersonal system which is at the foundation of the adult language?

This is the point at which Nigel provided an interesting and unexpected clue. Like all children (cf. Leopold 1939–49 III: 1–30) he had made systematic use of intonation from the start, all his expressions being characterized by particular pitch contours: typically, varieties of falling tone, though with some exceptions—all personal names, for example, were high level. Early in Phase II, Nigel introduced within one week (NL 7, $19\frac{1}{4}$–$19\frac{1}{2}$ months) a systematic opposition between rising and falling tone; this he maintained throughout the remainder of Phase II with complete consistency. Expressed in Phase I terms, the rising tone was used on all utterances that were instrumental or regulatory in function, the falling tone on all those that were personal or heuristic, while in the interactional function he used both tones but with a contrast between them. We can generalize this distinction by saying that Nigel used the rising tone for utterances demanding a response, and the falling tone for the others. The few exceptions were themselves systematic: for example, demands for music had, as expected, a rising tone unless they were accompanied by the music gesture, in which case the tone was falling, showing that the gesture was an alternative realization of the option 'request for music'—and that the falling tone is to be regarded as the unmarked term in the system. The important point to note here is that Nigel is *not* using intonation as it is used in adult English— since the contrasts in meaning that are expressed by intonation in English (Halliday 1967) are still outside his functional potential. He is adapting the elementary opposition between rising and falling, which he knows to be significant, to a functional system that is within his own limitations—and one which, as it happens, is perfectly transitional between Phase I and Phase III. This is the distinction that was referred to earlier, between the pragmatic function, or language as doing, Nigel's rising tone, and the mathetic function, or language as learning, Nigel's falling tone. The one aspect that lies outside this system is the imaginative or play function of language, which at this stage takes the form of chants and jingles with special intonation patterns of their own.

This distinction between two broad generalized types of language use, the mathetic and the pragmatic, that Nigel expresses by means of the contrast between falling and rising tone, turns out to be the one that leads directly in to the abstract functional distinction of ideational and interpersonal that lies at the heart of the adult linguistic system. In order to reach Phase III, the child has to develop two major zones of meaning potential, one ideational, concerned with the representation of experience, the other interpersonal, concerned with the communication process as a form and as a channel of social action. These are clearly marked out in the grammar of the adult language. It seems likely that the ideational component of meaning arises, in general, from the use of language to learn, while the interpersonal arises from the use of language to act. The fact that Nigel made the distinction between the mathetic and the pragmatic fully explicit by means of intonation was, of course, merely his own route through Phase II; it is not to be expected that this distinction will be expressed in the same way by all children, or even that it will necessarily be made explicit at all. But for Nigel this was a major step in his development of a grammatical system, as he progressed from the simple duality of content and expression that is characteristic of Phase I.

It is not to be thought that Phase II 'mathetic' is synonymous with ideational, or 'pragmatic' with interpersonal. Pragmatic and mathetic are generalized functional categories of the content, in the developmental system of the child, in which every utterance is, in principle, either one or the other. Ideational and interpersonal are abstract functional components of the grammar, in the developed, tristratal system of the adult; here every utterance is, in principle, both one and the other at the same time. What changes is the concept of 'function'; and from this point of view, Phase II is the developmental process whereby 'function' becomes distinct from 'use'. In other words, the notion 'function of language' splits into two distinct notions, that of 'use of language' and that of 'component of the linguistic system'. We shall try to summarize this process, together with other aspects of the entry into Phase III, in the final section that follows (Figure 2).

Summary of Functional Development

1. The origins of language development can be interpreted as the learning of a set of functions, each with its associated 'meaning potential'. The system is a functional one, in which function is identical with use: each utterance has one function only, and the meanings are such as 'give me that', 'I'm interested', 'let's be together'. The initial functions are instrumental, regulatory, interactional and personal; these are then followed by the heuristic and the imaginative. Each item in the language is a simple content-expression pair; there is no level of linguistic 'form' (no grammar).

2. At a certain stage, the child begins to use language in a 'mathetic' function, for the purpose of learning. This arises as a generalization from the personal and the heuristic: language in the identification of the self and, as a corollary, in the exploration of

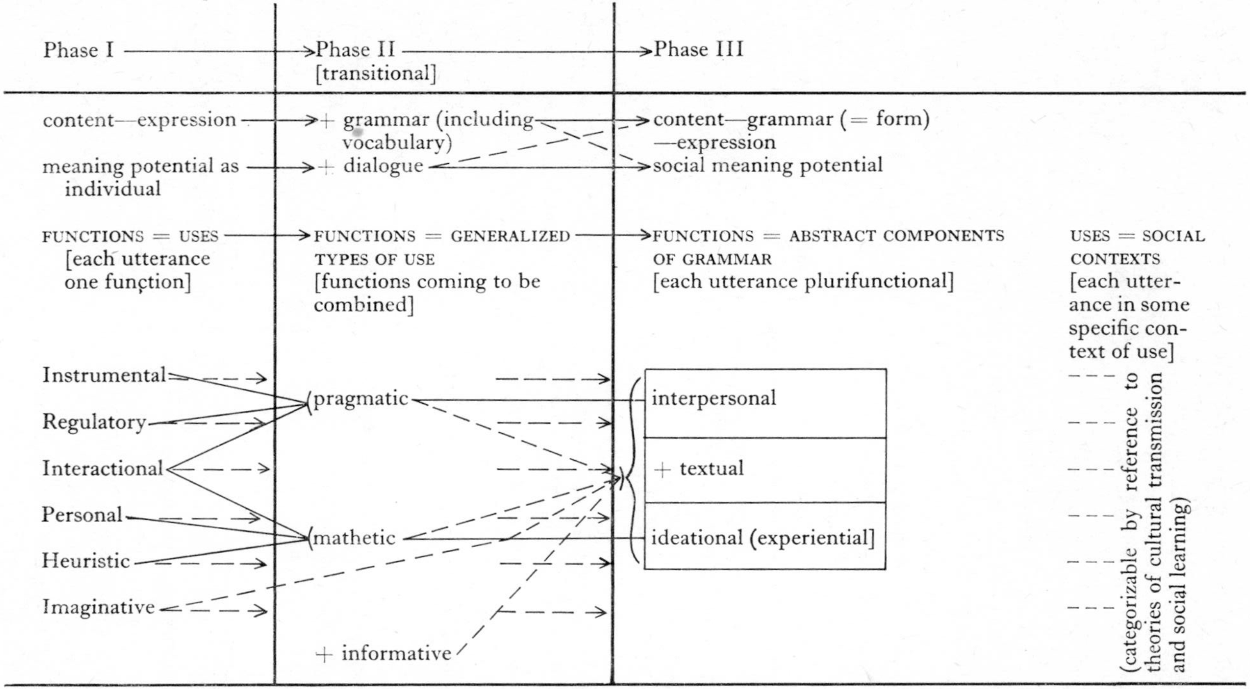

Phase I ─────────→Phase II ─────→Phase III
[transitional]

content─expression   content─grammar (= form)
                                  ─expression
meaning potential as   + grammar (including   social meaning potential
individual   vocabulary)
                          + dialogue

FUNCTIONS = USES   FUNCTIONS = GENERALIZED   FUNCTIONS = ABSTRACT COMPONENTS   USES = SOCIAL
[each utterance   TYPES OF USE   OF GRAMMAR   CONTEXTS
one function]   [functions coming to be   [each utterance plurifunctional] [each utter-
                          combined]   ance in some
                                                                                       specific con-
                                                                                       text of use]

                                                        interpersonal   (categorizable by reference to
                          pragmatic   theories of cultural transmission
                                                        + textual   and social learning)
Instrumental
Regulatory   ideational (experiential)
Interactional
                          mathetic
Personal
Heuristic
Imaginative

                          + informative

Figure 2

the non-self. This function is realized through verbal observation and recall (and, later, prediction). It generates a range of new meanings for which the child needs resources of vocabulary (e.g. names of objects and processes) and of structure (e.g. class and property, process and participant).

3. Simultaneously there appears to take place a generalization of the remaining functions under a 'pragmatic' rubric, which includes the use of language both to satisfy one's own needs and to control and interact with others (subsuming what is sometimes called 'manipulative' language). This also generates new meanings, for which other structures are required (e.g. request plus object of desire), and also other lexical items. With Nigel, however, only a minority of words was first learnt in this function, perhaps because often the specific meaning is recoverable from the situation (e.g. 'I want *that*').

4. The grouping into mathetic and pragmatic functions appeared, with Nigel, as the dominant characteristic of Phase II, the transitional phase. The distinction is that between language as learning and language as doing; between *separating* the self from the environment, thus identifying the one and interpreting the other, and *interacting* with the environment so as to intrude on the things and people in it, manipulating them and expressing attitudes towards them. With Nigel, nearly all words and structures were first used to express meanings in either one or the other of these two functions but not in both; after an interval, the resources that had been mastered in the one function were then transferred to the other. But, at the same time, all utterances were becoming plurifunctional; see 10 below.

5. In its inception, the mathetic–pragmatic distinction corresponds to one of 'response required' (pragmatic) versus 'response not required' (mathetic). This probably accounts for the remarkably explicit form given to this distinction by Nigel, who used rising tone to express the pragmatic meaning and falling tone for the mathetic. The question whether the mathetic–pragmatic distinction represents a general Phase II strategy must be left open at this stage; the use of intonation to express the distinction is, of course, Nigel's own idea.

6. As far as the linguistic system is concerned, Phase II consists in learning grammar; that is, in introducing into the system a

level of linguistic form, interposed between content and expression and made up of sets of options realized as structure and vocabulary. The need for a grammar arises out of the pragmatic and the mathetic functions; the latter, which is probably of greater significance for cognitive development, seems to provide the main impetus, at least for the learning of vocabulary. The introduction of grammatical structure makes it possible, however, to combine both functions in one utterance.

7. At the same time as learning grammar, the child also learns dialogue. This is the other major step characterizing Phase II. Here the main impetus probably comes from the pragmatic functions, with their emphasis on involvement. With dialogue, the child acquires a potential for adopting and assigning linguistic roles, which in turn calls for further resources in the grammar (e.g. a set of options in mood—declarative, interrogative and so on—and the structures which are used to realize them).[1]

8. Functionally speaking, the grammar of the adult language comprises the two major components (i) ideational, embodying the speaker's experience and interpretation of the world that is around him and inside him, and (ii) interpersonal, embodying his own involvement in the speech situation—his roles, attitudes, wishes, judgements and the like. To express this another way, the linguistic system has evolved so as to serve, for the speaker, on the one hand, the 'observer' function and on the other hand the 'intruder' function. These two 'meta-functions', together with a

---

[1] It is the system of mood that is eventually going to determine the patterns of rising and falling tone. How does Nigel adapt this to his own interpretation of rise and fall? At this stage, he has no system of mood other than that which is expressed by his own use of the distinction of rise and fall, i.e. the pragmatic/mathetic system; the demand for a new name, [ǽdȳdà] 'what's that?' cannot really be regarded as an interrogative—it is true that it always has a falling tone but this is *not* because it is a wh- question (he has no wh- question at this stage), but because it has a mathetic function. When he does learn the wh-question form *where* + personal name, this at first has either tone, with (it seems) a difference in meaning between the two; but subsequently this and all other wh- questions take on the rising tone, presumably on the grounds that an answer is a form of response (even though a purely linguistic one), and that demanding an answer is therefore a type of pragmatic function. Later still he learns the yes/no interrogative form; but this is not used for asking questions at all—it is used solely as the realization of the informative function, to communicate experience to be shared by the hearer, e.g. *did you fall down* 'I want you to know that I fell down—you didn't see the event', contrasting with *you fell down* 'I fell down—as you saw'.

third, the 'textual' function, are incorporated in the system of the adult language as distinct sets of options, each having strong internal but weak external constraints (i.e. a choice within one function affects other choices within the same function but not, in general, those outside it). Each set of options is realized through distinct structures which are mapped on to one another in the production of utterances.

9. It follows that, in the Phase III (the adult system), 'function' is no longer synonymous with 'use'. The adult has indefinitely many uses of language; but the typical utterance of the adult language, whatever its use, has both an ideational and an interpersonal component of meaning. For example, every main clause embodies selections—and therefore is structured—simultaneously in transitivity (ideational) and in mood (interpersonal).

10. It appears, then, that the 'meta-functions' of the Phase III grammatical system arise, indirectly but unmistakably, out of the primary uses of language that the child develops in Phase I. On the evidence of Nigel, the transition takes place by a process of generalization from these primary functions, which yields the two broad function types of pragmatic and mathetic. The pragmatic is oriented towards meanings such as 'I want', 'will you?', 'may I?', 'let's'; so it provides the context for the interpersonal systems of the grammar, typically those of mood, modality, person, attitude and the like. The mathetic is oriented towards experiential meanings, and so provides the context for ideational systems such as those of transitivity (the grammar of processes), time and place, qualifying and quantifying, and so on.

11. Hence the child's Phase I functional system, which is a system of the *content* in a 'content, expression' language, evolves along the familiar lines of generalization followed by abstraction, into the Phase III (adult) functional system, which is a system of the *form* in a 'content, form, expression' language. The concept of function has itself evolved in the process (cf. Figure 2). In Hjelmslevian terms, the functional basis of language has shifted from the 'content substance' (in a system having no level of form) into the 'content form'. The child, at Phase II, makes the crucial discovery that, with language, he can both observe and interact with the environment at the same time; this is the significance of Nigel's 'that's cake—and I want some!'. By the time he enters Pahse III

the child has a great many 'uses' of language; but all of them are actualized through the medium of the ideational and the inter-personal 'functions'; in other words, through his two-fold meaning potential as observer and as intruder.

12. Meanwhile therefore the original Phase I functions have not just disappeared. It is these that have become the uses of language —or rather, perhaps, they have become the generalized contexts of language use. In addition to those that seem to have been the key to the transition process, two others had been postulated, the imaginative and the informative. The imaginative, or play, func-tion of language is present already in Phase I; by the end of Phase II, the child is playing not only with sounds but with forms and meanings as well, reciting, distorting and inventing rhymes, rou-tines and stories. Eventually—but not until well into Phase II—he adds the informative function, the use of language to communicate experience to someone who did not share it with him; this is a highly complex function, since it is one that is solely defined by language itself.[1] At the same time, language still serves, for the child, the uncomplicated functions for which he first learnt it. Only, their scope is now immeasurably enlarged, in breadth and in depth: in other words, in the meaning potential that is asso-ciated with each.

Conclusion

By the end of Phase II, the child has entered the adult language. He has built up a system that is multistratal (content, form, expression) and multifunctional (ideational, interpersonal, text-ual). From this point on, he is adding to what he already has. He has learnt *how* to mean; his language development now consists in extending the range of his meaning potential to broader cultural horizons.

In order to follow this process further, we should have to go

---

[1] The imaginative and informative functions call for the narrative mode (within the ideational component) as distinct from simple observation and recall. This in turn requires discourse, i.e. text which is structured so as to be relevant not only to the situation but also to the verbal context, to what is said before and after. What we referred to as the 'textual' component in the linguistic system can be seen developing, with Nigel, in response to the needs of dialogue and of narrative.

outside the linguistic system and into the culture. The child's uses of language are interpretable as generalized situation types; the meanings that he can express are referable to specific social contexts, and at least in some instances may be approached through a context-specific semantic analysis such as is exemplified in Turner (1973).

Bernstein (1971a, b) has shown that certain types of social context are critical to the process of cultural transmission; the language of these contexts plays a crucial part in the child's socialization. Now, as we have seen, all language behaviour, including that which characterizes these critical contexts, is mediated through the basic functions of language, the observer function and the intruder function; and the meanings that are expressed are linked, in this way, to what Malinowski (1923) called the 'context of situation'. But because these functions are not simply aspects of the use of language, but are part of—indeed, are the heart of—the linguistic system, the specific meanings expressed are at the same time instances of general semantic categories, and hence are interpreted in the 'context of culture' (to use another of Malinowski's concepts).

What is the significance of this for the child? The significance is that, because of the functional basis of language, the particular, concrete meanings that are expressed in typical everyday situations become, for him, the primary source for building up the context of culture. By the time he reaches Phase III, each instance of 'I want' or 'may I?' or 'let me take part' or 'what's going on?' is encoded in words and structures which serve in some measure to categorize the social order and the child's own part in it. So it happens that the child's own early uses of language impose certain requirements on the nature of the linguistic system, determining, the functional basis on which it is organized; with the result that, as these early uses evolve into generalized social contexts of language use, the linguistic system is able to act through them as the primary means for the transmission of the culture to the child. In this way language comes to occupy the central role in the processes of social learning.

References

Bellugi, Ursula and Brown, Roger (eds.) (1964) *The Acquisition of Language*. Monographs of the Society for Research in Child Development, 29.1.

Bernstein, Basil (1969, 1970) 'A sociolinguistic approach to socialization: with some reference to educability'. Reprinted in Bernstein, 1971c. pp. 143–69.

— (1971a) 'Social class, language and socialization'. In A. S. Abramson (ed.) *Current Trends in Linguistics XII*, The Hague: Mouton. Reprinted in Bernstein 1971c, pp. 170–89.

— (1971b) 'A critique of the concept of Compensatory Education'. In Bernstein 1971c, pp. 190–201.

— (ed.) (1971c) *Class, Codes and Control, Volume I: Theoretical studies towards a sociology of language*, London: Routledge & Kegan Paul.

— (ed.) (1973) *Class, Codes and Control, Volume II: Applied studies towards a sociology of language*, London: Routledge & Kegan Paul.

Bloom, Lois (1970) *Language Development — form and function in emerging grammars*, Cambridge, Mass.: M.I.T. Press.

Braine, Martin D. S. (1971) 'The acquisition of language in infant and child'. In C. E. Reed (ed.) 1971, pp. 7–95.

Britton, James N. (1970) *Language and Learning*, London: Allen Lane Press.

Brown, Roger (1974) *A First Language*, London: Allen & Unwin.

Brown,Roger and Bellugi, Ursula (1964) 'Three processes in the child's acquisition of syntax'. In Lenneberg (ed.) 1964, pp. 131–61

Bühler, Karl (1934) *Sprachtheorie: die Darstellungsfunktion der Sprache*, Jena: Fischer.

Doughty, Peter, Pearce, John and Thornton, Geoffrey (1971) *Language in Use*, London: Edward Arnold (Schools Council Programme in Linguistics and English Teaching).

— (1972) *Exploring Language*, London: Edward Arnold (Schools Council Programme in Linguistics and English Teaching).

Ervin, Susan M. and Miller, Wick R. (1963) 'Language development'. In *Child Psychology*, Chicago: the National Society for the Study of Education (Sixty-second Year-book), pp. 108–43.

Fillmore, Charles J. (1968) 'The case for case'. In Emmon Bach and Robert T. Harms (eds.) *Universals in Linguistic Theory*, New York: Holt, Rinehart, Winston, pp. 1–88

Firth, J. R. (1950) Personality and language in society. *The Sociological Review*, 42. Reprinted in J. R. Firth, *Papers in Linguistics 1934–1951*, London: Oxford University Press, 1957.

— (1957) 'A synopsis of linguistic theory'. In *Studies in Linguistic Analysis* (Special Volume of the Philological Society), Oxford: Blackwell. Reprinted in F. R. Palmer, *Selected Papers of J. R.*

Firth 1951–1959, London: Longman (Longmans' Linguistics Library), 1968.

Gruber, J. S. (1967) 'Topicalization in child language' *Foundations of Language*, **3**, 37–65.

Halliday, M. A. K. (1967) *Intonation and Grammar in British English*, The Hague: Mouton (Janua Linguarum Series Practica 48).

— (1969) 'Relevant models of language' *Educational Review*, **22**, 26–37.

— (1970) 'Language structure and language function'. In John Lyons (ed.), *New Horizons in Linguistics*, Harmondsworth: Penguin Books.

— (1973) *Explorations in the Functions of Language*, London: Edward Arnold.

Ingram, David (1971) 'Transitivity in child language' *Language*, **47**. 888–910.

Lamb, Sydney M. (1970) 'Linguistic and cognitive networks'. In Paul Garvin (ed.) *Cognition: a mutiple view*, New York: Spartan Books.

Lenneberg, Eric (1964) 'A biological perspective of language'. In Lenneberg (ed.) 1964, pp. 65–88.

— (ed.) (1964) *New Directions in the Study of Language*, Cambridge, Mass.: M.I.T. Press.

— (1966) 'The natural history of language'. In Smith and Miller (eds.) 1966, pp. 219–52.

— (1967) *Biological Foundations of Language*, New York: Wiley.

Leopold, Werner F. (1939–49) *Speech Development of a Bilingual Child: a linguist's record*, Volumes I–IV. Evanston and Chicago: Northwestern University.

Lewis, M. M. (1947) *Language in Society*, London: Nelson.

Mackay, David, Thompson, Brian and Schaub, Pamela (1970) *Breakthrough to Literacy: Teacher's Manual*. London: Longman (Schools Council Programme in Linguistics and English Teaching).

Malinowski, Bronislaw (1923) 'The problem of meaning in primitive languages'. Supplement I to C. K. Ogden and I. E. Richards, *The Meaning of Meaning*, London: Routledge & Kegan Paul (International Library of Psychology, Philosophy & Scientific Method).

— (1935) *Coral Gardens and their Magic*, Volume II. London: Allen & Unwin; New York, American Book Co.

Morris, Desmond (1967) *The Naked Ape*, London: Cape.

Osser, Harry (1970) 'Three approaches to the acquisition of language'. In Frederick Williams (ed.) *Language and Poverty: perspectives on a theme*, Chicago: Markham Publishing Co.

Reed, Carroll E. (ed.) (1971) *The Learning of Language*, New York: Appleton-Century-Crofts.

Reich, Peter A. (1970) 'Relational networks' *Canadian Journal of Linguistics*, **15**, 95–110.

Schlesinger, I. M. (1971) 'Production of utterances and language acquisition'. In Dan. I. Slobin (ed.) *The Ontogenesis of Grammar: some facts and several theories*, New York: Academic Press.

Smith, Franklyn L. and Miller, George A. (eds.) (1966) *The Genesis of Language—a psycholinguistic approach*, Cambridge, Mass.: M.I.T. Press.

Turner, Geoffrey J. (1973) 'Social class and children's language of control at age five and age seven'. In Bernstein (ed.) 1973.

16

ERIC H. LENNEBERG

Understanding Language without Ability to Speak: A Case Report

In Reading 15 Halliday stresses the importance of the active participation by the child in his environment especially as it concerns language. In this reading Lenneberg presents a case report on an eight-year-old boy who, although unable to speak, was able to understand language. An experiment was devised whereby the child was asked to follow certain tape-recorded instructions. These the child carried out. Lenneberg concludes that the active use of language is not essential for the development of understanding it. How do the conclusions of Halliday and Lenneberg compare? They seem at first sight to be fairly incompatible. I would only say that the word 'understanding' is used by them in different ways. Lenneberg has only measured an extremely small area of meaning—explicit meaning in which all the elements necessary for understanding are clearly present in the language. He is not concerned with the ambiguities and depths of connotative and contextual meaning which a speaking boy of eight would be able to use and understand. It would be interesting to read a report on the boy now that he is a man.

Infants' random babbling is generally considered to play a major —by some, an essential—role in the acquisition and development of language. In fact, many psychologists believe that the main reason for the failure of mammals other than man to learn to speak or even to bring their vocalizations under new and varied stimulus control is due to their scanty random vocalizations. Recently it was discovered that dolphins make a great variety of vocal tract produced noises and, to be sure, the hope was soon expressed that these animals may with proper training learn to converse

Eric H. Lenneberg: Extract from 'Understanding language without ability to speak: A case report' *Journal of Abnormal and Social Psychology*, 65, 1962, pp. 419–25. © American Psychological Association, 1962.

with their trainers in English. Incidentally, this hope was shared by Dr. Doolittle, Hugh Lofting's charming literary creation.

Our understanding of human behaviour is often greatly enlightened by careful investigations of clinical aberrations and in many instances disease or congenital abnormalities provide conditions that may replace the crucial experiments on children that our superego forbids us to plan and perform. No psychological theory on verbal behaviour can be successful unless it takes into consideration and accounts for the pathological variations that may be observed clinically. In the present paper I will present the case of a child who is typical of a large group of children with deficits in their motor execution of language skills but who can learn to understand language even in the total absence of articulation. This and similar clinical material forces us to review our theoretical formulations concerning the role of babbling and echoic responses in the acquisition of language and to review once more the relationship between understanding and speaking a language.

Case Report

This is an 8-year-old boy who has a congenital disability for the acquisition of motor speech skills (anarthria) which, however, has not impaired his ability to learn to understand language.

Family history
The family history is non-contributory. The subject is the second of three children: both siblings are intelligent and well. The mother is now divorced and lives with the subject's grandmother. A home visit revealed a warm and socially adequate climate.

Physical and laboratory examinations
When first seen by the author the child had been brought to a neurological service with a chief complaint of failure to develop speech. He was then 3 years and 9 months, of markedly small stature but with a head circumference normal for his chronological age. Anomalies of the eyes had been corrected surgically. He had single palmar creases in both hands but no other mongoloid stigmata. The only other abnormal finding on examination was an enlarged heart; no murmurs were heard. His oral cavity was of normal configuration and he had no difficulties in chewing,

swallowing, sucking, blowing, or licking. Laryngoscopy was negative. On radiological evidence his bone age was 2 : 8 according to Todd's standards. A skull series was normal. All laboratory tests were negative, and there were no signs of hypothyroidism or inborn errors of metabolism. An electroencephalogram was read as non-diagnostic though it was noted that activity in the right temporal area was less rhythmic than in the left.

Psychological tests
Tests were performed at 4, 5, and 8 years. Merrill-Palmer, WISC, Bender Visual Motor Gestalt, and Leiter International Performance tests were used, the examinations being administered by three different psychologists and at two different clinics. The subject always related easily to the examiner and gave no signs of emotional disturbance or psychiatric disease. IQ's were consistently in the 72–83 range but might have been consistently biased by the subject's inability to express himself verbally. He always gives an alert impression, reacts quickly to verbal instructions, and has always shown an adequate concentration span with little signs of distractability or hyperactivity. At his most recent test no evidence of 'organic' deficits was obtained although some 'immaturity in his drawings' was noted. He is slightly retarded in his mental development but the deficit is definitely in the educable range and cannot explain his inability to speak.

Voice and speech
The child's crying and laughter have always sounded normal. He is also able to make other noises, for instance short cough-like grunts accompanying his pantomimed communications. While playing alone he will readily make noises that sound somewhat like Swiss yodelling (though he has never had any experience with these sounds!) and which do not resemble any kind of vocalization heard among normal American children. (Samples of these sounds are reproduced in a documentary film.) When the author first saw him he appeared to have some difficulty in bringing his voicing mechanism under voluntary control. For instance, he was unable to make the pointer of the VU meter in an Ampex tape recorder jump by emitting grunts into a microphone even though he was fully aware of the logical connection between sound and

deflection of the pointer and was fascinated by it. He would hold on to the microphone and move his head and lips towards it as if to prompt himself for the action; after a few futile attempts and with signs of rising frustration he would in desperation end up gesturing to the examiner's mouth inviting him to make the needle jump, or else simply resort to clapping his hands and accomplish his end this way. In recent years he seems to have learned to control his vocal apparatus to a greater extent. He has had speech training for a considerable length of time and can now repeat a few words after the speech therapist or his mother but the words are still barely intelligible and are never produced without the support from the speech correctionist or the mother (samples are reproduced in the film).

Some of the spontaneous sounds emitted by the patient at 4 years were analysed spectrographically. The spectrograms are grossly abnormal for a child of this age and resemble those of a neonate in a number of respects, such as the unsteadiness in the formant pattern, the intermittent bursts of non-harmonic overtones, and the almost random change in resonance distribution over the spectrum (Lenneberg 1961). The spectrograms may be interpreted either as grossly immature or as evidence of a fixed central nervous system abnormality implicating the basic mechanisms for speech synergism.

From the patient's first visit to the clinic it has been obvious that he had a normal and adequate understanding of spoken language. He has been seen more than 20 times since then and the finding of full comprehension has been confirmed by neurologists, psychologists, speech therapists, medical residents, and other hospital personnel. A number of tape recordings have been made of interviews including a visit to the patient's home. Most of the examinations were done without the presence of his mother. At one time a short series of instructions were tape-recorded and transmitted to the patient through earphones. He followed the instructions without being able to see the examiner.

Interpretation
It is tempting to explain the patient's responses to verbal instructions by extralinguistic means. Perhaps he is merely responding to visual cues given by the examiner and has, in fact, not

learned to understand English! Could children with his type of abnormality develop perceptual skills such as were observed in von Osten's famous horse, der kluge Hans, who supposedly could stamp his hoof in response to questions posed to him in German, but who, upon close examination by the psychologist Pfungst, had merely learned to observe the questioner, picking up minute motor cues related to posture and respiratory patterns which signalled to him whether to stop or to continue to stamp his hoof? There is direct evidence against this hypothesis. The child described can react to tape-recorded instructions in the absence of any observer. Further, his responses do not merely consist of nodding but also of doing things which could under no circumstance be conveyed by inadvertent motor cues. In the film which documents the case, it is clear that the child frequently follows commands without looking at the examiner. Out of the 45 responses only 3 times was there vacillation between correct and incorrect answers and the last answer in each case is correct. On the other hand, there was no hesitation in the 3 instances when incorrect answers were given. There is no reason to assume that this child has superhuman ability to respond to visual cues instead of assuming that he has learned what every other child of his age has learned, namely to understand English. Table 1 summarizes the child's performance. It is the result of a panel of three judges who scrutinized the film, viewing each command and its execution individually and with as many repetitions as was necessary in

TABLE 1

Number of subject's correct, indecisive, and incorrect responses.

	Classification of subject's response						
	Correct		Indecisive		Incorrect		
Type of reponse required	No cue possible	Cue possible or certain	No cue possible	Cue possible or certain	No cue possible	Cue possible or certain	Total
Action	19	5	0	0	2	2	28
Yes-no nodding	2	11	0	3	0	1	17
Total	21	16	0	3	2	3	45

order to determine by unanimous agreement whether there was any likelihood of extralinguistic cuing.

Finally, we must consider the possibility that this patient had no understanding of syntactic connections but merely responded to key words in the commands and questions. This possibility is extremely unlikely in the face of his understanding of such sentences as 'Take the block and put it on the bottle.' 'Is it time to eat breakfast now?' 'Was the black cat fed by the nice lady?'

Diagnosis
The hospital's clinical diagnosis is multiple congenital anomalies, which, however, is a wastebasket classification and of no heuristic value. Certainly it does not explain the absence of motor speech. The two most common causes for this deficit, peripheral deafness and severe emotional disturbance, may be readily ruled out on clinical evidence. Nor may we assume that the patient's mental retardation is a sufficient cause since the degree of deficiency revealed in his psychological tests is not ordinarily accompanied by any marked speech deficit. Patients with an IQ as low as 25 to 35 have a wide repertoire of sounds and frequently use a vocabulary of 50 or more words. Some authorities would classify this patient as having congenital or developmental motor aphasia. I am not in favour of such a classification on terminological grounds. Aphasia has come to designate loss of speech in persons who had been fluent before the onset of disease or trauma. The condition occurs in children (Guttmann 1942) as well as in adults and presents a symptomatology that is distinct from any developmental condition. However, the most important reason for rejecting the term aphasia for cases such as described here is that aphasia has traditionally been applied to cortical and subcortical lesions. The present case, on the other hand, gives every indication of an abnormality on a lower level, probably mesencephalic, because of the association with the ocular abnormalities and the discoordination as seen in the spectrograms. The term congenital anarthria better characterizes the condition. Psychological tests make cortical or subcortical damage also unlikely and his excellent understanding of language supports this view.

Discussion

Failure to learn to understand despite babbling and imitative facility
The case reported makes it clear that hearing oneself babble is not a necessary factor in the acquisition of understanding; apparently, hearing oneself babble is also not a sufficient factor. In a language acquisition study on home-raised mongoloid children (research in progress) I have gathered empirical evidence that these children are excellent imitators who babble abundantly and freely. In all cases they have a speaking command of at least single word utterances; yet their understanding of complex commands and questions (such as used in the demonstration film) is frequently defective (usually if their IQ is about 50 or below). Here the vocal play is present and motivation is provided through interaction with parents, but it does not enable these children to overcome their inborn cerebral deficit.

Relationship between speaking and understanding
We must now pose the problem: if the secondary reinforcement provided by hearing oneself babble is neither necessary nor sufficient for an acquisition of understanding of language, could learning to speak be an entirely independent task, justifying a theory that applies to it alone, but not to the learning of understanding? We will see that the answer to this question is a qualified *no*.

The case presented here—by no means unique—is particularly dramatic because of the vast discrepancy between understanding and speaking; a similar phenomenon in more attenuated form is extremely common. Understanding normally precedes speaking by several weeks or even months. The discrepancy is regularly increased in literally all types of developmental speech disorders and is best illustrated in a condition known in the profession as Delayed Speech. Pertinent are also those children who have structural deformities in the oral cavity or pharynx and who produce unintelligible speech for years—sometimes throughout life—without the slightest impairment of understanding. Congenitally deaf children also learn to comprehend language in the absence of vocal skills. Understanding in all of these circumstances is definitely prior to and in that sense independent from speaking.

However, there is no clear evidence that speaking is ever present in the absence of understanding. Speaking is to be understood here as the production of utterances that are bona fide examples of a natural language (such as English) with presumptive evidence of autonomous composition of grammatically acceptable sentences. An empirical test of speaking without understanding might be as follows: a child acquires nothing but words that have no meaning to him (by blind imitation) and learns the formal principles governing the generation of sentences. He will now utter sentences out of context and irrelevant to situations by established common-sense standards; he would also have to be demonstrably incapable ever to respond appropriately to commands formulated in natural language. My assertion is that such a condition has never been described as a congenital, developmental problem (Mark 1962). (Adventitious conditions such as sensory aphasia in the adult are problems in 'partial loss', not 'partial acquisition' of language and are therefore not relevant to this discussion. Nor could case reports of psychotic children be adduced reliably because even if their utterances are primarily echolalic, there are usually indications that the child does understand, at least at times, what is said to him. In fact, this is usually the basis of the therapy given them.) It is thus likely that the vocal production of language is dependent upon the understanding of language but not vice versa. Though there is no conclusive proof of this hypothesis, there are theoretical considerations that make this likely. In order to make this latter point clear, a few general remarks on the nature of grammar are indispensable. My discussion will lean heavily on Chomsky's (1957) and Chomsky and Miller's (1962) work.

Wherever the word 'imitation' is used in connection with language-learning it is assumed that subjects learn more than passive mirroring of sentences heard. The novel creation of sentences is a universally accepted fact. At first it was thought that this phenomenon could be accounted for by postulating that grammar simply reflected transitional probabilities between words. In this model the learning of grammar was thought to be like the learning of probabilities. Such learning has been demonstrated to occur for a great many mammals. If this model were acceptable, a child's exposure to certain contingencies should enable him to learn grammar in the absence of 'understanding' the relationship between words. Chomsky has offered formal proof against left-to-right probabilistic models, and has shown how a different model can overcome some of the basic difficulties encountered by Markovian grammars. We shall not concern ourselves here with the mathematical detail but shall merely demonstrate by a few examples (most of them suggested by Chomsky) that grammar simply cannot be explained in terms of learned sequential contingencies, and that therefore the understanding and producing of sentences cannot be equated with probability learning.

Consider the following two strings of words,

a colourless green ideas sleep furiously

b furiously sleep ideas green colourless.

In terms of transitional probabilities they are indistinguishable. Both sentences can only occur in a zero order of approximation to English. However, we can discriminate between them from the point of view of grammaticality. Sentence *a* strikes us as a possible sentence, whereas *b* does not. The difference between *a* and *b* could not possibly be due to association by contiguity for obvious reasons (Miller, Galanter, and Pribram 1960). Nor is the sequence of form class markers -*less*, -*s*, -*ly* the hallmark of grammaticalness as shown by the sentence,

c friendly young dogs seem harmless

which is grammatical though it reverses the order of the markers.

In order to account for the difference in our perception of *a* and *b* we might try to see whether sequential contingencies do exist, but instead of on the level of words, on the level of parts of speech (actually proposed by Jenkins and Palermo 1961). If this were so the essence of the transitional probability model would be saved and the principle underlying the formation of sentences would still be simple enough to allow of the possibility of speaking without understanding. Unfortunately this model is no more successful in accounting for 'sentencehood' than any other Markovian device. If we compare the strings,

d occasionally call warfare useless

e useless warfare call occasionally

we find that now *d* is perceived as more grammatical than *e* though the order of parts of speech in *d* is that of *b* above which we rejected as less grammatical. This example shows that the traditional categorization in terms of parts of speech is certainly not successful in reinstating a Markovian model.[1]

Mowrer (1960) has proposed that simple contiguity of words is sufficient explanation for the complex meaning that is conveyed by a sentence. Osgood (1957) on the other hand believes that grammatical order can be set aside by motivational factors and that with an increase of motivation word order would correlate with order of importance of words. Doubt is cast on both views, however, by comparison of sentences such as,

f the fox chases the dog

g the dog chases the fox

which clearly make either position untenable. A child whose task it is to learn to produce sentences such as *f* and *g* in the appropriate physical environment must necessarily learn some principle of concatenation which goes *beyond* recognition of contiguity. It would be tempting to maintain that the principle to be learned is something like 'First noun phrase is the actor or subject in a sentence.' Yet, the patterning involved must be more complex and in a sense more abstract still, for even a preschool child would understand the sentence,

h the fox is chased by the dog

as belonging to *g* and not to *f*. To explain this phenomenon we would now have to postulate that in addition to the principle above, the child would also have to learn that the presence of the morphemes *is*, *-ed*, *by* signals a reversal of the original principle. But sentence

i the fox is interested by virtue of his nature in chasing the dog

eliminates this possibility because this sentence is understood as similar in meaning to *f* instead of *g* despite the presence of morphemes *is*, *-ed*, *by* occurring in essentially the same sequential order as in *h*. In other words, if we must learn to compose sentences that conform to English grammar, we can only learn to apply the structural principles of sentence formation by first

---

[1] Nor is there any hope that eventually more efficient categories might be discovered since Chomsky's (1957) criticism is levelled against all finite-state sentence-generating devices. Compare his argument concerning mirror-image languages, and Miller's (1960) argument.

learning to understand and to group sentences in accordance with similarity or differences in meaning. It is not possible to explain the grammatical phenomena demonstrated in the test sentences above by assuming that the entire sentence is in one way or another associated with the complex natural situation to which it refers. Sentences without any referential meaning such as,

j A v's C
k C v's A
l C is v'ed by A
m A is v'ed by C

can easily be grouped in terms of similarity and dissimilarity of meaning. Therefore, the word 'meaning' in this context refers to grammatical understanding and not to an association between a symbol and a physical stimulus.

Obviously, we do not yet have a satisfactory model that might explain how grammar is learned. All we can say is that a child learns to produce novel sentences after hearing a number of utterances which were produced by formal laws of generation in addition to a number of other determining factors: he must be able to abstract the formal laws through observation (or be equipped to accept sentences as an input and recognize invariant patterns of complex relationship) before he can apply them to the production of new sentences. It is particularly important to realize that what the child learns during acquisition of grammar is the peculiar formal relationship that obtains between a number of different grammatical patterns, i.e., the relationship between active-passive, declarative-interrogative-negative, and many other similar relationships called 'rules of transformation' (Chomsky 1957; Harris 1957). It is this latter ability—and only this—that enables any speaker of English to group the sentences *f* through *i* according to similarity in meaning. The psychological process involved here is more similar to the operation by which we know that

$$w \left(\sqrt{w} \times \sqrt{w} \right)$$

and

$$\frac{w^6}{w^4}$$

can both be represented by w^2 than to an operation by which we know that the symbol S_4 is next in line to be generated after a train of symbols, S_1, S_2, S_3, has been produced. This point is illustrated by Chomsky's examples of structural ambiguity. There are rules of transformations which convert sentences of the form

　　n one visits relatives

　　o relatives are visiting

into a phrase,

　　p visiting relatives.

Because of the two different transformational origins this phrase is ambiguous and, when used in a sentence, may render that entire sentence ambiguous:

　　q visiting relatives can be a nuisance.

The conclusion of this discussion is that 'knowing a language' may be, and ordinarily is, manifested by two distinct behavioural manifestations: understanding and speaking. Upon careful analysis however, both of these manifestations depend upon the application and use of a single set of grammatical rules; in the case of understanding, the rules are applied to the analysis, i.e., processing and organizing of input data; in the case of speaking, the same rules are applied to the organization of output data or responses. In the process of language-learning, the acquisition of grammatical rules must occur first in connection with analysing incoming sentences; then with producing outgoing sentences. The most important point here is, however, that knowing a natural language is dependent upon the acquisition of a single set of organizing principles and that this set of principles is merely reflected in understanding and speaking but is not identical with these skills.

Summary

A case was presented, typical of a larger category of patients, where an organic defect prevented the acquisition of the motor skill necessary for speaking a language, but evidence was presented for the acquisition of grammatical skills as required for a complete understanding of language. Theories on the acquisition of speech and language must account for both motor and grammatical skills. Present theories assert that babbling, hearing oneself vocalize, and imitation are the cornerstones of speech development.

These phenomena primarily relate to the development of the motor skills involved which, however, never develop in isolation, i.e., without simultaneous acquisition of grammatical skills. The case presented together with the language deficit in certain Mongoloids clearly shows that babbling, hearing oneself talk, and imitation are neither sufficient nor necessary factors in the acquisition of grammar, and since the motor skills alone are never shaped into 'speaking without grammar', i.e., parroting without understanding, it is concluded that the present theories are inadequate.

References

Chomsky, N. (1957) *Syntactic Structures*, The Hague: Mouton.
— and Miller, G. A. (1963) 'Introduction to the Formal Analysis of Natural Languages'. In R. D. Luce, R. R. Bush, and E. Galanter (eds.) *Handbook of Mathematical Psychology*, Volume II, New York and London: John Wiley, 269–321.
Guttmann, E. (1942) 'Aphasia in Children' *Brain*, LXV, 205–19.
Harris, Z. S. (1957) 'Co-occurrence and Transformation in Linguistic Structure' *Language*, XXXIII, 283–340.
Jenkins, J. J. and Palermo, D. S. (1961) 'Mediation Processes and the Acquisition of Linguistic Structure'. Paper read at SSRC conference in Cambridge, Mass., October 1961.
Lenneberg, E. H. (1961) 'Speech as a Motor Skill with Special Reference to Nonaphasic Disorders'. Paper read at SSRC conference in Cambridge, Mass., October 1961.
Mark, H. J. (1962) 'Elementary Thinking and the Classification of Behavior' *Science*, CXXXV, 75–87.
Miller, G. A. (1960) 'Plans for Speaking'. In G. A. Miller, E. Galanter, and K. H. Pribram (eds.) pp. 139–58.
—, Galanter, E., and Pribram, K. H. (eds.) (1960) *Plans and the Structure of Behavior*, New York: Holt, Rinehart, Winston.
Mowrer, O. H. (1960) *Learning Theory and the Symbolic Processes*, New York: John Wiley.
Osgood, C. E. (1957) 'Motivational Dynamics of Language Behavior'. In M. R. Jones (ed.) *Nebraska Symposium on Motivation: 1957*, Lincoln: University of Nebraska Press, pp. 348–424.

17 HEINZ WERNER and EDITH KAPLAN
The Contexts of Meaning

In this empirical study, Werner and Kaplan are concerned with how children aged 8½–13½ years acquire the meanings of nonsense words through the agency of verbal contexts. This research indicates some of the problems inherent in the child's mastery of the semantic system of his language; he has to learn particularly how to extend his cognitive formulations to include the new word and at the same time he has to establish a new relationship in the network of relationships amongst word meanings.

A. The Test

In the main, a child learns the meaning of a word in two ways. One way is direct and explicit, i.e., the adult names a thing or defines a word for the child. The other way is indirect and implicit, through experience with concrete and/or verbal contexts.

This study is concerned with the acquisition of word meanings through verbal contexts. The children participating in this investigation ranged from 8½ to 13½ years of age and were divided into five age groups with 25 children at each age level. The interquartile *IQ* range was from 101 to 111.

The test was as follows: The child's task was to find the meaning of an artificial word, which appeared in six different verbal contexts. In all, there were 12 sets of six sentences each. The 12 artificial words denoted either an object or an action. For example, the artificial word in the first set of six sentences was *corplum*, for which the correct translation was 'stick' or 'piece of wood'. The contexts for *corplum* were as follows:

1. A *corplum* may be used for support.
2. *Corplums* may be used to close off an open place.
3. A *corplum* may be long or short, thick or thin, strong or weak.

Heinz Werner and Edith Kaplan: Extract from 'Development of word meaning through verbal context: An experimental study' *Journal of Psychology*, **19**, 1950, pp. 251–7.

4. A wet *corplum* does not burn.
5. You can make a *corplum* smooth with sandpaper.
6. The painter used a *corplum* to mix his paints.

B. Procedure

The experimental procedure was as follows: After the child was made thoroughly familiar with the task, he was presented with a card on which Sentence 1 of Series I was printed. After the child responded to the first sentence, he was asked how and why the meaning he gave for the word fit into the sentence. He then was presented with the second sentence while the first context was still in view. After having given his interpretation of the word as it appeared in the second sentence (which may or may not have differed from his first response) the child was again asked how and why it fit and also whether it could be applied to the preceding sentence. This procedure was carried out until all six contexts had been presented to the child. The child's responses were carefully recorded.

C. Analysis and Results

Although correctness was not the major aspect of the study, it may be briefly mentioned that correctness of responses increased significantly from age level to age level.

Our main concern was with the ways children gave signification to the artificial words; we were especially interested in the development of the signification process. For the purpose of analysis, three judges derived 60 criteria from a preliminary inspection of the protocols. These criteria, pertaining to linguistic as well as semantic characteristics, were then employed by the three judges in the final analysis.

Studying the protocols one is impressed with the great variety of processes by which children acquired and generalized word meanings from verbal contexts. Many responses of the youngeı children indicate a lack in the differentiation between the meaning of the word and the given verbal context. Instead of conceiving the word as referring to a circumscribed meaning, many of the younger children regarded the artificial word as carrying the meaning of the whole or part of the context in which it appeared. We may call this type of conception a SENTENCE-CORE CONCEPT. For instance, one sentence, containing the artificial word, *bordick*, (faults) was the following: *people talk about the bordicks of others and don't like to talk about their own.* One child, dealing with this sentence, remarked: 'Well, *bordick* means "people talk about others and don't talk about themselves", that's what *bordick* means.' That this child seriously thought that *bordick* meant the whole sentence became clear when he tried to fit this meaning into the context: *people with bordicks are often unhappy.* The child fitted his sentence-core concept into this context as follows: 'People talk about others and don't talk about themselves—they are often unhappy.' To this question: 'How does this meaning fit?', the child had this answer: 'Say this lady hears that another lady is talking about her, so she'll get mad at her and that lady will be very unhappy.'

A frequent method of fitting a sentence-core concept, formed for one sentence, into another context was by a process we have termed ASSIMILATION. The child interprets the context of a new sentence as the same or similar to the context of the previous sentence. Through such assimilation, the concept for the previous sentence now fits into the new sentence. To illustrate, in one series the artificial word is *hudray* (for which such concepts as 'increase', 'enlarge' or 'grow' are adequate). Sentence 6 of this series read: *you must have enough space in the bookcase to hudray your library.* One child said: 'Hudray means "to have enough space".' He took a part of the context as the referent for *hudray*. Returning to the previous sentences, he said that the concept, 'to have enough space', fits all six sentences. For example, it fits Sentence 1 (*if you eat well and sleep well you will hudray*): 'If you eat well, that is, if you do not overeat, you will have enough room in your stomach and won't get too chubby; if you sleep well, but not too much, you don't get overlazy; so you leave some room for more sleep—so you leave space—like.'

Not infrequently, the child derived two independent sentence-core concepts pertaining to two successive sentences. In attempting to apply the second solution to the first sentence, he often combined the two solutions. For instance, for the two sentences:

Jane had to hudray the cloth so the dress would fit Mary.

You hudray what you know by reading and studying.

one child gave as respective solutions: 'Jane had to "let out the hem" of the cloth' and 'You "learn by books" what you know.' Coming back from the second to the first sentence the child said: ' "Learn by books" fits here. Jane had to "learn by books" how to "let out the hem" in the cloth. Jane used an encyclopedia of sewing.' For this girl, the first solution 'let out the hem' was so completely embedded in the sentence context that it became a part of the sentence and no longer a substitute for *hudray*. The child could now introduce the subsequent solution ('learn by books') above and beyond the first, original solution. At times, we obtained as many as three independent solutions combined in one sentence.

Another indication that word and sentence were not clearly differentiated at the earlier levels was the frequent manifestation of what we have called HOLOPHRASTIC GRADIENT. Here, the concept was not limited to the unknown word, but spread to neighbouring parts, thus carrying pieces of the sentence with it; e.g., for the word *lidber* (collect, gather), one child stated for the sentence: *Jimmy lidbered stamps from all countries*, 'Jimmy "collected" stamps from all countries.' The concept was extended from 'collect' to 'collect stamps'. Thus the concept, 'collect stamps' was applied to another sentence: *The police did not allow the people to lidber on the street*, in the following manner: 'Police did not permit people to "collect stamps" on the street.'

Thus far, we have considered only those forms of signification of a word which are based on an intimate fusion of word and sentence (or sentence-parts). In our analysis, we found other forms of signification, in which the concepts, though they did not display sentence-word fusion, were still lacking the circumscribed, stable character of the more mature concepts. We called such products SIMPLE CONTEXTUAL or SIMPLE HOLOPHRASTIC CONCEPTS. Here the word meaning was definitely set apart from the context of the sentence; nevertheless, it differed from conventional word meanings in that it bore a wide situational connotation rather than a circumscribed, stable one. The artificial word did not refer, for the child, to a single object or action, but to a more inclusive context. Sometimes the broad situational connotation of the word was explicitly stated by the child, i.e., he employed a whole phrase to express the meaning of the word. In other cases, the child used a single word, seemingly delimited in its meaning, which on probing was found to be far more inclusive than it appeared on the surface. The following may serve as examples of explicitly stated holophrastic concepts.

The artificial word *ashder* (obstacle) appears in the sentence, *The way is clear if there are no ashders*. One child responded: 'The way is clear if there are no "parts of a radio that don't fit in right" (together).' In the mind of this child, the word, *ashder*, referred to a radio-repair situation.

In the case of the sentence: *The police did not allow the people to lidber on the street*, one child's translation of *lidber* was 'throw paper around' (i.e., cluttering up the street by throwing paper around).

An illustration of implicit holophrastic concepts is the following, involving the word *ontrave* (hope): *ontrave sometimes keeps us from being unhappy*. A child substituted for *ontrave* the seemingly, circumscribed word 'want'. However, on probing, it became apparent that 'want' referred to a broad contextual situation, 'If you "want a bow and arrow set and you get it", that keeps you from being unhappy.'

For this same sentence, another child came to the solution, 'mother'. ' "Mother" keeps you from being unhappy.' However, 'mother' actually meant 'mother when she gives you things you want'.

One may note an important characteristic attached to such situational word meanings; the word has not only a broad situational content, but this content is fluid and lacks closure: i.e., the concept may change in range from sentence to sentence, elements being added or subtracted etc. This can be seen from the way children quite typically expanded a concept in order to fit it into another sentence. This process of expansion, denoting fluidity of conceptualization, we have termed CONTEXTUAL or HOLO-PHRASTIC EXPANSION. An example of this holophrastic expansion is the following: One child had developed the concept 'books to study' for *hudray*. 'Books' became expanded to 'throwing books' when the child attempted to fit the concept into the sentence:

Mrs. Smith wanted to hudray her family. The child stated: 'Mrs. Smith wanted to "throw books", at her family.'

Another child, who had arrived at the concept 'long' for one sentence, expanded it to 'get long hair' in another: *The older you get the sooner you will begin to soldeve,* '. . . the sooner you will begin to "get long hair" '.

On occasion the contextual expansion was more systematically employed. The child formed a conceptual nucleus, which remained constant throughout the six contexts; and added to this nucleus elements varying with each sentence. We have termed this procedure PLURALIZATION. For example, one child formed a nucleus for all the sentences of one series containing the artificial word, *lidber.* This nucleus was 'collect'. In one sentence *lidber* meant 'collect ribbons' (*all the children will* 'collect ribbons' *at Mary's party*); in another sentence, it was 'collect autographs' (*The people* 'collected autographs' from *the speaker when he finished his talk*); in a third sentence, it meant 'collect information' (*People* 'collect information' *quickly when there is an accident*), and so on.

We should like to mention two other forms of signification of a word, that were essentially based on contextual or holophrastic conceptualization. One we have termed GENERALIZATION BY JUXTAPOSITION; the other GENERALIZATION BY CHAIN.

In the case of juxtaposition, a concept of an object *A* obtained in one sentence is applicable to a second sentence through the mediation of a concept of an object *B* that is spatially contiguous to the object *A*. For instance, a child gave the solution 'plaster' for *contavish* in the sentence: *before the house is finished, the walls must have contavishes.* 'Plaster' also fits into the sentence, *A bottle has only one contavish.* Here the child used 'label' for *contavish*, saying: 'A bottle has only one "label".' Nevertheless 'plaster' was retained as the solution because 'plaster', as the child explained, 'is used to put on the "label" '. In other words, the concept of an object such as 'plaster' could be used as an over-all solution because the juxtaposed object ('label') fits into the sentence. Most likely, the concept was contextual: not just 'plaster' but 'plaster +'.

A similar mechanism seemed to be operative in generalization by chain. This type of generalization probably differs from juxtaposition only in so far as the two objects in question are conceived of as temporally rather than spatially connected (e.g., cause and effect). As an example, 'honour' was substituted for *sackoy* in one sentence: *We all admire people who have much sackoy*. In the next sentence, 'guts' was the meaning attributed to *sackoy*. 'You need "guts" to fight with a boy bigger than you.' But 'honour' still fits because, as the child explained, 'If you have "guts", you are "honoured" aren't you?'

Finally, the two main groups of immature signification discussed in this paper may be briefly compared statistically. As will

TABLE 1

Age	$8\frac{1}{2}$–$9\frac{1}{2}$	$9\frac{1}{2}$–$10\frac{1}{2}$	$10\frac{1}{2}$–$11\frac{1}{2}$	$11\frac{1}{2}$–$12\frac{1}{2}$	$12\frac{1}{2}$–$13\frac{1}{2}$
I Sentence-contextual	11·9	9·2	1·8	0·2	0·5
II Non-sentence-contextual	11·7	10·8	7·9	4·6	3·3

be recalled, in the first group, the word carries with it the whole or parts of the sentence context; in the second group, the word is clearly differentiated from the sentence context, though it still possesses a broad contextual meaning. Table 1 summarizes the occurrence of these two types of contextual word meanings at the various age levels.

The figures represent the mean occurrence per child at each age group. Both forms of word meanings decreased as age increased; however, there is a clearcut difference between the two developmental curves. Signification based on sentence-word fusion (Type I) decreased most sharply between the second and third age levels (around 10–11 years), with practically no occurrence after the third age level. The other type of contextual signification (in which there is no fusion of word meaning and sentence) showed an entirely different developmental trend: it gradually decreased, and even at the 13-year level there were as many as 3·3 such solutions per child.

The abrupt decrease of Type I, the most immature form of signification, around the 10- to 11-year level suggests a rather fundamental shift in language attitude, towards a task, which, as in our test, is on a relatively abstract verbal plane.

In closing, we should like to mention briefly that there are aspects of language development other than semantic, discussed in this paper, which showed similar abrupt changes at the same age levels. This is particularly true with respect to grammatical structure. The data indicate that there is a growing comprehension of the test sentence as a stable, grammatical structure. Younger children manipulated the sentence as a fluid medium, lacking closure; that is, in the case of giving meaning to the artificial word they frequently altered the grammatical structure of the test sentence. The frequency of such manipulation showed an abrupt drop at the end of the second age level with practically no occurrence at the fourth and fifth levels.

One of the most significant and little explored problems of language development concerns the relationship between the semantic and grammatical aspects of language. The close correspondence of the developmental curves, indicated by our data, between two seemingly independent aspects of language lends support to those theories that assume a genetic interdependence of meaning and structure.

10 36 pp.

CATHY HAYES
Non-human Language

This reading is taken from one of the several research projects which have been attempted to teach a higher primate such as a chimpanzee human language. The Hayes kept an ape from birth in their home and tried to bring it up as they would a human infant. This chapter contains the discussion about Viki's language.

It is interesting because it contains a discussion of the dependence of understanding by Viki on the actual situation. What Viki does not seem able to do is to understand language when it is free of the immediate context in which it is uttered. She cannot understand language in a way that Lewis shows that a child can; she cannot use language without the supplementary cues provided by the situation, except for a very small list of commands.

The work on these higher primates illustrates by comparison just how much children learn when they acquire their maternal language and the wide range of functions that language has.

The Hayes taught Viki in an intensive programme. The Kelloggs, on the other hand, allowed their chimpanzee Gua the opportunity to acquire human language *incidentally* in the same way as human children acquire it. By comparing the two accounts, Viki comes ahead on points: she could say three words—'mama', 'papa', and 'cup'—whereas Gua could not. (See W. N. & L. A. Kellogg (1933) *The Ape and the Child*, New York: McGraw-Hill).

Of all the questions we are asked by new acquaintances, the one we dread most to hear is: 'How many words does Viki understand?' A definite answer is next to impossible for a number of reasons: (1) Failure to obey a command is no test of comprehension in our contrary Viki. (2) She understands in a fluctuating way—some days she 'knows' a word perfectly, other days not at all. (3) Any list of understood words can be endlessly lengthened by including

Cathy Hayes: Extract from *The Ape in Our House*, Gollancz, 1952, chapter 27, pp. 224–31. © Cathy Hayes and McIntosh and Otis, Inc., 1952.

variations of the basic form. (4) Almost any expression includes a great deal more than the words themselves; and these other elements of the language complex—situation, gesture, the inflection, pitch, and loudness of the speaker's voice—are so bound up with the words as we commonly use them, that it is very hard to say for sure just what an animal (or a person) is responding to.

An example of this difficulty may be seen in the ritual by which Viki visits the bathroom: Glancing at the clock, I say, 'Viki, it's time to go to the bathroom. *Go* to the *bathroom.*'

Viki reluctantly heads for the little room, crawling over and under furniture on the way, tumbling and doing somersaults. Eventually, in spite of all her stalling, she arrives at the bathroom door. Then I give the second command, 'Get *up* on the *board.*'

She climbs onto the diaper-changing board, which lies across the bathtub, and plays with the contents of the soapdish until I say, 'Lie down, Viki!'.

She lies down, I unpin her. If she is clean, I say 'Get over on your potty', and she steps from the rim of the tub to the potty.

When a suitable time has elapsed or action has taken place, I tell her to '*flush* the toilet', 'get over on the board', and 'lie down'. Then I ask her to '*give* me a *pin*'. When she is securely fastened, I say, 'Turn off the *light*'. She does so and we leave the bathroom. Now I give the final command. Viki is by now busy with some toy, but when I say, 'Close the door', she returns to the bathroom door and slams it emphatically shut.

At first glance this performance seems to involve considerable language comprehension; but on second thought we wonder if she might not be simply following a set routine. Would not a string of brusque but uninformative 'Hup!'s be enough to run her through this series of activities? When we test this possibility, we find that this is indeed the case. But it's not that simple either: if I now switch the order of the various items—tell her to get on the potty *before* I remove her diaper, or ask her to give me her pins while she is still on the potty—she does obey these inappropriate commands. She is hesitant, however, and searches my face, as if puzzled by the conflict between my words and the requirements of the situation.

On the other hand, when she is inattentive, she does the thing which makes sense at the time, apparently not noticing that I have asked for something else. (I also do this when a person's words do not match the situation. The fact that Viki does it more often probably reflects her low level of interest in language.)

There are some cases where we see no evidence of comprehension unless our words fit the situation. For instance, at bedtime Viki has a cup of cocoa, which we refer to as her 'party'. When we say, 'Is it time for a party?' Viki makes food barks and heads for the kitchen. If we dally, she may get the can of cocoa from the pantry by herself. However, it is hard to say whether she is reacting to our words or has simply acquired a sense of the day's routine events. Certainly if I ask her if she wants a party at any other time of the day, she simply stares at me.

Early in the evening, we sometimes say, 'Do you want to go to the *show?*'. With great excitement, she dashes to the front door, and into the car. But here also, there are other clues than the words. There is the time of day again, and also the fact that we begin turning off the lamps, and gathering up extra diapers, sweaters, and so on. Testing her, we find that she gives the show-going reaction only at the appropriate time of day. At nine o'clock in the morning, however, our invitation draws a blank stare (I must admit that if I were invited to a movie at nine o'clock in the morning, I might also stare blankly.

We have seen that the situation sometimes gives Viki a clue as to what we are asking of her. She responds to numerous other spoken words where understanding may depend on still other cues. For instance, a number of sharp words get her instant attention. Said with urgency, 'Look!' or 'Hey!' cause her to look first at us, and then at the object to which we are pointing or which has captured our gaze.

Better than any scolding is a scornful 'You bad girl!'. Impatient with her table manners, I mutter, 'Stupid little ape!'. She puts down her fork, looks in my eyes with a great sadness, and steals into my arms.

Sometimes loudness seems to be the only criterion for obedience. For instance, the words 'come' or 'come here' are ignored if uttered conversationally. Said with the slightest smile, 'come' starts a game of tag in which I am constantly 'it'. I chase her round and round the furniture, up and down the house, while she slithers out of reach like a wet football. Finally, when she completely exasperates me by scuttling under the bed, I bellow, 'COME!'. Then she comes.

She often seems ignorant or deaf to a certain command until a sharp 'Viki!' brings a delayed but proper response. When I complain that it is hard to say whether Viki *can't* or *won't* understand, Keith reminds me that, in either case, chimps are not selectively bred for obedience to verbal commands, as are horses, dogs and people.

Are there any words which Viki comprehends without need of supplementary cues? There are a few, though the list is limited by her youth and her chimpanzee language deficit. She obeys the commands: '*Go* to your *room*', '*Go outside*', and '*Go upstairs*' without error. She will bring a cup when we tell her to. If she removes a taboo object from its proper place, we say, '*Put it back!*' and she does so immediately and gently. She will 'turn on the *light*' or 'turn on the *water*', but may turn them off instead, if they happen to be on already. When told to, she will go find her shirt and put it on. If someone says 'Goodbye' or 'Bye bye', Viki waves. I depend on the command '*Give* it to me!' to get pins, buttons and scissors away from her. She obeys this even when we are not holding out our hands to receive the object.

As far as we are concerned, the most important word in Viki's vocabulary is 'No!'. We first used this expression when she was six months old, and books were her favourite teething rings. As Viki grew larger and our patience wore thin, the variations of 'No! No!' to be heard in our house were limited only by her genius for mischief and our invective vocabulary. There came to be 'Don't do this' and 'Don't do that' for specific crimes, a low menacing, 'Vikiiii', a rapid-fire 'Hey hey hey hey', and between clenched teeth, 'Viki, I'm warning you!'. More elaborate 'No! No!' variations include: 'Viki, get off those blinds before you pull them down and brain your papa!' 'Must you bulb-snatch from every lamp in the house?' and 'Don't flush the soap down the potty, dear.'

Her typical response to all varieties of 'No! No!' is to cease her sinning abruptly. Sometimes she throws herself prone and rocks. Again she will stamp her foot and sass us back. Most often she makes us feel silly by diverting her attention to something else, and listening in wide-eyed innocence to our rebukes, since she is obviously busy on another matter. Once the coast is clear, she returns to her favourite mischief (which is currently pounding on the windows with her feet, while she swings from the blinds).

When an object is delicate, but not forbidden, we calm her sudden bursts of animal spirits with *'Gently!'* or *'Careful!'*. She does not inhibit completely at these commands, but merely calms down.

If she is impatient to have a thing which we are making ready, we say, *'Wait!'* and she waits patiently until we break the spell with 'Here you are!'. Here again, since 'waiting' is basically inhibiting of activity, we consider it merely another shade of 'No! No!'.

From time to time we have tried to speed Viki's education by teaching her the meanings of words. Our greatest success, and that which has proved the most valuable to Viki as an experimental animal, has been *'Do this!'*. We believe that she had a certain amount of imitative ability in the first place, and that we were able to direct and enhance it by teaching her to follow our 'Do this!'.

On the whole, however, we have found it even harder to teach her language understanding than to test it. After more than eighteen months of coaching, we have not yet taught Viki to identify her nose, ears, eyes, hands and feet. Some days, to be sure, she can point to all these parts without error, but at other times, she is completely lost. When we try to teach her a few new words, she may start to learn them; but then, suddenly, she can't even remember the old ones. Too many words apparently lead to confusion—and for Viki, a very few are too many.

In contrast to the artificial situation of identifying her parts, Viki reacts very dependably to certain words used in play. She always brings her toy dog when we say, 'Go get your *dog*!' even if it is out of sight in the next room. When we say, *'Listen!'* she bends an ear to the nearest wrist watch. *'Kiss* me' is enthusiastically obeyed, although she does not always honour the proper parent when we say 'Kiss mama', or 'Kiss papa'. In language comprehension, as in most of Viki's behaviour, situations which combine motor activity and social interplay are the most successful.

By now it should be clear why we dread the question: How many words does she understand? Ruling out as much as we can of situation, gestures, glances, and inflection, and taking Viki at her most obedient, I should estimate that she understands not more than fifty word groupings in the form of expressions or commands.

However, we allow the possibility that we may be under-estimating her powers as we often do in other areas. Incidents like the following occur quite frequently. One night Keith found himself without a receptacle for his cigarette ashes. Trying to be funny, he said, 'Hand me an ashtray, will you, Viki?'. And she did.

To give a second example, on our trip we met a man named Carnochan who had collected apes in Africa. Within Viki's hearing he told us about his chimps who picked pockets with their feet. Later as I was showing him our photo albums, Viki amazed me with an entirely new trick. With her hands in plain sight and the glaze of innocence in her eyes, she reached out and snatched a picture with one chimpy foot.

Although Viki is generally poor at understanding words, she recognizes a surprising number of non-language sounds. When a cap is removed from a bottle of coke, the fizzing noise draws food barks from the next room. At the first metallic swish of a lipstick being opened, she comes running for her sample. When we first began to play our 'bring-me-the-dog' game, she simply stared at the word 'dog', but when we barked, 'Rhow! Rhow!' she ran straight to the toy.

Perhaps the thing that makes it difficult for her to learn words is that this type of symbol is not typically a discrete sound, but rather a combination of several basic sound units. These same elements appear time after time in different words, which are distinguished from one another by different arrangements of the elements— sometimes a very slight difference. If the words of our language were each as different from one another as a footstep is from a dog's bark, for example, perhaps Viki would learn them as easily as we do.

We have recently tested her ability to understand recom-binations of familiar words within a sentence. For instance, she performs perfectly on 'Kiss me' and 'Bring me the dog'. When we first said, '*Kiss* the *dog*', Viki did nothing at all. We coached her so that she might see what we were expecting her to do. Then we presented the second group: 'Bring me a cup. Kiss me. *Kiss* the *cup.*' This took fewer coachings, which indicated that some learning had taken place. Subsequent series took increasingly less time until 'Kiss me. Give me your hand. *Kiss* your *hand*' was almost instantly comprehended. We will do more of this work as more nouns and action verbs become available to her.

We anticipate that Viki will understand more and more of what we say as time goes on, but we doubt that her comprehension will ever go further than simple commands and the names of things. And without more involved language, with only gestural demonstrations, a teacher can transmit very little knowledge to his pupil. It is only when I consider how much we rely on the few words she does understand that I realize how much less we will be able to teach her than could be given to a human child her age.

One can become educated without talking. But listening and understanding opens to a man the wisdom of the ages. It adds to his meagre personal talents and experience the accumulated thought of countless men before him. Where does that leave one small ape who can't quite remember which are her ears and which are her eyes?

Language and the Environment

Readings 19 and 20 are taken from the same book entitled *Language and Poverty*. The title suggests the area of this last section, in which we shall be dealing with the language problems of children from deprived backgrounds—the so-called disadvantaged children.

In Reading 19 Osser puts the particular problems facing any debate on the development of language and the environment—especially social class—into a theoretical perspective. Osser attempts to put over a point of view that is neither innatist nor behaviourist; instead he stresses that the many complex processes in language acquisition are related to, if not to say dependent upon, social factors.

19 Biological and Social Factors in Language Development

HARRY OSSER

Presumably, many of the language problems of the so-called disadvantaged child should be susceptible to interpretation relative to contemporary research and theory in the area of language acquisition. On the contrary, however, what this appeal to research and theory reveals to us is that the contemporary picture is in a state of substantial flux. If we are to benefit at all from consulting this changing picture, it is important to have some knowledge of the various positions which it incorporates. In this paper, we will review some of these positions, and at the same time show how they lead to contrasting emphases and implications regarding the language of the disadvantaged child.

In contemporary psycholinguistics a predominant point of view is that the child is 'prewired' for language behaviour, so that his linguistic abilities depend largely on the unravelling of maturational processes. This clearly nativistic view is postulated by a number of linguists and psycholinguists, including, for example, Chomsky (1965), Lenneberg (1967), and McNeill (1966). The theoretical counterpart of their views appears in the work of Skinner (1957) and Mowrer (1960) who, in stressing the role of environmental, or social, factors, argue that the child acquires language by being reinforced for imitating the speech patterns of the people around him. A somewhat different environmentalist position, which is neutral with respect to the controversy between the nativists and empiricists over the origin of language behaviour, is derived from the research and theorizing of the sociolinguists who are primarily interested in the role of social structural factors, such as social-class membership, type of family structure, and role relations between speaker and listener, on the use of language in particular situations. We will next consider these positions in some detail.

Harry Osser: Extract from F. Williams (ed.) *Language and Poverty: Perspectives on a theme*, Institute for Research on Poverty, 1970, chapter 13, pp. 248–264. Reprinted by permission of Rand McNally College Publishing Company.

The Nativist Position

A Biolinguistic Viewpoint

One of the most detailed arguments in support of the nativist position is presented by Lenneberg (1967), who proposes that language development is a function of maturational factors, and that human language is a species-specific phenomenon. He argues that non-humans can never be trained to use language in a human manner because underlying speech there are a number of anatomical and physiological features that do not exist in species below the level of man. These include differences in oropharyngeal morphology, cerebral dominance, specialization of cerebrocortical typography, special coordination centres for motor speech, specialized temporal pattern perception, special respiratory adjustment, and tolerance for prolonged speech activities. All of the special features together permit speech reception and the precise and very rapid movements of the articulators that are necessary for speech production.

In arguing that language development is a function of maturational factors, Lenneberg (1967, pp. 128–30) refers to the parallels between language and motor development in children from twelve weeks through four years. His interpretation of this information is that there is a synchrony between the attainment of each language milestone and the development of particular motor skills. Language cannot begin to develop until the child has attained a certain level of physical maturation and growth. This view is vulnerable, of course, to the discovery of a lack of synchrony between the two types of development in individual cases.

Language development is often divided into two major stages, prelinguistic and linguistic. During the prelinguistic stage, approximately from birth up to twelve months, the infant produces a number of different kinds of vocalizations, e.g., cooing, chuckling, and babbling. When the child enters the linguistic stage (at about 12 months), he begins to use individual words. Lenneberg, Rebelsky, and Nichols (1965) have studied the prelinguistic sound making of both deaf and hearing infants. The deaf infants not only went through the same sequence of vocalizations as the hearing infants, but they also produced as much noise. This suggests that the emergence of prelinguistic behaviour does not depend upon social factors such as training or reward, but instead is a function of maturational factors.

Lenneberg also argues that the transition from prelinguistic to linguistic behaviours occurs as a function of maturational processes. He states that there is no evidence that the onset of speech in the child is correlated with the initiation of any special language training by the mother. In support of this claim, Lenneberg refers to the research results of Morley (1957), who carried out a large-scale longitudinal study of the language development of children whose backgrounds were heterogeneous. She found that notwithstanding considerable differences in social milieu, the onset of speech occurred at about the same time for the great majority of the children. Lenneberg may be correct in his statement that the onset of language is unrelated to training, but since our information on the verbal interactions between parents and children is very sparse, the opposite argument could, of course, be proposed. That is to say, there is no evidence to suggest that the onset of speech is independent of social factors, for as Morley observed, not all children begin to speak at the same time. Lenneberg's view would probably be that individual differences in time-of-speech onset are correlated with individual differences in rate of motor development; that is, he would explain such differences as biologically based.

Not only is the onset of speech a very regular event for most children, but according to Lenneberg's (1967, pp. 133–4) own research, children also attain other milestones of language development in a fixed sequence and at a relatively constant chronological age. He found that 450 out of 500 children were able, at thirty-nine months, to name a large number of objects in their houses, to comprehend spoken instructions, and to produce structurally complex sentences spontaneously and fairly intelligibly.

Lenneberg derives additional evidence for the maturational viewpoint from studies of abnormal children. He found, for example, that in mongoloid children, as in normal children, there was the same synchrony between motor and language milestones of development. The difference between the two groups was that the developmental process was stretched out beyond the usual time limits for the mongoloid group. Lenneberg interprets such evidence as the strongest support for the argument that language development is regulated by maturational phenomena.

Lenneberg argues that speech acquisition is unlike the acquisition of many skills where large individual differences exist which depend upon genetic factors, yet considerable training is also necessary before the skill develops maturely. He claims that language as a skill is different from, say, piano playing, in that equal aptitude for it is exhibited in a much larger number of individuals than for the latter. In addition, the onset of language skill occurs very early, and appears not to need particular training.

There is a problem with Lenneberg's argument that language as a skill is unlike many other skills in that many more people show equal aptitude in it; this is that the term 'language skill' remains undefined. A similar problem exists in the psycholinguistic and linguistic literature where the statement is made that by three years (or in some instances by four, or five, or six years) the child has acquired the basic structures of his language; again a key term remains undefined. There are probably a large number of language skills, and the question is whether there are small or large differences in such skills.

Lenneberg's argument, in summary form, is that the child's capacity to learn language is a consequence of maturation. The evidence he provides is that the milestones of language development are normally interlocked with stages of motor development which are themselves distinctly related to physical maturation. Such synchrony is preserved even when the whole maturational schedule is slowed down, as in cases of pathology. There is no evidence that the onset of language is related to special training. The capacity for language acquisition is intimately related to the maturation of uniquely human anatomical and physiological characteristics. Language is a species-specific behaviour.

Lenneberg acknowledges the existence of individual differences in language ability, and he suggests that they relate to complex interactions between biological and social factors. He offers two interpretations of the frequent experimental finding that disadvantaged (i.e., lower-class) children exhibit poorer language performances than middle-class children. Lenneberg (1967, p. 136) speculates that such observed differences may be a function of nutritional factors, or due to the experimenter's inadequate sampling techniques.

Lenneberg's interest in the commonalities of language performance, rather than individual and group differences, has not led him to examine closely the role of social factors in language development. The two major research suggestions relating to the language problems of the disadvantaged that derive from Lenneberg's biolinguistic viewpoint are: (1) to search for biological factors (e.g., early nutritional deficiencies) that may account for such problems, and (2) to obtain more adequate speech samples in contrastive studies of lower-class and middle-class children than has previously been the case. There are only limited suggestions in the biolinguistic viewpoint for the remedial treatment of the disadvantaged child.[1] Perhaps the main suggestion is to ensure adequate nutritional support for the child's physical development. The value of such a suggestion is severely curtailed by our ignorance of the role of nutritional factors in language development.

A Linguistic Viewpoint

The linguist Chomsky (1965) maintains that the child's ability to produce and understand novel sentences can only be understood by assuming that he has an innate language capacity. In particular, Chomsky posits the existence of a language acquisition device, which is, of course, an abstraction, so that he can account for the disparity between the linguistic input to the child, and his output. This device therefore refers to a hypothetical set of innate mechanisms that permit the child to analyse incoming linguistic data, and to produce messages. Chomsky asserts that linguistic principles are not learned at all, but are simply part of the innate conceptual capacities brought to the language-learning situation by the child.

Chomsky asserts that the child acquires language by discovering

[1] We should acknowledge the feeling currently expressed by some that intersections between a biolinguistic perspective and Jensen's (1969) arguments about genetically-based restrictions upon intellectual development should be explored. As of this writing, however, most of the concern with this issue is focused upon Jensen's position itself, and until some of the questions on this are resolved it will probably not be profitable to explore the significance of his position relative to biolinguistic theory, let alone to combine the two when considering the disadvantaged child.

its underlying system of grammatical rules. The processes characterized by the language acquisition device incorporate a built-in
set of specifications for correct grammars, plus a testing capability
which permits the child to discover which particular grammar,
from out of a small set of correct grammars, is appropriate for
the language he is exposed to. The device receives a sample of
the possible sentences in the language, and the child abstracts the
regularities from them; or, in other words, he acquires the rules
of the language. Once the child has done this, he can now go far
beyond the particular sample of sentences he has heard, so that
he can produce and understand novel sentences.

The role of experience in Chomsky's model of language acquisition is quite limited. The child uses language input solely to
eliminate his false hypotheses about the rules of a language. This
position is that all the child requires for developing language is
exposure to a small amount of the language he is to learn. That
which is defined as the language acquisition device provides him
with a preknowledge of language universals, i.e., the rules and
constituents which underlie all languages. The child's remaining
task is to learn the unique rules of his own language. It is clear
that Chomsky's model of language acquisition provides only a
passive role for environmental, or social, factors, whereas the
child is assigned a very active role in his own language development.

Chomsky (1965) asserts that the child inevitably acquires the
language of his culture. Such learning relates to his intrinsic
cognitive resources, and is only minimally dependent upon ex-
trinsic supports. Chomsky emphasizes the basic human equality
with regards to linguistic competence (i.e., knowledge of the
language) by contrast to linguistic performance (i.e., actual
behaviour). Chomsky's position contains virtually no suggestions
for the remediation of the language problems of disadvantaged
children. He does suggest one general direction which research
on children's language should take, and this suggestion has
implications for studies of both advantaged and disadvantaged
children. Chomsky (1964) argues that valid assessments of language development require the use of many different kinds of
measurements. One example of recent research on disadvantaged
children which attempts to meet requirements is that of Osser,

Wang, and Zaid (1969), who compared the linguistic performances of a group of lower-class Negro preschoolers with those of a group of middle-class white children. Two tasks were employed, including one of speech imitation and one of speech comprehension. These tasks were designed to evaluate the child's control over different syntactic structures of standard English. It was assumed that there were differences in the linguistic environments of the two groups, which would result in differences being observed in their performances on the experimental tasks. In general, the findings were consistent with this expectation. However, on one of a number of different indicators of performance—namely, 100 per cent correct responses to a syntactic structure for either the imitation task or the comprehension task—the differences beween the two groups, with regard to control over the test structures, were insignificant. Does this evidence allow the interpretation that both groups are equal in linguistic development, at least with respect to the test structures? The answer depends upon the definition of *linguistic control*. Some investigators may accept the single use of a grammatical structure as evidence of control, whereas others may demand more stringent conditions be met before the child is assumed to exhibit control over that structure. However this definitional dilemma is resolved, it seems clear that Chomsky's suggestion concerning multiple measurements of language performance is extremely valuable.

A Psycholinguistic Viewpoint

Chomsky's (1965) formulation of the major features of child language acquisition is accepted by McNeill (1966) who looks at the theoretical problems of language development from the different perspective of a psycholinguist. He is concerned, for example, with specifying the child's innate linguistic rules, and also with the description of the particular set of rules that the child uses at different stages of his development. McNeill, like other developmental psycholinguists, is interested in the convergence of the child's language system onto the adult model.

McNeill views the language acquisition device as necessarily highly structured, because the input to it is unstructured (e.g., incomplete sentences, typically disfluent speech), yet its output, which conforms to grammatical rules, is highly structured. He envisages the internal organization of the device as being made up of two components. One component consists of certain kinds of linguistic information in the category of language universals, and the other is a set of procedures that enable the child to analyse his linguistic input.

By this view the child knows the ways in which a language can be structured; that is, he has knowledge of language universals, which are the general forms of human language. Such general forms have presumably developed to match human capacities, and if this is in fact the case, then it is reasonable to expect that a description of language universals would illuminate the character of the acquisition device. Every language uses the same syntactic categories, arranged in the same way—the syntactic categories of sentences, noun phrases, and verb phrases. The same grammatical relations obtain among these categories as, for example, the subject and predicate of a sentence, verb and object of a verb phrase, and so on. These basic grammatical relations correspond to the traditional grammatical functions of subject, predicate, verb, object modifier, and head. If such relations are universal, what is the evidence that they are present in children's early speech?

If all children are endowed with language universals, then their early linguistic outputs should be very similar, and only later would they show divergence towards their particular grammars. The examination of cross-cultural data would therefore provide a direct test of McNeill's view that the child who begins to learn a language already knows the major syntactic categories, which appear universally in human languages. There is a small amount of supportive information for this position. It has been observed that children from several different language communities use two similarly functioning form classes when they begin to speak in two-word sentences, notwithstanding large differences in the respective adult languages. Slobin (1966) refers to a Russian child who had a pivot class (P) and an open class (O) that coincided with the same classes of words that were used by an English-speaking child investigated by Brown and Fraser (1964). Both children included in their P-class demonstratives, personal pronouns, various adjectives, and several determiners. The P-class seems to subserve a modifier function, and there is no single class of modifiers in Russian or English which corresponds to the two children's P-class. McNeill suggests that children come equipped to notice a general function of modification when it occurs in the speech of adults, so that they learn to categorize words which serve this function.

McNeill (1970) later offered a more elaborate view of the development of the P- and O-classes. He thought originally that each represented a very generalized grammatical category, but he now views the construction of the two classes as evidence of the child's learning of syntactic features. This change in interpretation was necessary to take into account the occasional finding that adjectives, as well as members of other form classes, have been found in both P- and O-classes (the O-class consists usually of nouns only), and was also attributable to changes in linguistic theory regarding the nature of word categorization. These views consist of a discussion of the syntactic features of various categories and subcategories of words. For example, nouns can be cross-classified in terms of many distinguishing features, such as common, proper, inanimate, so that words in the same form class can have different syntactic features.

McNeill's proposal is that the very young child responds perhaps to one syntactic feature of a word, and places all words with this syntactic feature into the same class. McNeill assumes that in very early speech, children have two categories, one of which is a modifier category (the P-class) and the other is a modified category (the O-class). If the child also responds to another feature of the same word, he may then place it into more than one category. In order to develop the modifier and modified categories, the child must, according to McNeill, be able to understand the basic grammatical relations between them, which then permits him to identify which of the two words has the modifier function and which one has the modified function. Such knowledge, according to McNeill's interpretation, depends upon the innate characteristics of the language acquisition device.

McNeill's view of the process of language acquisition has led him, like Lenneberg (1967), to focus upon the similarity in linguistic performance among very young children, and, of course, the confirmation that similarities do exist in the early syntax of Russian and American children has buttressed his theoretical viewpoint. McNeill's stress on nativistic factors does not offer any obvious suggestions either for research into the linguistic problems of the disadvantaged, nor for programmes of remediation.

Evaluation of the Nativist Position

It has not been customary in psychology to posit a great deal of internal organization as the basis for behaviour, although some innate mechanisms are postulated by most theorists. The behaviourists, for example, have accepted the capacities of association formation, and stimulus and response generalization as native properties of the organism. The nativists go much beyond this description of innate capacities and claim many more endowments for the child. Their view is that the child has available unlearned procedures for analysing speech input, and abilities for hypothesis testing, as well as an inborn preknowledge of the universal features of language structure. Without such capacities, the nativists assert, the child could not acquire a language. They argue that without the postulation of such capacities there cannot be developed any adequate explanation for what we observe as the child's productive use of language.

The evidence for the nativist position is, with the exception of the information provided by cross-cultural comparisons of early speech, largely of an indirect nature. There is one kind of support in Lenneberg's arguments that language is a species-specific phenomenon and is genetically determined. Another type of supportive evidence derives from the study of language universals. The nativist view of language universals is that all human languages share these features because all humans share specific learning capacities.

None of the arguments put forward by the nativists proves their case for elaborate language-information-processing abilities. The nativists however, provide the basic question that any substantial theory of child language acquisition will have to answer: How does a child go beyond the examples of sentences he hears in the speech around him?

The Environmentalist Position

Psychologists who work within the framework of behaviourism (e.g., Skinner 1957; Mowrer 1960) have talked about language development in terms of the traditional categories of explanation derived from learning theory—namely, reinforcement and generalization—rather than invoking the learning of rules and innate supportive mechanisms. The beginning of language behaviour, as described by Mowrer (1960), can be summarized as follows. The infant begins to learn language by associating the sounds of the human voice, particularly his mother's, with need-satisfying circumstances (e.g., milk drinking). The result of this is that when he hears his own random babbling, he is more likely to repeat those sounds that are similar to the pleasurable sounds made by his mother. Thus the pleasure associated with the mother's voice now becomes transferred to the child's own vocalizations. Mowrer's argument may be extended as follows: As the mother tends to reward the infant's sounds, particularly if they approximate adult speech patterns, the child learns that his imitations are generally reinforced, and thus he is on his way to learning those speech patterns. This model of language acquisition may be designated the imitation-reinforcement model. So far the explanation is only applicable to the child's acquisition of sounds, words, and sentences that he has heard. Since a child produces for the most part novel sentences (ones that he has not heard or produced before), an additional explanation is necessary.

The problem of explaining novel behaviours has usually led behaviourists to suggest that the speaker is reinforced for certain behaviours, so that he generalizes his responses to new stimulus situations. There is a major problem in using the explanatory concept of generalization in the interpretation of novel linguistic behaviour. In a typical generalization experiment, an organism is said to have shown generalization when after being trained to respond to one stimulus, it also responds to a second stimulus. Response transfer is usually explained by referring to the similarity between the two stimuli, where the similarity is specifiable along a physical dimension, such as intensity of sound, and so on. In trying to use the generalization argument to explain, say, the child's acquisition of the plural forms for English, it is not only extremely difficult to define the stimulus situations which result in such learning, but it is equally difficult to see how arguments that relate to responses based on physical similarities can be carried over to situations where physical similarity is not involved. The morphological signals for the noun plural in English are physically quite different, for example, glass*es*, boy*s*, doughnut*s*, and pant*s* (which has no singular form, so is considered to embody a 'zero-morpheme').

Newer views of generalization have been proposed by Jenkins and Palermo (1964), and Braine (1963a, b). They explain novel linguistic behaviour as a contextual generalization phenomenon, which means basically that a child learns to use a word in a particular position, and then generalizes the use of this word to similar sentence positions. This viewpoint has some very serious defects, as Bever, Fodor, and Weksel (1965) have pointed out. In essence, the contextual generalization hypothesis does not take into consideration that the same word can appear in a large number of different contexts, so that if the child had to acquire language by contextual generalization, he would probably need considerably longer than he seems to take in achieving mature usage.

What is the role of reinforcement in language acquisition? The Lenneberg, Rebelsky, and Nichols (1965) study of the pre-linguistic vocalizations of deaf children strongly suggests that at least for the first few months of vocalization no social reinforcement is necessary. Can the same be said for the development of linguistic behaviour? Brown, Cazden, and Bellugi (1969) have evidence that bears upon this question. They analysed the conversations between mother and child to determine whether there is anything like grammatical training by the mother going on. In inspecting the grammatical correctness of the child's utterances which were followed by some expression of approval (positive social reinforcement), they found that grammatical contingencies did not govern the mother's approval or disapproval of the child's speech. Instead, the truth or falsity of the utterance defined such approval or disapproval. For example, when Eve said, 'Mama isn't boy; he a girl', the mother answered, 'That's right'. Eve used the wrong pronoun, but her mother knew what she meant, and what she meant was in fact true. However, when Adam said in perfectly grammatical English, 'Walt Disney comes on, on Tuesday', his mother said 'That's not right', because the child was wrong about the day of the week. Brown, Cazden, and Bellugi note that the parents they studied typically rewarded true statements and punished false ones, which results paradoxically in speakers who are highly grammatical, but not notably truthful. Even if the child were reinforced, for grammatical statements, and punished for non-grammatical statements, such parent behaviour only provides the child with information on the acceptability of particular sentences. The fact that the child can generate novel sentences for which he has not been rewarded remains unexplained.

What is the role of imitation in language acquisition? There is evidence that imitation is not necessarily involved in speech comprehension. Lenneberg (1962) describes a child who could not talk because of a congenital disability that affected the development of motor speech skills. This child nevertheless could understand elaborate instructions, for example, 'Take the block and put it on the bottle'; 'Is it time to eat breakfast now?' and (after being told a story) 'Was the black cat fed by the nice lady?' This child obviously could not imitate speech, nor could he have ever been reinforced for speech production.

Does imitation have any role in language development? In a general sense the answer has to be yes, for without being provided with samples of the language to be learned, and unless he operated on these samples in some way, the child could not learn his language. Slobin (1968) suggests a specific role for imitation in language development. He examined the child's imitations of the parent's expansions, where an expansion is the parent's imitation of what the child says, but with additional elements supplied. For example, the child says, 'Papa name Papa', the mother expands this to 'Papa's name is Papa, uhhum', and the child imitates the mother's utterance, and in doing so adds something not in his original sentence, for example, 'Papa name *is* Papa'. Slobin found that Adam and Eve (children studied by Brown and Fraser 1964) in imitating expansions added something to their original utterances 50 per cent of the time. The new items added included articles, the copula, a pronoun, a preposition, an inflection —that is, the forms that were missing from their spontaneous speech. Slobin argues that such imitation very likely helps the child advance in his grammatical development, although Slobin acknowledges that there is no direct evidence that adult expansions of children's speech play an essential or even a facilitative role in normal grammatical development.

Other evidence suggests that the imitation-reinforcement position cannot provide an adequate interpretation of language development. Children's speech, particularly in the early stages of development, contains examples which deviate from the adult model of the language, for example, 'The children*s* are here', and 'We went*ed*', as well as other combinations which never occur in adult speech, and which therefore could never have been heard and imitated, such as 'All gone shoe' and 'More car' (Braine 1963b). Such deviations from adult usage are more parsimoniously interpreted as instances of linguistic productivity which derive from the child's acquisition of a rule system, or in other words, they illustrate the child's implicit grammatical theory.

The Sociolinguistic Position

Psycholinguists have been preoccupied with studying the child's acquisition of grammatical structures—that is, the forms of language—and have neglected the set of equally important questions of how the child learns the social uses of language. The developing subdiscipline, sociolinguistics, does concern itself with such questions. One of the articles of faith to the sociolinguist is that a considerable diversity exists in the way in which language can be used to meet needs demanded by individual social structures. Many of the central problems in developmental sociolinguistics have been summarized in the statement that in addition to the child's acquisition of the structural rules of his language, he also must learn another set of rules which refer to when he should speak, when he should remain silent, which linguistic code he should use, and to whom (Hymes 1967).

The major theoretical work in developmental sociolinguistics has been carried out by Bernstein (1964). He assumes that linguistic output, or certain kinds of linguistic output, are not as highly valued in some subcultures and in some family structural types as in others. Bernstein describes two general kinds of lin-

guistic codes, the restricted and the elaborated that are isomorphic
to social subgroups. The habitual restricted-code user usually
but not always comes from a lower social class than the elaborated-
code user, and by contrast to the predominantly elaborated-code
user, is quite limited in the range of his possible selections from
the total population of lexical and structural options. Bernstein
suspects that social groups differ significantly in the range of
situations in which they use elaborated speech.

Hess and Shipman (1965) have reported an experiment that
derives directly from and supports Bernstein's theorizing. They
analysed the content of mothers' communication to their children,
where the mothers came from different social class backgrounds.
Findings indicated that whereas the middle-class mothers tended
to give their children informationally adequate messages, with
occasional supportive statements, the lower-class mothers, by
contrast, tended not to be explicit, and conveyed very little information in their messages.

The main directions of research on the language of the disadvantaged child suggested by the various environmentalist
positions can be summarized as follows. One direction is the
necessary closer examination of the child's environment in order
to locate possible sources of support for details of his language
development. For example, in analysing the verbal interchanges
between a child and his parents, one needs a detailed specification
of the kinds of linguistic information (both structural and functional) being provided for the child; then one also needs to specify
the child's use (or lack of use) of such information. A second
direction is the analysis of the correlations between communicative
demands in certain situations and the language used to meet such
demands. Williams and Naremore (1969) have carried out one of
the first major studies on this problem. They investigated the way
in which children brought language to bear upon specific situations
to meet the different communicative demands imposed by a
linguistic field worker. Language samples in this research had
been obtained from the corpus of the Detroit Dialect Study
(Shuy *et al.* 1967) and included the responses to questions (e.g.,
'What games do you play around here?') given by fifth- and
sixth-grade children of varying socioeconomic status and ethnicity.
Social-class differences in the elaboration of responses were

greatest when a field worker's question could be answered minimally but adequately by a simple yes or no (or 'uh huh'); here the
lower-status children tended to give such minimal (but com-
municatively acceptable) responses as against the middle-class
children's going beyond this minimum. Status differences in the
incidence of elaboration, however, all but vanished when the
question required elaboration (e.g., 'Tell me how you play base-
ball?'). Also as might be expected, but seldom studied, there were
substantial within- and between-group variations according to the
topics (games, television, aspirations) discussed. On a more
general level, the lower-class child had a tendency to talk in the
first person, communicating from his own perspective, thus using
a self-focused mode of discourse. The middle-class child, by contrast, tended to employ a variety of perspectives in his remarks.
He used the third person more frequently than the lower-class
child, which increased his options in constructing subject-noun
phrases, so that he could incorporate many communication perspectives in one message. Williams and Naremore found that
maximal differences in modes of communication were obtained
for the two social-class groups when they responded to the
television topic (see also, Williams 1969).

The environmentalist position is sharply differentiated from the
nativist position with regard to remediation of the language problems of the disadvantaged. To begin with, the environmental
position usually assumes that such problems actually exist, and
that observed social-class differences are not totally explainable by
referring to faulty sampling techniques, which is the suggestion
offered by many nativists. The environmentalist position, in
addition, implies that language behaviour can be changed by
developing appropriate training procedures. It is the case, however, that so far most research has been concerned with diagnosis
of problems rather than with their remediation.

Integration of Nativist and Environmentalist Positions

The nativist position, as exemplified in the work of Chomsky
(1965), Lenneberg (1967), and McNeill (1966), focuses our
attention on what is assumed to be a set of indisputable facts,

namely that prelinguistic behaviour and early linguistic behaviour unfold under the influence of maturational processes, and are relatively independent of experiential influences. The nativists propose that an adequate explanation of language development must be predicated upon a range of sophisticated innate structures. They claim that models of language acquisition which rest upon the explanatory concepts of imitation and reinforcement (e.g., that of Mowrer 1960), or word position learning (e.g., that of Braine 1963a) fail to account for the complexity of linguistic knowledge. The nativists argue that the child is not taught language but learns it rather effortlessly, largely because the general features of language structure reflect the general character of the human capacity to acquire knowledge.

The environmentalists, in sharp contrast to the nativists, assume environmental factors exert considerable influence on language development, so they suspect that careful analysis of these factors will reveal important information on the nature of the processes of language acquisition. Given that the environmentalist and the nativist positions seem to be radically different, the question is whether there is any common ground between them.

One point of convergence between the two positions is that both agree that language is acquired in a social context. A second point of agreement is on the existence of individual and group differences in linguistic performance. Among the nativists, Lenneberg (1967) makes the most explicit statements about such differences. He remarks that they occur at the time of speech onset, as well as at the time the various speech milestones are reached. His interpretation of these differences is that they result from complex interactions between social and biological factors in development. On the environmentalist side, there is much literature related to the role of environmental factors in determining individual and group differences (McCarthy 1954; Cazden 1966).

Yet another point of intersection between the two positions concerns the appropriate methods to study child language. Chomsky (1964) and the sociolinguists (e.g., Bernstein 1964; Hymes 1967) would all agree that a broad spectrum of tasks, situations, and linguistic analytic procedures are necessary to validly assess the child's language capabilities. Novel modes of assessment have recently been developed by Williams and

Naremore (1969), and Osser, Wang and Zaid (1969), among many others.

In explaining language development the environmentalists stress the role of forces acting upon the child, i.e., external agents; whereas the nativists stress internal mechanisms of the speaker-listener himself. These two viewpoints are in conflict but are not necessarily irreconcilable. It is clearly possible to integrate these two models so that the coexistence of both social factors and biological factors in determining linguistic behaviour would be admitted. It is possible, for example, to hold the view that all humans are by their nature equal with respect to language competence, and simultaneously to accept the existence of individual and group differences in language performance.

The information that has been collected thus far in studies of language development suggests that no single position, nativist or environmentalist, can explain all developmental language phenomena. There are four kinds of problems for which explanations have to be developed; we need to account for: (1) the development of prelinguistic vocalization; (2) the acquisition of basic language structures; (3) the acquisition of elaborated language sequences; (4) the acquisition of different modes of communication (the ability to use different styles of speech, such as a narrative, or an explanatory style, when it is appropriate in a particular social situation).

It is quite possible that social factors play a lesser role in the development of the skills represented in (1) and (2), but a greater role in those skills defined by (3) and (4). There is, at present, very little evidence on the precise role of either social or biological factors in the acquisition of linguistic structures and their use. The promise shown by such research as that of Bernstein (1964) and Hess and Shipman (1965) suggests that our knowledge of the role of social factors in language development will be vastly improved as more fine-grained analyses are carried out on child-adult verbal interactions. It is assumed by those who propose a nativist view on language development that the child need only be provided with a small sample of sentences and he will 'invent' the remainder of the language. It is therefore very likely that the study of child-adult verbal interactions will permit the definition of the characteristics of the linguistic input to the child, which together with studies of the child's output will provide insights into the role of biological and social factors and their interactions in language development.

References

Bernstein, B. (1964) 'Elaborated and restricted codes: their social origins and some consequences'. In J. J. Gumperz and D. Hymes (eds.) *The Ethnography of Communication, American Anthropologist*, 66, No. 6, Part 2, 55–69.

Bever, T. G., Fodor, J. A., and Weksel, W. (1965) 'On the acquisition of syntax: a critique of *contextual generalization*' *Psychological Review*, 72, 467–82.

Braine, M. D. S. (1963a) 'On learning the grammatical order of words' *Psychological Review*, 70, 323–48.

— (1963b) 'The ontogeny of English phrase structure: the first phase' *Language*, 39, 1–13.

Brown, R. and Fraser, C. (1964) 'The acquisition of syntax'. In Ursula Bellugi and R. Brown (eds.) *The Acquisition of Language*. Monograph of the Society for Research in Child Development, Vol. 29.

Brown, R., Cazden, Courtney, and Bellugi, Ursula (1969) 'The child's grammar from I to III'. In J. P. Hill (ed.) *The 1967 Minnesota Symposium on Child Psychology*, Minneapolis: University of Minnesota Press.

Cazden, Courtney B. (1966) 'Subcultural differences in child language: an interdisciplinary review' *Merrill-Palmer Quarterly*, 12, 185–219.

— (1967) 'On individual differences in language competence and performance' *J. Special Education*, 1, 135–150.

Chomsky, N. (1964) 'Formal discussion'. In Ursula Bellugi and R. Brown (eds.) *The Acquisition of Language*. Monograph of the Society for Research in Child Development, Vol. 29.

— (1965) *Aspects of the Theory of Syntax*, Cambridge, Mass.: M.I.T. Press.

Hess, R. D., and Shipman, Virginia C. (1965) 'Early experience and the socialization of cognitive modes in children' *Child Development*, 36, 869–86.

Hymes, D. (1967) 'Models of the interaction of languages and social setting' *J. Social Issues*, 23, 8–28.

Jenkins, J. J., and Palermo, D. S. (1964) 'Mediation processes and the acquisition of linguistic structures'. In Ursula Bellugi and R. Brown (eds.) *The Acquisition of Language*. Monograph of the Society for Research in Child Development, Vol. 29.

Jensen, A. R. (1969) 'How much can we boost IQ and scholastic achievement?' *Harvard Educational Review*, 39, 1–123.

Lenneberg, E. H. (1962) 'Understanding language without ability to

speak: a case report' *J. Abnormal and Social Psychology*, **65**, 419–25.
— (1967) *Biological Foundations of Language*, New York: Wiley.
—, Rebelsky, F. G., and Nichols, I. A. (1965) 'The vocalization of infants born to deaf and hearing parents' *Vita Humana*, **8**, 23–37.
McCarthy, Dorothea (1954) 'Language development in children'. In L. Carmichael (ed.) *Manual of Child Psychology*, New York: Wiley.
McNeill, D. (1966) 'Developmental psycholinguistics'. In F. Smith and G. A. Miller (eds.) *The Genesis of Language: A Psycholinguistic Approach*, Cambridge, Mass.: M.I.T. Press.
— (1970) 'The development of language'. In P. A. Mussen (ed.) *Carmichael's Manual of Child Psychology*, New York: Wiley.
Morley, Muriel, E. (1957) *The Development and Disorders of Speech in Childhood*, London: Livingstone.
Mowrer, O. H. (1960) *Learning Theory and the Symbolic Processes*, New York: Wiley.
Osser, H., Wang, Marilyn D., and Zaid, Farida. (1969) 'The young child's ability to imitate and comprehend speech: a comparison of two sub-cultural groups' *Child Development*, **40**, 1063–75.
Shuy, R. W., Wolfram, W. A., and Riley, W. K. (1967) 'Linguistic correlates of social stratification in Detroit speech'. U.S. Office of Education Cooperative Research Project No. 6-1347.
Skinner, B. F. (1957) *Verbal Behavior*, New York: Appleton-Century-Crofts.
Slobin, D. I. (1966) 'The acquisition of Russian as a native language'. In F. Smith and G. A. Miller (eds.) *The Genesis of Language: A Psycholinguistic Approach*, Cambridge, Mass.: M.I.T. Press.
— (1968) 'Imitation and grammatical development in children'. In N. S. Endler, L. R. Boulter, and H. Osser (eds.) *Contemporary Issues in Developmental Psychology*, New York: Holt, Rinehart, Winston.
Williams, F. (1969) 'Social class differences in how children talk about television: some observations and speculations' *J. Broadcasting*, **13**, 345–57.
— and Naremore, Rita C. (1969) 'On the functional analysis of social class differences in modes of speech' *Speech Monographs*, **36**, 77–102.

20

ELLIS G. OLIM
Maternal Language Styles and Cognitive Development

After Osser's consideration of the theoretical implications of language and social class, we turn to Olim's discussion of the practical educational problems facing schools teaching disadvantaged children. The problems of such children's education in the United States may be more intractable than in England, because the problems of deprived areas are exacerbated by the existence of different ethnic groups, the Negroes, Puerto Ricans, Mexicans and so on. But in England the work of Bernstein has shown the validity of Halliday's remark that 'educational failure is often, in a very general and rather deep sense, language failure'. Olim suggests, as Bernstein does in Reading 21, that language failure judged from an educational point of view is partly a result of social class differences.

Among the many variables that contribute to the creation and maintenance of poverty is maternal language style. In brief, the argument is this: The behaviour which leads to social, educational, and economic poverty is learned; it is socialized in early childhood. This socialization takes place in large measure by way of language. Since the mother is the primary socializing agent in most instances, the learning takes place in the context of the mother-child communication system. The deprivation that leads to poverty is a lack of cognitive meaning and cognitive and linguistic elaboration in this communication system. The family control system of the socially deprived is one in which appeals to status and role predominate and this type of system, by offering the child predetermined solutions and a narrow range of alternatives of action and thought, limits the child's cognitive development.

The converse of the foregoing situation suggests one way of

Ellis G. Olim: Extract from F. Williams (ed.) *Language and Poverty: Perspectives on a theme*, Institute for Research on Poverty, 1970, chapter 11, pp. 212–28. Reprinted by permission of Rand McNally College Publishing Company.

ameliorating some of the problems of poverty. In culturally advantaged families, the family control system more often includes an orientation towards persons rather than to status, and/or an orientation towards consequences, viewing behaviour as antecedent to more or less predictable outcomes. In person- and consequence-oriented families, the dominant language code is more particular, more differentiated, and more precise. It permits and encourages in the child a wider range of alternatives of action and thought, leading towards greater elaboration, discrimination, and differentiation of cognitive and affective content.

However, cognitive development alone is not enough to guarantee the elimination of social inequity. In both types of family control systems there exist language codes in which meanings are transmitted primarily through extraverbal and nonverbal channels. These codes emphasize the communal rather than the individual, the concrete rather than the abstract, the present rather than the future. Such codes have the potential of enhancing the aesthetic, of encouraging the development of interpersonal sensitivity. In the present condition of our schools, this type of code is largely dysfunctional.

Before we develop the general argument presented above, however, let us delineate some of the dimensions of the problem and underscore the urgency of its solution.

Dimensions of the Problem

For the foreseeable future, it seems clear that society, culture, and human behaviour will continue to move towards ever greater elaboration, complexity, and subtlety. The dreams of even the most utopian among us can no longer contemplate seriously a return to pristine simplicity. If we do have a vision of finding the good life and of solving the problems created by the incredible growth of our cities, the seething new nationalism over half the earth's surface, and the destructive potentialities of our technology, such a vision is likely to embrace the conviction that man cannot retreat but must press ever harder towards the goal of expanding his potential as a human being and of maximizing the opportunities of all for optimal growth and development.

We have little reason to suppose that the accumulation and dissemination of knowledge and information will abate. The economy is expanding most rapidly in those service industries that demand high educational attainment and highly developed skill in the use of symbol systems. At the same time, as a result of increased productivity, there has been only moderate expansion in manufacturing employment in the United States in the past twenty years. Unskilled jobs are rapidly disappearing as more and more physical work is assigned to machines. The economy is being converted from one in which workers produce physical products to one in which they produce services. Many of the new services deal with the management of information. Society, therefore, is accelerating its need and demand for persons who have developed highly skilled and elaborate methods of processing information and who are able to manipulate the environment, not directly as in factory work, but representationally, by symbolic means—the means essential for coping with the conditions of an advanced technological civilization.

Even if we assume that technological advances will decrease the manpower needs of the information industries or if we assume that, for whatever the reason, society learns to become a learning society, in which people will spend most of their time in the cultivation of leisure (in the Greek sense of that concept), the need for high levels of symbol-processing skills will continue to increase.

It is disturbing that while the movement towards information gathering and processing is proceeding at an exponential rate, a large segment of the population is being left further and further behind. These are the poverty people, the socially disadvantaged, the people who have been migrating from rural areas to swell the densely crowded metropolises. Most of these reside in the ghettos, where they are not being acculturated to urbanism. These new migrants must bridge a far wider cultural gap than their predecessors—European immigrants who had to be assimilated by the manufacturing industries in which the demand was for physical labour at standardized tasks. Some of these earlier migrants responded to the need for the establishment of small businesses. Often in a rapidly expanding economy, such enterprises became large. Because readily accessible avenues of economic mobility were available to many second- and third-generation

Americans, they were able to acquire the social and cognitive skills that a less-sophisticated urbanism then demanded, thereby rising to political, governmental, managerial, and professional occupations.

The task facing the new migrants is far more difficult, the cultural gap far greater, because life and society have become far more complex than for the earlier immigrants. This enormous expansion and elaboration of the physical and social worlds must be accompanied by a correlative expansion of the cognitive world of the new migrants, if they are to adapt successfully to the conditions of modern life.

In the search for the elimination of poverty and disadvantage in general many solutions are being offered: educational, economic, social and psychological.

Since the schools traditionally have been the major means for socializing children to the mores of our society, it is understandable that early attention would be directed to the schools, their possibilities for improvement, and their failures. The schools have indeed lagged behind in adapting to the changing needs of a changing society. One indispensable condition of educability today is the achievement of abstract, conceptual intelligence and a stance that encourages an ever-expanding level of intellectual competence. For those interested in improved education for the socially and culturally disadvantaged child, the challenge to the educational system takes on particular poignancy because this kind of competence has never been achieved by a majority of our children, let alone the underprivileged. Even after we prevented the majority of children from becoming early dropouts by extending the number of years of mandatory school attendance, most of them remained intellectual dropouts—they have not been educated by any reasonable definition of that term. Hence, the current concern with improving opportunities for the under-privileged has laid bare a problem that has been for a long time latent. We are now observing that in the great urban centres a large proportion of the children in the early grades are not being adequately educated even by traditional standards and are being grossly undereducated in relation to the demands which society will place upon them when they reach late adolescence and enter the labour market.

However, it would be an oversimplification to place primarily on the schools blame for the failure of the socially disadvantaged to achieve adequate levels of intellectual competence. Even after all the inadequacies of the American school system are acknowledged, there still remains the stubborn fact that in economically depressed areas of the large metropolitan cities a sizeable proportion (sometimes estimated to be as high as two-thirds) of the children arrive at the first grade without the basic cognitive, motivational, and social skills necessary to undertake the tasks ordinarily presented in a first-grade curriculum. It is too early to evaluate correctly the effects of intervention and remediation programmes (such as Head Start and Follow Through)—particularly the long-term effects—but to date there is not sufficient evidence for self-congratulation on the success of such programmes.

Some feel that the solution to poverty is essentially economic—that rising employment in the context of an ever-expanding economy is the answer. Economists of this persuasion hold that there must be a continuous increment in the gross national product in order to create employment opportunities and purchasing power for the expanding population and the presently unemployed.

But not all agree that continuous increments in the gross national products or in the provision of services are unmixed blessings. Some would wish to slow down or call a halt to the continuous production of commodities and the emphasis on sustained technological innovation. Some would prefer to devote a major share of the nation's energy to eliminating air and water pollution, conserving natural beauty, beautifying the environment in which we live, advancing medical knowledge, expanding the role of education, eliminating poverty, attaining world peace, and cultivating leisure. And it may be argued that the knowledge explosion is not an explosion of wisdom so much as it is an explosion of information gathering and processing to achieve more and more effects without too much attention to the value for humanity of such effects. The predominant view in the nineteenth century was that scientific research, by unlocking the secrets of nature, would usher in the abundant life for all and provide the opportunity for the cultivation of leisure. Contrary to this expectation, the explosion of scientific knowledge has created an ironical situation in which much of technology is engaged in trying to find solutions to problems brought about by the continued application of science to society.

An even more serious consequence of the unbridled techno-logical application of science to the expansion of the economy has been the resulting alienation of man both from himself and from others. It is more than a metaphor to say that man is becoming more and more like the computers he has invented. It is a truism that our culture has tended for a long time to promote con-formity, triviality, and dehumanization. In an affluent society, things have become the measure of man. Why are so many per-sons, brought up with elaborated and complex language and cog-nitive structures, turning to extraverbal and nonverbal channels of communication, both intrapersonally and interpersonally?

This is not to suggest that linguistic impoverishment and mindlessness are the antidote to dehumanization and alienation. On the contrary, I would contend that maximization of one's human potential, by which I include intrapersonal and inter-personal sensitivity and nonverbal and extraverbal communication, is contingent upon the development of an elaborated language code. The dehumanization and alienation of today's society argue, additionally, for the encouragement of greater sensitivity of human beings in extraverbal and nonverbal channels of communication.

In turning to the problems of the socially and culturally dis-advantaged, we see, then, that there are two problems, not one. The first is that social and cultural disadvantage are correlated with retardation and restriction in intellectual growth. The second is that the disadvantaged suffer also from the evils of dehumanization and alienation that characterize society as a whole. Important as it is to alleviate and eliminate cognitive underdevelopment, it is important also to find ways of increasing intrapersonal and interpersonal sensitivity, affective development, motivation, and an awareness of what it means to be human in a community of human beings—not only for the disadvantaged but also for the socially and economically advantaged.

Language and Cognitive Development

Let us return, now, to the development of the argument set forth at the outset. It is not sufficient to say that social and cultural disadvantage (with its attendant psychological constriction) depresses the underprivileged child's academic potential. This is true enough. But the more basic problem is to understand how cultural experience is translated into cognitive behaviour and educability. We need to know how cultural disadvantage acts to shape and depress the potential of the human mind and when cultural disadvantage exercises its most critical influence (Hess and Shipman 1965).

One of the views implicit in the summary argument I presented at the outset is that language, in some way, has a determining influence on cognitive development. This view has been advanced by a number of theorists. Vygotsky (1962, p. 51) states:

> Thought development is determined by language, i.e., by the linguistic tools of thought and by the sociocultural experience of the child. . . . The development of logic in the child, as Piaget's studies have shown, is a direct function of his socialized speech. The child's intellectual growth is contingent on his mastering the social means of thought, that is, language.

According to Vygotsky, the process of intellectual development starts with a dialogue of speech and gesture between child and parent. One of the most important roles adults play in promoting the child's cognitive development is to demarcate the relevant and important dimensions of experience (Luria and Yudovich 1959; Vygotsky 1962). From significant adults in his environment, the child learns what is important for him to attend to; how to give order, structure, and meaning to the relevant environmental stimuli; and how to process, both directly and representationally (symbolically), the information he attends to. The mother's first words, when she shows her child objects and names them, have a decisive influence on the formation of the child's mental processes. The word isolates the essential features of an object or event and inhibits the less essential properties (Luria and Yudovich 1959). Berlyne (1963) has summarized the Soviet position on the nature of the child's intellectual development. As children acquire language, they test their tentative notions about the meanings of words chiefly through verbal interaction with more-verbally-mature speakers (John and Goldstein 1964). Excellent discussions on the mediating role of language have been presented by Brown

(1958, 1965). Bloom, Davis, and Hess (1965, p. 13) describe the usefulness of affixing labels to objects as follows:

> As the child comes to perceive the world about him, he is able to 'fix' or hold particular objects and events in his mind as he is given words or other symbols to 'attach' to them. 'Mama' and 'Dadee' become representations of the important adults in his life. 'Bottle', 'cup', 'dog' become symbols for appropriate objects in the environment.

This view of the language-thought relationship draws upon the work of those anthropologists who have affirmed a determinative relationship between language and cognitive development, notably, Sapir (1929) and Whorf (1956), and upon the work of Bernstein (1965), who has advanced a sociolinguistic approach to social learning. Thus Sapir (1929, pp. 209–10) has stated:

> Language is a guide to 'social reality'. . . . It is quite an illusion to imagine that one adjusts to reality essentially without the use of language and that language is merely an incidental means of solving specific problems of communication or reflection. The fact of the matter is that the real world is to a large extent unconsciously built up on the language habits of the group. . . . We see and hear and otherwise experience very largely as we do because the language habits of our community predispose certain choices of interpretation.

This is a reversal of the older, traditional view that all languages deal with the same 'reality' and that thought is independent of, and prior to, language. Whorf (1956, pp. 212–13), a student of Sapir, explicates the Sapir–Whorf hypotheses as follows:

> . . . the background linguistic system (in other words, the grammar) of each language is not merely a reproducing instrument for voicing ideas but rather is itself the shaper of ideas, the programme and guide for the individual's mental activity. . . . Formulation of ideas is not an independent process, strictly rational in the old sense, but is part of a particular grammar. . . . We dissect nature along lines laid down by our native languages. The categories and types that we isolate from the world of phenomena we do not find there because they stare every

observer in the face; on the contrary, the world is presented in a kaleidoscopic flux of impressions which has to be organized by our minds—and this means largely by the linguistic systems in our minds. We cut nature up, organize it into concepts, and ascribe significances as we do, largely because we are parties to an agreement that holds throughout our speech community and is codified in the patterns of our language. . . .

Brown and Lenneberg (1954, p. 454) have stated the Sapir–Whorf hypothesis succinctly:

> The world can be structured in many ways, and the language we learn as children directs the formation of our particular structure. Language is not a cloak following the contours of thought. Languages are molds into which infant minds are poured.

A caveat is in order. Brown (1965, p. 315) points out that for concepts that are universal, 'social mediation is not likely to be important', that is, they are learned from direct commerce with the physical world. Nevertheless, he agrees that the most important form of concept learning is probably socially and linguistically mediated.

Let us summarize the argument to this point. Much of reality is not what is 'out there', independent of conceptualization of reality, but consists of what is verbally schematized. Central, therefore, to the individual's grasp of reality is the use of language. Without it, complex information could not be processed since such processing requires (1) abstraction, from the infinite welter of events in the world, of categories of events sharing common defining attributes, (2) a code to enable recovery (recollection) of concepts pertinent to the processing of information, and (3) a constant reshuffling of events into different categories with different focal-defining attributes. The necessity for this constant development of new categorizations of experience apparently is embedded in the fact that some of reality is capable of being restructured (conceptualized) in an infinite number of ways. Without categorization the ongoing stream of events would have to be ignored, or if perceived, handled individually (as infrahuman animals must). By means of a limited number of words standing for concepts and by means of the combinatorial possibilities of words, it is possible for man to assimilate experience in manageable ways that are far beyond the reach of animals.

Social Structure and Language

In Whorf's view, the language habits (integrated fashions of speaking) of a community are seen as acting directly upon the individuals, rather than being mediated through the social structure. 'On the contrary, they are seen as determiners of social relations through their role in shaping the culture' (Bernstein 1965). Bernstein (1965, p. 149) offers a sociological modification of the Whorfian view:

> . . . a number of fashions of speaking . . . are possible in any given language and . . . these fashions of speaking, linguistic forms, or codes, are themselves a function of the form social relations take. According to this view, the form of the social relation or—more generally—the social structure, generates distinct linguistic forms or codes and *these codes essentially transmit the culture and so constrain behaviour.*

Bernstein's view is that in the context of a common language there will arise distinct linguistic forms—fashions of speaking—which induce in the speakers different ways of relating to objects and persons. Language 'is a set of rules to which all speech codes must comply, but which speech codes are generated is a function of the system of social relations' (Bernstein 1965, p. 151).

Bernstein (1959, 1960, 1961a, 1961b, 1964, 1965) has expounded the view that the language code of a specific social structure conditions what the child learns and how he learns, and sets limits within which future learning may take place.

> Different social structures will emphasize or stress different aspects of language potential, and this in turn will create for the individual particular dimensions of relevance. As the child learns his speech, so he will learn his social structure, and the latter will become the sub-stream of his innermost experience through the effects of linguistic processing (Bernstein 1961a, pp. 322-3).

Many investigators have shown that the structure and level of the language which a child acquires are related to variables associated with social class (Anastasi 1958; Cazden 1966; Irwin 1948; John 1963; Lawton 1963; Milner 1951, Templin 1957). Jensen (1968), Gordon (1965), and Raph (1965) have summarized much of the work in this area.

Bernstein has discussed these 'different aspects of language potential' in terms of differential codes. He has identified two kinds of communication codes, or styles of language, which have a direct bearing on how language helps shape thought: restricted and elaborated codes. Restricted codes are stereotyped, limited, and condensed, lacking in specificity and the exactness for precise conceptualization, differentiation, and discrimination. The individual limited to a restricted code is sharply constricted in range and detail of concepts and information processing. A major purpose of restricted codes is to promote solidarity and to ease tensions within a group—not to promote cognitive elaboration. Restricted codes arise where the form of the social relation is based upon closely shared identifications and common assumptions. Restricted codes reinforce the form of the social relation rather than explicit meanings and intentions of the speakers. Orientation is less towards the verbal and more towards the extraverbal channel of speech. Restricted codes are status-oriented. But, as Bernstein has indicated, they should not be disvalued. A restricted code contains a vast potential of meanings, particularly metaphorical. It is a form of speech which symbolizes a communally based culture.

In elaborated codes, communication is individualized and the message is specific to a particular situation, topic, or person. It is more differentiated, more precise, permitting expression of a wider and more complex range of thought. Meanings are elaborated and more explicit and specific. Intelligibility of the message is important. An elaborated code is person- or object-oriented rather than status-oriented. Verbal planning requires a high level of syntactic organization and lexical selection since the conveyance of relatively explicit meaning is the major function of an elaborated code (Bernstein 1965). Though meanings are not necessarily abstract, abstraction is facilitated. Also, the code facilitates the verbal transmission and elaboration of the individual's unique experience.

Now, the significance of these two forms of code in terms of socioeconomic status level is this: Restricted codes are available to both upper and lower socioeconomic groups. But lower socioeconomic groups tend to be limited in their language styles mainly to restricted codes. As previously mentioned, the mechanism by which the child is socialized to his language code or codes is in the communicative interaction between mother and child. It follows therefore, that the mother's language style has decisive consequences for the language development of the child.

Family Control Systems and Language Styles

How does the mother's language style—that is, whether her mode of communication to the child is based primarily on an elaborated or a restricted code—manifest itself in different family control systems and how are these systems related to socioeconomic status? Following Bernstein (1964), Hess and Shipman (1965) hold that the kind of family control and regulation used determines the type of code used. Three types of family control have been distinguished by Hess (Hess *et al.* 1968). One type is oriented towards control by status or position appeal or by appeal to ascribed role norms. A second type is oriented towards the subjective states of individual persons. A third is oriented towards consequences, towards rational considerations involving antecedent conditions and consequent effects. Families differ in the extent to which they use each of these types of regulatory appeal. We might say that the relative proportion of each of the three types of orientation used defines (in principle, at least) the style of the family.

In status-oriented families, behaviour is generally regulated in terms of role expectations. The appeal to the child is based on tradition and authority (as publicly defined). This approach is essentially imperative and status-normative in character. 'You must do this because I say so', or 'Girls don't act like that' (Bernstein 1964). Mothers in status-oriented families tend to favour inhibitory and input-control techniques in the control of the child. Inhibitory techniques are intended to prevent a response from recurring or to prevent the child from considering or selecting certain types of alternatives for action and thought. Input-control techniques are used to restrict information and alternatives open to the child. Where intentional, its purpose is to prevent certain types of response from happening by preventing the initial stimulating circumstances from occurring. In the deprived family, this type of control is likely to be inadvertent, rather than intentional, stemming from the disadvantaged mother's inability to provide the symbols and patterns of thought and communication necessary for developing the cognitive potential of the child. This is because she has a limited fund of ideas and information on which to draw in her attempts to cope with the environment. The result is the oft-noted paucity of linguistic and symbolic interaction in culturally deprived families.

The consequences for the child of the mother's use of inhibitory and input-control techniques are to promote the development of a nonrational, nonverbal stance towards the environment. By cutting off the opportunity of the child to engage in linguistic and symbolic interaction the results for the child are a limited repertoire of information and ideas, a low level of differentiation and complexity in his linguistic and cognitive structure, a failure to develop a sense of competence and pleasure in the use of his mind as a way of coping with the environment, and an inability to deal with situations and problems that call for the use of abstract concepts and complex problem-solving strategies (Olim, Hess, and Shipman 1967).

A third type of technique, whose effect is to internalize cognitive control in the child, consists of the attempt to regulate the child's behaviour through appeal to logical considerations and consequences ('If you run out into the street, you may get hurt'), and to subjective consequences and feeling states ('If you go to bed late, you will be tired and sleepy tomorrow'). This approach involves the presentation to the child of a wide range of logical alternatives to thought and action and, by pointing out the rationale of various courses, it encourages the child to choose correctly or wisely among the alternatives that are open to him.

Internalizing techniques are more likely to be associated with families who modify and moderate their appeals to status and role by the frequent use of techniques based upon personal-subjective or cognitive-rational orientations. In the personal-subjective orientation, the family is oriented more towards personal and individual considerations than towards group considerations. The individual characteristics of the child are taken into account. In situations of conflict, the feelings, preferences, reactions, and viewpoint of the child are given careful consideration. In the cognitive-rational orientation, justification of behaviour is sought in the elements of the situation, emphasizing antecedent-consequent considerations. This orientation is not necessarily inconsistent with the personal-subjective approach, but need not include personal considerations in its appeal to logical considerations.

The consequences for the child of the use of personal-subjective and cognitive-rational approaches is to orient the child away from external standards as reference points and away from uncritical acceptance of authority and existing institutions. They orient the child, rather, towards an awareness of the existence of more options for thought and action, exploration of the environment in order to maximize comparisons among possibilities, and the development of elaborated and complex language and cognitive structures. Where the status-orientation approach is dominant, the child is led to attend to authority figures for direction, to develop a compliant, passive approach to learning (until he learns, as a result of failure and frustration in school, either to tune out the school or to adopt a defiant, rebellious attitude towards it), and to reach solutions to problems impulsively rather than reflectively. In personal-subjective-oriented systems, the child is directed towards expressive, subjective responses in others and in himself and towards greater responsivity to interpersonal aspects of behaviour. The cognitive-rational approach tends to orient the child to logical principles as a guide to behaviour. Both the personal-subjective and the cognitive-rational approaches encourage the child to develop a more active stance towards engagement with the environment and a more assertive approach to learning.

The various family control systems and strategies described above are related to maternal language styles and to socioeconomic status level. Mothers who are predominantly status-normative oriented are likely to come from the lower socioeconomic levels and to be limited to restricted codes. Status-oriented statements are often imperative in form, are arbitrary, and restrict the range of alternatives of thought and action. The mother-child communicative interaction system does not require an elaborated code since the system is designed to promote role-conforming rigidity. It is a system that promotes group and status solidarity rather than individuation of personal development. Mothers who are predominantly oriented towards personal-subjective and cognitive-rational approaches are more likely to come from the higher socioeconomic status levels and will manifest elaborated language styles because these orientations not only permit but demand an elaborated code to deal with the wide range of alternatives of behaviour and thought that are involved.

Implications for Children's Cognitive Development

If the arguments presented in this essay are sound, there are a number of practical implications and applications for those en-engaged in attempting to eliminate poverty and its attendant evils. First, on a psychological level, any programme of remediation or change must start in the preschool years and be related to the mother-child communication interaction system. The child is exposed to a great deal of potential information in his environment. What he assimilates and accommodates to, how he interprets the stimuli to which he attends, and the responses he develops are learned in interaction with the environment, which in most instances is the maternal environment. Patterns of linguistic and cognitive activity are developed which become the basis upon which further cognitive development proceeds. The opportunity and encouragement to begin the process of developing an elaborated code are usually available to the higher-socioeconomic-status child but generally denied to the lower-socioeconomic-status child (i.e., the socially and culturally deprived). Bloom (1964) concludes that as much intellectual growth is achieved between birth and age four as is achieved between age four and age seventeen. Remediation, then, should begin in the home. Some efforts have been made along this line. However, there is considerable ground for pessimism that the problem can be handled on an individual basis (Bloom, Davis, and Hess 1965, p. 16) when 'the total syndrome of poverty, broken homes, slum living, large families, and illiteracy all conspire against the intellectual development of the child'.

How can a mother, who is limited to a restricted code, be the means for making it possible for her child to develop an elaborated code? And if the social structure and the structure of the disadvantaged family shape and promote the development of restricted codes and if 'language is used by participants of a social network to elaborate and express social and other interpersonal relations' (Hess and Shipman 1965, p. 871), how can the bind be broken? Two obvious solutions come to mind.

The first is to extend the school age downward to the early critical years of language and cognitive development. Preschool and early childhood programmes, preservice and in-service teacher training for disadvantaged areas, and development of more effective instructional materials for use with the disadvantaged are all being tried. Whether such programmes can rescue the disadvantaged child from the crushing effects of the total syndrome of poverty is a moot question.

The second solution would call for drastic social reform. Since the structure of the family and the attendant family control systems are embedded in the larger structure of society, it may be that nothing short of a major transformation in the economic and social world of the disadvantaged will suffice to bring about a major change in their cognitive world.

Of course, one need not back either of these alternatives to the exclusion of the other. Since behaviour and social structure interact, those interested in the eradication of poverty may work at various levels simultaneously—educational, economic, social, and psychological.

I have already indicated that the socially and culturally deprived suffer from a serious disadvantage cognitively but that they also suffer from what may be a far worse problem—one that is shared by the whole society—that is, the problem of dehumanization and alienation. Although elaborated codes maximize the range of alternatives of thought and action, and the possibility of this maximization should be open to all, the acquisition and use of an elaborated code does not require that the user have either an exquisite sense of his own identity and worth as a human being, or a highly developed sense of community. What else can we conclude from the litany of troubles besetting us today: social unrest, the repolarization of racial attitudes, the disarray and underfinancing of our public school system and public health services, student revolts, dissent and civil disobedience, the pollution of our air and water supplies, experimentation with drugs, and experimentation with new forms of social structure? Surely, those responsible for these troubles are not those limited to a restricted code. On the contrary they are the responsibility of those who have developed an elaborated code and complex cognitive strategies. We should also ask ourselves how it has come about that the young who have mastered an elaborated language code and who have been reared in relatively open family systems—open both in the Bernstein sense and in the Rogerian sense (Rogers 1961)—are sometimes just those who are most sensitive to their alienation from themselves and from other human beings.

The growth of Black Power and racial separatism in America is, I believe, symptomatic of the unwillingness of the disadvantaged black to give up his (admittedly tenuous) grip on what little identity and community he has in exchange for the alienated depersonalization of the white society. Bernstein (1961b, pp. 308-9) indicates that the solution for the person limited to a restricted code is not to eliminate it but to create for him the possibility of utilizing an elaborated code as well. For survival and success in an advanced society, this prescription seems unassailable. But Bernstein (1961b, p. 308) also points out that a restricted code:

> . . . contains its own aesthetic—a simplicity and directness of expression, emotionally virile, pithy, and powerful, with a metaphoric range of considerable force and appropriateness. It is a language which symbolizes a tradition and a form of social relationship in which the individual is treated as an end, not as a means to a further end.

Is it not appropriate to conclude that it is just as important for the socially advantaged to develop to a high degree the use of restricted codes and concomitantly to develop a sense of community with their fellow human beings? Is it not just as important to construct social relations in which persons are not treated as objects and commodities, where competition and conquest are not the dominant values, and where affective intrapersonal and interpersonal development are as important as the development of proficiency in scientific-rational-symbolic thought? The current emphases on human development (as opposed to merely cognitive competence) reflect the tremendous dissatisfaction many feel with the under-development of extraverbal and nonverbal channels of communication and modes of relationship (see, for example, *Psychology Today*, December 1967).

In so far as we rely on our educational system to be the vehicle for overcoming some of the effects of poverty, we must face the fact that to provide remedial and compensatory education for the socially disadvantaged is not enough. From the standpoint of developing human potential, it is necessary to face up to the fact that we have failed in all our institutions (including the school) to see the urgency of fostering the humanness of citizens. Hutchins (1965) has posed the question as to whether we are not educating our children for the wrong future. With ever-increasing techno-logical efficiency and productivity, are we not confronted with the terrifying prospect that, no matter how much we increase the complexity and level of our training, there may still be a declining number of job opportunities for which even complex skills will be needed? In a society which is evolving towards less work and more leisure, educating, not training, should be the proper goal of our schools. It is a truism that education requires attention to the total man—his aesthetic and moral aspects as well as his cognitive. To these ends, our schools should emphasize the development of human sensitivity as well as cognitive competence, though the latter should not be disvalued since the future society may be a learning society (Hutchins 1965). To the extent that the schools and, indeed, our society do not engage in such emphases, all our children may progressively become culturally disadvantaged.

References

Anastasi, Anne (1958) *Differential Psychology*, New York: Macmillan.
Berlyne, D. E. (1963) *Soviet Research on Intellectual Processes in Children*. Monograph of the Society for Research in Child Development, Vol. 28.
Bernstein, B. (1959) 'A public language: some sociological implications of a linguistic form' *British J. Sociology*, **10**, 311–26.
— (1960) 'Language and social class' *British J. Sociology*, **11**, 271–6.

— (1961a) 'Aspects of language and learning in the genesis of the social process' *J. Child Psychology and Psychiatry*, **1**, 313–24.

— (1961b) 'Social class and linguistic development: a theory of social learning'. In A. H. Halsey, J. Floud, and A. Anderson (eds.) *Education, Economy, and Society*, New York: Free Press.

— (1964) 'Family role systems, communication, and socialization'. Paper presented at Conference on Development of Cross-National Research on Education of Children and Adolescents, February, 1964, University of Chicago.

— (1965) 'A socio-linguistic approach to social learning'. In J. Gould (ed.) *Penguin Survey of the Social Sciences*, Penguin Books.

Bloom, B. S. (1964) *Stability and Change in Human Characteristics*, New York: Wiley.

—, Davis, A., and Hess, R. D. (1965) *Compensatory Education for Cultural Deprivation*, New York: Holt, Rinehart, Winston.

Brown, R. W. (1958) *Words and Things*, New York: Free Press.

— (1965) *Social Psychology*, New York: Free Press.

— and Lenneberg, E. H. (1954) 'A study in language and cognition' *J. Abnormal and Social Psychology*, **49**, 454–62.

Cazden, Courtney B. (1966) 'Subcultural differences in child language: an interdisciplinary review' *Merrill-Palmer Quarterly*, **12**, 185–219.

Gordon, E. W. (1965) 'Characteristics of socially disadvantaged children' *Review of Educational Research*, **35**, 377–88.

Hess, R. D., and Shipman, Virginia (1965) 'Early experience and the socialization of cognitive modes in children' *Child Development*, **36**, 869–86.

Hess, R. D., Shipman, Virginia, Bear, Roberta M., and Brophy, J. (1968) *The Cognitive Environments of Urban Preschool Children*, Chicago: University of Chicago Press.

Hutchins, R. M. (1965) 'Are we educating our children for the wrong future?' *Saturday Review*, September 11, 1965, 66–7, 83.

Irwin, O. C. (1948) 'Infant speech: the effect of family occupational status and of age on use of sound types' *J. Speech and Hearing Disorders*, **13**, 224–6.

Jensen, A. R. (1968) 'Social class and verbal learning'. In M. Deutsch *et al. Social Class, Race, and Psychological Development*, New York: Holt, Rinehart, Winston.

John, Vera (1963) 'The intellectual development of slum children: some preliminary findings' *American J. Orthopsychiatry*, **33**, 813–22.

— and Goldstein, L. S. (1964) 'The social context of language acquisition' *Merrill-Palmer Quarterly*, **10**, 265–75.

Lawton, D. (1963) 'Social class differences in language development: a study of some samples of written work' *Language and Speech*, **6**, 120–143.

Luria, A. R., and Yudovich, F. (1959) *Speech and the Development of Mental Processes in the Child*, London: Staples Press.

Milner, Esther (1951) 'A study of the relationships between reading readiness in grade one school children and patterns of parent-child interaction' *Child Development*, **22**, 95–112.

Olim, E. G., Hess, R. D., and Shipman, Virginia (1967) 'Role of mothers' language styles in mediating their preschool children's cognitive development' *The School Review*, **75**, 414–24.

Raph, Jane B. (1965) 'Language development in socially disadvantaged children' *Review of Educational Research*, **35**, 389–400.

Rogers, C. (1961) 'The implications of client-centered therapy for family life'. In *On Becoming a Person*, Boston: Houghton Mifflin.

Sapir, E. (1929) 'The status of linguistics as a science' *Language*, **5**, 207–214.

Templin, Mildred C. (1957) *Certain language skills, in children, their development and interrelationships*. Institute for Child Welfare Monograph Series, No. 26. Minneapolis: University of Minnesota Press.

Vygotsky, L. S. (1962) *Thought and Language*. Eugenia Hanfmann and Gertrude Vakar (ed. and trans.), Cambridge Mass.: M.I.T. Press.

Whorf, B. L. (1956) 'Science and linguistics'. In J. B. Carroll (ed.) *Language, Thought, and Reality: Selected Writings of Benjamin Lee Whorf*, Cambridge, Mass.: M.I.T. Press.

21

BASIL B. BERNSTEIN
Language and Socialization

Bernstein's original work was concerned with an examination of the
development of different language styles in different social classes; these
different language styles—he called them 'restricted' and 'elaborated'
codes—have some correlation, he suggested, with the child's perception
and conceptualization of the environment. More recently he and his
colleagues have suggested that the type of language used by the child
would be more highly correlated with the mother's behaviour and
attitudes than with the totality of social class. It is worth remembering,
though, that correlation in this instance does not necessarily imply a
causal relationship.

In this reading taken from Bernstein's lecture given in a series on
linguistics by distinguished linguists at the Institute of Contemporary
Arts in the winter of 1969–70, he argues that his research has implications beyond the role of language in the gradual processes of socialization and his dichotomization into distinct language styles can be a
basic factor in our social structure.

I want first of all to make clear what I am not concerned with.
Chomsky in 'Syntactic Structures' neatly severs the study of the
rule system of language from the study of the social rules which
determine their contextual use. He does this by making a distinction between competence and performance. Competence refers to
the child's tacit understanding of the rule system, performance
relates to the essentially social use to which the rule system is put.
Competence refers to man abstracted from contextual constraints.
Performance refers to man in the grip of the contextual constraints
which determine his speech acts. Competence refers to the Ideal,
performance refers to the Fall. In this sense Chomsky's notion of
competence is Platonic. Competence has its source in the very
biology of man. There is no difference between men in terms of

Basil B. Bernstein: Extract from 'Language and socialization' in N. Minnis
(ed.) *Linguistics at Large*, Gollancz, 1971, pp. 229–45. Reproduced by permission of Routledge & Kegan Paul.

their access to the linguistic rule system. Here Chomsky, like many other linguists before him, announces the communality of man; all men have equal access to the creative act which is language. On the other hand, performance is under the control of the social—performances are culturally-specific acts, they refer to the choices which are made in specific speech encounters. Thus from one point of view, Chomsky indicates the tragedy of man, the potentiality of competence and the degeneration of performance (Hymes 1966).

Clearly, much is to be gained in rigour and explanatory power through the severing of the relationship between the formal properties of the grammar and the meanings which are realized in its use. But if we are to study speech, *la parole*, we are inevitably involved in a study of a rather different rule system; we are involved in a study of rules, formal and informal, which regulate the options we take up in various contexts in which we find ourselves. This second rule system is the cultural system. This raises immediately the question of the relationship between the linguistic rule system and the cultural system. Clearly, specific linguistic rule systems are part of the cultural system, but it has been argued that the linguistic rule system in various ways shapes the cultural system. This very briefly is the view of those who hold a narrow form of the linguistic relativity hypothesis. I do not intend this evening to get involved in that particular quagmire. Instead, I shall take the view that the code which the linguist invents to explain the formal properties of the grammar is capable of generating any number of speech codes, and there is no reason for believing that any one language code is better than another in this respect. On this argument, language is a set of rules to which all speech codes must comply, but which speech codes are realized is a function of the culture acting through social relationships in specific contexts. Different speech forms or codes symbolize the form of the social relationship, regulate the nature of the speech encounters, and create for the speakers different orders of relevance and relation. The experience of the speakers is then transformed by what is made significant or relevant by the speech form. This is a sociological argument because the speech form is taken as a consequence of the form of the social relation or, put more generally, is a quality of a social structure. Let me qualify this immediately. Because the speech form is initially a function of a given social arrangement, it does not mean that the speech form does not in turn modify or even change that social structure which initially evolved the speech form. This formulation, indeed, invites the question—under what conditions does a given speech form free itself sufficiently from its embodiment in the social structure so that the system of meanings it realizes points to alternative realities, alternative arrangements in the affairs of men. Here we become concerned immediately with the antecedents and consequences of the boundary-maintaining principles of a culture or sub-culture. I am here suggesting a relationship between forms of boundary maintenance at the cultural level and forms of speech.

I am required to consider the relationship between language and socialization. It should be clear from these opening remarks that I am not concerned with language, but with speech, and concerned more specifically with the contextual constraints upon speech. Now what about socialization? I shall take the term to refer to the process whereby a child acquires a specific cultural identity, *and* to his responses to such an identity. Socialization refers to the process whereby the biological is transformed into a specific cultural being. It follows from this that the process of socialization is a complex process of control, whereby a particular moral, cognitive and affective awareness is evoked in the child and given a specific form and content. Socialization sensitizes the child to various orderings of society as these are made substantive in the various roles he is expected to play. In a sense then socialization is a process for making people safe. The process acts selectively on the possibilities of man by creating through time a sense of the inevitability of a given social arrangement, and through limiting the areas of permitted change. The basic agencies of socialization in contemporary societies are the family, the peer group, school and work. It is through these agencies, and in particular through their relationship to each other, that the various orderings of society are made manifest.

Now it is quite clear that given this view of socialization it is necessary to limit the discussion. I shall limit our discussion to socialization within the family, but it should be obvious that the focusing and filtering of the child's experience within the family in a large measure is a microcosm of the macroscopic orderings of society. Our question now becomes: what are the sociological factors affecting linguistic performances within the family which are critical to the process of socialization?

Without a shadow of doubt the most formative influence upon the procedures of socialization, from a sociological viewpoint, is social class. The class structure influences work and educational roles and brings families into a special relationship with each other and deeply penetrates the structure of life experiences within the family. The class system has deeply marked the distribution of knowledge within society. It has given differential access to the sense that the world is permeable. It has sealed off communities from each other and has ranked these communities on a scale of invidious worth. We have three components, knowledge, possibility, invidious insulation. It would be a little naive to believe that differences in knowledge, differences in the sense of the possible, combined with invidious insulation, rooted in differential *material* well-being, would not affect the forms of control and innovation in the socializing procedures of different social classes. I shall go on to argue that the deep structure of communication itself is affected, but not in any final or irrevocable way.

As an approach to my argument, let me glance at the social distribution of knowledge. We can see that the class system has affected the distribution of knowledge. Historically and now, only a tiny percentage of the population has been socialized into knowledge at the level of the meta-languages of control and innovation, whereas the mass of the population has been socialized into knowledge at the level of context-tied operations.

A tiny percentage of the population has been given access to the principles of intellectual change whereas the rest have been denied such access. This suggests that we might be able to distinguish between two orders of meaning. One we could call universalistic, the other particularistic. Universalistic meanings are those in which principles and operations are made linguistically explicit whereas particularistic orders of meaning are meanings in which principles and operations are relatively linguistically implicit. If orders of meaning are universalistic, then the meanings are less tied to a given context. The meta-languages of public forms of thought, as these apply to objects and persons, realize meanings of a universalistic type. Where meanings have this characteristic then individuals have access to the grounds of their experience and can change the grounds. Where orders of meaning are particularistic, where principles are linguistically implicit, then such meanings are less context-independent and *more* context-bound. That is tied to a local relationship and to a local social structure. Where the meaning system is particularistic, much of the meaning is embedded in the context and may be restricted to those who share a similar contextual history. Where meanings are universalistic, they are in principle available to all because the principles and operations have been made explicit and so public.

I shall argue that forms of socialization orient the child towards speech codes which control access to relatively context-tied or relatively context-independent meanings. Thus I shall argue that elaborated codes orient their users towards universalistic meanings, whereas restricted codes orient, sensitize, their users to particularistic meanings; that the linguistic realization of the two orders are different, and so are the social relationships which realize them. Elaborated codes are less tied to a given or local structure and thus contain the potentiality of change in principles. In the case of elaborated codes the speech is freed from its evoking social structure and takes on an autonomy. A university is a place organized around talk. Restricted codes are more tied to a local social structure and have a reduced potential for change in principles. Where codes are elaborated, the socialized has more access to the grounds of his own socialization, and so can enter into a reflexive relationship to the social order he has taken over. Where codes are restricted, the socialized has less access to the grounds of his socialization and thus reflexiveness may be limited in range. *One of the effects of the class system is to limit access to elaborated codes.*

I shall go on to suggest that restricted codes have their basis in condensed symbols whereas elaborated codes have their basis in articulated symbols. That restricted codes draw upon metaphor whereas elaborated codes draw upon rationality. That these codes constrain the contextual use of language in critical socializing contexts and in this way regulate the orders of relevance and relation which the socialized takes over. From this point of view, change in habitual speech codes involves changes in the means by which object and person relationships are realized.

I want first to start with the notions of elaborated and restricted speech variants. A variant can be considered as the contextual constraints upon grammatical-lexical choices.

Sapir, Malinowski, Firth, Vygotsky, Luria have all pointed out from different points of view that the closer the identifications of speakers the greater the range of shared interests, the more probable that the speech will take a specific form. The range of syntactic alternatives is likely to be reduced and the lexis to be drawn from a narrow range. Thus, the form of these social relations is acting selectively on the meanings to be verbally realized. In these relationships the intent of the other person can be taken for granted as the speech is played out against a back-drop of common assumptions, common history, common interests. As a result, there is less need to raise meanings to the level of explicitness or elaboration. There is a reduced need to make explicit through syntactic choices the logical structure of the communication. Further, if the speaker wishes to individualize his communication, he is likely to do this by varying the expressive associates of the speech. Under these conditions, the speech is likely to have a strong metaphoric element. In these situations the speaker may be more concerned with how something is said, and when it is said—silence takes on a variety of meanings. Often in these encounters the speech cannot be understood apart from the context and the context cannot be read by those who do not share the history of the relationships. Thus the form of the social relationship acts selectively on the meanings to be verbalized, which in turn affect the syntactic and lexical choices. The unspoken assumptions underlying the relationship are not available to those who are outside the relationship. For these are limited, and restricted to the speakers. The symbolic form of the communication is condensed yet the specific cultural history of the relationship is alive in its form. We can say that the roles of the speakers are communalized roles. Thus, we can make a relationship between restricted social relationships based upon communalized roles and the verbal realization of their meaning. In the language of the earlier part of this talk, restricted social relationships based upon communalized roles evoke particularistic, that is, context-tied meanings, realized through a restricted speech variant.

Imagine a husband and wife have just come out of the cinema

and are talking about the film: 'What do you think?' 'It had a lot to say.' 'Yes, I thought so too—let's go to the Millers, there may be something going there.' They arrive at the Millers, who ask about the film. An hour is spent in the complex, moral, political, aesthetic subtleties of the film and its place in the contemporary scene. Here we have an elaborated variant, the meanings now have to be made public to others who have not seen the film. The speech shows careful editing, at both the grammatical and lexical levels, it is no longer context-tied. The meanings are explicit, elaborated and individualized. Whilst expressive channels are clearly relevant, the burden of meaning inheres predominantly in the verbal channel. The experience of the listeners cannot be taken for granted. Thus each member of the group is on his own as he offers his interpretation. Elaborated variants of this kind involve the speakers in particular role relationships, and *if you cannot manage the role, you cannot produce the appropriate speech.* For as the speaker proceeds to individualize his meanings, he is differentiated from others like a figure from its ground.

The roles receive less support from each other. There is a measure of isolation. *Difference* lies at the basis of the social relationship, and is made verbally active, whereas in the other context it is *consensus*. The insides of the speaker have become psychologically active through the verbal aspect of the communication. Various defensive strategies may be used to decrease potential vulnerability of self and to increase the vulnerability of others. The verbal aspect of the communication becomes a vehicle for the transmission of individuated symbols. The 'I' stands over the 'We'. Meanings which are discreet to the speaker must be offered so that they are intelligible to the listener. Communalized roles have given way to individualized roles, condensed symbols to articulated symbols. Elaborated speech variants of this type realize universalistic meanings in the sense that they are less context-tied. Thus individualized roles are realized through elaborated speech variants which involve complex editing at the grammatical and lexical levels and which point to universalistic meanings.

Let me give another example. Consider the two following stories which Peter Hawkins, Assistant Research Officer in the Sociological Research Unit, University of London Institute of

Education, constructed as a result of his analysis of the speech of middle-class and working-class five-year-old children. The children were given a series of four pictures which told a story and they were invited to tell the story. The first picture showed some boys playing football, in the second the ball goes through the window of a house, the third shows a woman looking out of the window and a man making an ominous gesture, and in the fourth the children are moving away.

Here are the two stories:

(1) Three boys are playing football and one boy kicks the ball and it goes through the window   the ball breaks the window and the boys are looking at it   and a man comes out and shouts at them   because they've broken the window   so they run away   and then that lady looks out of her window and she tells the boys off.

(2) They're playing football   and he kicks it and it goes through there   it breaks the window and they're looking at it   and he comes out   and shouts at them   because they've broken it   so they run away   and then she looks out   and she tells them off.

With the first story the reader does not have to have the four pictures which were used as the basis for the story, whereas in the case of the second story the reader would require the initial pictures in order to make sense of the story. The first story is free of the context which generated it, whereas the second story is much more closely tied to its context. As a result the meanings of the second story are implicit, whereas the meanings of the first story are explicit. It is not that the working-class children do not have in their passive vocabulary the vocabulary used by the middle-class children. Nor is it the case that the children differ in their tacit understanding of the linguistic rule system. Rather, what we have here are differences in the use of language arising out of a specific context. One child makes explicit the meanings which he is realizing through language for the person he is telling the story to, whereas the second child does not to the same extent. The first child takes very little for granted, whereas the second child takes a great deal for granted. Thus for the first child the task was seen as a context in which his meanings were required to be made explicit, whereas the task for the second child was not seen as a task which required such explication of meaning. It would not be difficult to imagine a context where the first child would produce speech rather like the second. What we are dealing with here are differences between the children in the way they realize in language use apparently the same context. We could say that the speech of the first child generated universalistic meanings in the sense that the meanings are freed from the context and so understandable by all. Whereas the speech of the second child generated particularistic meanings, in the sense that the meanings are closely tied to the context and would be only fully understood by others if they had access to the context which originally generated the speech.

It is again important to stress that the second child has access to a more differentiated noun phrase, but there is a restriction on its *use*. Geoffrey Turner, Linguist in the Sociological Research Unit, shows that working-class, five-year-old children, in the same contexts examined by Hawkins, use fewer linguistic expressions of uncertainty when compared with the middle-class children. This does not mean that working-class children do *not* have access to such expressions, but that the eliciting speech context did not provoke them. Telling a story from pictures, talking about scenes on cards, *formally framed* contexts, do not encourage working-class children to consider the possibilities of alternate meanings and so there is a reduction in the linguistic expresssions of uncertainty. Again, working-class children have access to a wide range of syntactic choices which involve the use of logical operators, 'because', 'but', 'either', 'or', 'only'. The constraints exist on the conditions for their *use*. Formally framed contexts used for eliciting context-independent, universalistic meanings may evoke in the working-class child, relative to the middle-class child, restricted speech variants, because the working-class child has difficulty in managing the role relationships which such contexts require. This problem is further complicated when such contexts carry meanings very much removed from the child's cultural experience. In the same way we can show that there are constraints upon the middle-class child's use of language. Turner found that when middle-class children were asked to role play in the picture story series, a higher percentage of these children, when compared with working-class children, initially refused. When the middle-class children were asked 'What is the man saying?', or linguistically equivalent questions, a relatively higher percentage said 'I don't know'. When this question was followed by the hypothetical question 'What do you think the man might be saying?' they offered their interpretations. The working-class children role played without difficulty. It seems then that middle-class children at five need to have a very precise instruction to *hypothesize in that particular* context. This may be because they are more concerned here with getting their answers right or correct. When the children were invited to tell a story about some doll-like figures (a little boy, a little girl, a sailor and a dog) the working-class children's stories were freer, longer, more imaginative than the stories of the middle-class children. The latter children's stories were tighter, constrained within a strong narrative frame. It was as if these children were dominated by what they took to be the *form* of a narrative and the content was secondary. This is an example of the concern of the middle-class child with the structure of the contextual frame. It may be worthwhile to amplify this further. A number of studies have shown that when working-class black children are asked to associate to a series of words, their responses show considerable diversity, both from the meaning and form class of the stimulus word. In the analysis offered in the text this may be because the children for the following reasons are less constrained. The form class of the stimulus word may have reduced associative significance and so would less constrain the selection of potential words or phrases. With such a weakening of the grammatical frame a greater range of alternatives are possible candidates for selection. Further, the closely controlled middle-class linguistic socialization of the young child may point the child towards both the grammatical significance of the stimulus word and towards a tight logical ordering of semantic space. Middle-class children may well have access to deep interpretative rules which regulate their linguistic responses in certain formalized contexts. The consequences may limit their imagination through the tightness of the frame which these interpretative rules create. It may even be that with five-year-old children, the middle-class child will innovate more with the arrangements of objects (i.e.

bricks) than in his linguistic usage. His linguistic usage is under close supervision by adults. He has more autonomy in his play.

To return to our previous discussion, we can say briefly that as we move from communalized to individualized roles, so speech takes on an increasingly reflexive function. The unique selves of others become palpable through speech and enter into our own self, the grounds of our experience are made verbally explicit; the security of the condensed symbol is gone. It has been replaced by rationality. There is a change in the basis of our vulnerability.

So far, then, I have discussed certain types of speech variants and the role relationships which occasion them. I am now going to raise the generality of the discussion and focus upon the title of the paper. The socialization of the young in the family proceeds within a critical set of interrelated contexts. Analytically, we may distinguish four contexts.

1. The regulative context—these are authority relationships where the child is made aware of the rules of the moral order and their various backings.

2. The instructional context, where the child learns about the objective nature of objects and persons, and acquires skills of various kinds.

3. The imaginative or innovating context, where the child is encouraged to experiment and re-create his world on his own terms, and in his own way.

4. The interpersonal context, where the child is made aware of affective states—his own, and others.

I am suggesting that the critical orderings of a culture or sub-culture are made substantive—are made palpable—through the forms of its linguistic realizations of these four contexts—initially in the family and kin.

Now if the linguistic realization of these four contexts involves the predominant use of restricted speech variants, I shall postulate that the deep structure of the communication[1] is a restricted code having its basis in communalized roles, realizing context bound meanings, i.e., particularistic meaning orders. Clearly the specific

---

[1] i.e. the underlying principles which regulate performances in the four critical socializing contexts.

grammatical and lexical choices will vary from one context to another.

If the linguistic realization of these four contexts involves the predominant usage of elaborated speech variants, I shall postulate that the deep structure of the communication is an elaborated code having its basis in individualized roles realizing context-free universalistic meanings.

In order to prevent misunderstanding an expansion of the text is here necessary. It is likely that where the code is restricted, the speech in the regulative context may well be limited to command and simple rule-announcing statements. The latter statements are not context-dependent in the sense previously given for they announce general rules. We need to supplement the context-independent (universalistic) and context-dependent (particularistic) criteria with criteria which refer to the extent to which the speech in the regulative context varies in terms of its *contextual specificity*. If the speech is context-specific then the socializer cuts his meanings to the *specific* attributes/intentions of the socialized, the specific characteristics of the problem, the specific requirements of the context. Thus the general rule may be transmitted with degrees of contextual specificity. When this occurs the rule is individualized (fitted to the local circumstances) in the process of its transmission. Thus with code elaboration we should expect:

1. Some developed grounds for the rule.
2. Some qualification of it in the light of the particular issue.
3. Considerable specificity in terms of the socialized, the context and the issue.

This does not mean that there would be an absence of command statements. It is also likely that with code elaboration the socialized would be given opportunities (role options) to question.

Bernstein and Cook (1965), Cook (1971) have developed a semantic coding grid which sets out with considerable delicacy a general category system which has been applied to a limited regulative context. Turner (1971) is attempting a linguistic realization of the same grid.

We can express the two sets of criteria diagrammatically. A limited application is given by Henderson (1970).

Realization of the Regulative Context

Universalistic

Specific ——————|——————Non-specific

Particularistic

It may be necessary to utilize the two sets of criteria for all four socializing contexts. Bernstein (1967, published 1970) suggested that code realization would vary with context.

If we look at the linguistic realization of the regulative context in greater detail we may be able to clear up another source of possible misunderstanding. In this context it is very likely that syntactic markers of the logical distribution of meaning will be extensively used.

'If you do that, then . . .'
'Either you . . . or . . .'
'You can do that but if . . .'
'You do that and you'll pay for it.'

Thus it is very likely that young children may well in the *regulative* context have access to a range of syntactic markers which express the logical/hypothetical irrespective of code restriction or elaboration. However, where the code is restricted it is expected that there will be reduced specificity in the sense outlined earlier. Further, the speech in the control situation is likely to be well-organized in the sense that the sentences come as wholes. The child responds to the total frame. However, I would suggest that the informal *instructional* contexts within the family may well be limited in range and frequency. Thus the child, of course, would have access to, and so have available, the hypotheticals, conditionals, disjunctives, etc. but these might be rarely used in instructional contexts. In the same way, as we have suggested earlier, all children have access to linguistic expressions of uncertainty but they may differ in the context in which they receive and realize such expressions.

I must emphasize that because the code is restricted it does not mean that speakers will at no time use elaborated speech variants. Only that the use of such variants will be infrequent in the socialization of the child in his family.

Now, all children have access to restricted codes and their

various systems of condensed meaning, because the roles the code presupposes are universal. But there may well be selective access to elaborated codes because there is selective access to the role system which evokes its use. Society is likely to evaluate differently the experiences realized through these two codes. I cannot here go into details, but the different focusing of experience through a restricted code creates a major problem of educability only where the school produces discontinuity between its symbolic orders and those of the child. Our schools are not made for these children; why should the children respond? To ask the child to switch to an elaborated code which presupposes different role relationships and systems of meaning without a sensitive understanding of the required contexts must create for the child a bewildering and potentially damaging experience.

So far, then, I have sketched out a relationship between speech codes and socialization through the organization of roles through which the culture is made psychologically active in persons. I have indicated that access to the roles and thus to the codes is broadly related to social class. However, it is clearly the case that social class groups today are by no means homogeneous groups. Further, the division between elaborated and restricted codes is too simple. Finally, I have not indicated in any detail how these codes are evoked with families, and how the family types may shape their focus.

What I shall do now is to introduce a distinction between family type and its communication structure. These family types can be found empirically within each social class, although any one type may be rather more modal at any given historical period.

I shall distinguish between families according to the strength of their boundary-maintaining procedures. Let me first give some idea of what I mean by boundary-maintaining procedures. I shall first look at boundary maintenance as it is revealed in the symbolic ordering of space. Consider the lavatory. In one house, the room is pristine, bare and sharp, containing only the necessities for which the room is dedicated. In another there is a picture on the wall, in the third there are books, in the fourth all surfaces are covered with curious postcards. We have a continuum from a room celebrating the purity of categories to one celebrating the mixture of categories, from strong to weak boundary maintenance.

Consider the kitchen. In one kitchen, shoes may not be placed on the table, nor the child's chamber pot—all objects and utensils have an assigned place. In another kitchen the boundaries separating the different classes of objects are weak. The symbolic ordering of space can give us indications of the relative strength of boundary-maintaining procedures. Let us now look at the relationship between family members. Where boundary procedures are strong, the differentiation of members and the authority structure is based upon clear-cut, unambiguous definitions of the status of the member of the family. The boundaries between the statuses are strong, and the social identities of the members very much a function of their age, sex and age-relation status. As a shorthand, we can characterize the family as 'positional'.

On the other hand, where boundary procedures are weak or flexible, the differentiation between members and the authority relationships are less on the basis of position, because here the status boundaries are blurred. Where boundary procedures are weak, the differentiation between members is based more upon differences between persons. In such families the relationships become more egocentric and the unique attributes of family members more and more are made substantive in the communication structure. We will call these 'person-centred' families. Such families do not reduce but increase the substantive expression of ambiguity and ambivalence. In person-centred families, the role system would be continuously evoking, accommodating and assimilating the different interests, attributes of its members. In such families, unlike positional families, the members would be making their roles, rather than stepping into them. In a person-centred family, the child's developing self is differentiated by continuous adjustment to the verbally realized and elaborated intentions, qualifications and motives of others. The boundary between self and other is blurred. In positional families, the child takes over and responds to the formal pattern of obligation and privilege. It should be possible to see, without going into details, that the communication structure within these two types of family are somewhat differently focused. We might then expect that the reflexiveness induced by positional families is sensitized to the general attributes of persons, whereas the reflexiveness produced by person-centred families is more sensitive towards the particular aspects of persons. Think of the difference between Dartington Hall or Gordonstoun Public Schools in England, or the difference between West Point and a progressive school in the USA. Thus, in person-centred families, the insides of the members are made public through the communication structure, and thus more of the person has been invaded and subject to control. Speech in such families is a major medium of control. In positional families of course, speech is relevant but it symbolizes the boundaries given by the formal structure of the relationships. So far as the child is concerned, in positional families he attains a strong sense of social identity at the cost of autonomy; in person-centred families, the child attains a strong sense of autonomy but his social identity may be weak. Such ambiguity in the sense of identity, the lack of boundary, may move such children towards a radically closed value system.

If we now place these family types in the framework of the previous discussion, we can see that although the code may be elaborated, it may be differently focused according to the family type. Thus, we can have an elaborated code focusing upon persons or an elaborated code in a positional family may focus more upon objects. We can expect the same with a restricted code. Normally, with code restriction we should expect a positional family; however, if it showed signs of being person-centred, then we might expect the children to be in a situation of potential code switch.

Where the code is elaborated, and focused by a person-centred family, then these children may well develop acute identity problems, concerned with authenticity, of limiting responsibility— they may come to see language as phony, a system of counterfeit masking the absence of belief. They may move towards the restricted codes of the various peer group sub-cultures, or seek the condensed symbols of affective experience, or both.

One of the difficulties of this approach is to avoid implicit value judgements about the relative worth of speech systems and the cultures which they symbolize. Let it be said immediately that a restricted code gives access to a vast potential of meanings, of delicacy, subtlety and diversity of cultural forms, to a unique aesthetic whose basis in condensed symbols may influence the form of the imagining. Yet, in complex industrialized societies its differently focused experience may be disvalued, and humiliated within schools or seen, at best, to be irrelevant to the educational endeavour. For the schools are predicated upon elaborated code and its system of social relationships. Although an elaborated code does not entail any specific value system, the value system of the middle class penetrates the texture of the very learning context itself.

Elaborated codes give access to alternative realities yet they carry the potential of alienation of feeling from thought, of self from other, of private belief from role obligation.

In conclusion, I have tried to show how the class system acts upon the deep structure of communication in the process of socialization. I refined the crudity of this analysis by showing how speech codes may be differently focused through family types. I must point out that there is more to socialization than the forms of its linguistic realization.

Finally, it is conceivable that there are general aspects of the analysis which might provide a starting point for the consideration of symbolic orders other than languages.

References

Bernstein, B. (1970) 'Education Cannot Compensate for Society' *New Society* No. 387 (February 1970).
— (1970) 'Family Role Systems, Socialisation and Communication', Manuscript, Sociological Research Unit, University of London Institute of Education (1967). In D. Hymes, and J. J. Gumperz (eds.) 'A Socio-Linguistic Approach to Socialisation', *Directions in Sociolinguistics*, New York: Holt, Rinehart, Winston.
— and Cook, J. (1965) 'Coding Manual for Social Control', Sociological Research Unit,University of London, Institute of Education.
— and Henderson, D. (1969) 'Social Class Differences in the Relevance of Language to Socialisation' *Sociology*, Vol. 3, No. 1.
Bright, W. (ed.) (1966) *Sociolinguistics*, The Hague: Mouton.
Carroll, J. B. (ed.) (1956) *Language, Thought and Reality: selected writings of Benjamin Lee Whorf*, Cambridge, Mass.: M.I.T. Press.
Cazden, C. B. (1969) 'Sub-cultural Differences in Child Language: an inter-disciplinary review' *Merrill-Palmer Quarterly* **12.**
Chomsky, N. (1965) *Aspects of the Theory of Syntax*, Cambridge, Mass.: M.I.T. Press.
Cook, J. (1971) 'An Enquiry into Patterns of Communication and Control Between Mothers and their Children in Different Social Classes', Ph.D. Thesis presented to the University of London.

Coulthard, M. (1969) 'A Discussion of Restricted and Elaborated Codes' *Educational Review* **22**, No. 1.

Douglas, M. (1966) *Purity and Danger*, London: Routledge & Kegan Paul.

— (1970) *Natural Symbols*, London: Penguin.

Fishman, J. A. (1960) 'A Systematisation of the Whorfian Hypothesis' *Behavioural Science*, **5**.

Halliday, M. A. K. (1969) 'Relevant Models of Language' *Educational Review* **22**, No. 1.

Hawkins, P. R. (1969) 'Social Class, the Nominal Group and Reference' *Language and Speech*, **12**, No. 2.

Henderson, D. (1970) 'Contextual Specificity, Discretion and Cognitive Socialisation: with Special Reference to Language' *Sociology*, Volume 4, Number 3.

Hoijer, H. (ed.) (1954) 'Language in Culture' *American Anthropological Association Memoir No.* 79 (also published in Chicago).

Hymes, D. (1966) 'On Communicative Competence', Research Planning Conference on Language Development among Disadvantaged Children, Ferkauf Graduate School, Yeshiva University.

— (1967) 'Models of the Interaction of Language and Social Setting' *Journal of Social Issues* **23**.

— and Gumperz, J. J. (eds.) (1970) *Directions in Sociolinguistics*, New York: Holt, Rinehart, Winston.

Labov, W. (1965) 'Stages in the Acquisition of Standard English'. In Shuy, W. (ed.) *Social Dialects and Language Learning*, Champaign, Illinois: National Council of Teachers of English.

— (1966) *The Social Stratification of English in New York City*, Washington, D.C.: Center for Applied Linguistics.

Mandelbaum, D. (ed.) (1949) *Selected Writings of Edward Sapir*, University of California Press.

Parsons, T. and Shils, E. A. (eds.) (1951) *Toward a General Theory of Action*, Harper Torchbooks, Chapter 1, especially.

Turner, G. (1971) 'Social class and linguistic expressions of uncertainty', *Language and Speech*, **14**.

Williams, F. and Naremore, R. C. (1969) 'On the Functional Analysis of Social Class Differences in Modes of Speech' *Speech Monographs*, Vol. XXXVI, No. 2.